Heartsong

Two Hearts Beating as One Take Flight

JANAE THORNE-BIRD

iUniverse, Inc.
New York   Bloomington

Heartsong
Two Hearts Beating as One Take Flight

iUniverse books may be ordered through booksellers or by contacting:

iUniverse
1663 Liberty Drive
Bloomington, IN 47403
www.iuniverse.com
1-800-Authors (1-800-288-4677)

ISBN: 978-1-4401-8496-3 (pbk)
ISBN: 978-1-4401-8497-0 (ebk)

Printed in the United States of America

Library of Congress Control Number: 2009913127

iUniverse rev. date: 2/17/2010

For Dad, Jadon, Nolan, Patrick and John...preparing to be reunited

And lo, thou art unto them as a very lovely song of one that hath a pleasant voice, and can play well on an instrument: for they hear thy words, but they do them not.

And when this cometh to pass, (lo, it will come) then shall they know that a prophet hath been among them.

(Ezekiel 33:32, 33)

Special thanks to Paul and Rose Qualley (Andie McDowell) for the use of their computer to type my first manuscript on and to my editor, Lavina Fielding Anderson. Names and events have been changed for privacy and continuity.

Fly Away

All of her days have gone soft and cloudy
All of her dreams have gone dry
All of her nights have gone sad and shady
She's gettin' ready to fly...
Fly away...
Fly away...fly away

Life in the city can make you crazy
For sounds of the sand and the sea
Life in a high-rise can make you hungry
For things that you can't even see
Fly away...
Fly away...fly away

In this whole world there's nobody as lonely as she
There's no where to go and there's no where that she'd rather
be

She's lookin' for lovers and children playing
She's lookin' for signs of the spring
She listens for laugher and sounds of dancing
She listens for any old thing
Fly away...
Fly away...fly away

John Denver

Table of Contents

Vision Quest

It's early spring, 1998, when I climb the sacred summit seeking vision. My husband, Kurt, and I named the summit "Marriage Mountain" because of the numerous marriages we'd performed there. Not to mention it was one of our favorite spots to make love. Others say it's an energy vortex (like in Sedona)—a sort of gateway to heaven. All I knew for sure was on warm summer days I enjoyed watching the hawks and eagles circle about in extraordinary aerial displays as I lay on my back contemplating the Universe.

I'm breathless as I finally reach the plateau. As I pause to catch my breath, my eyes scan the panoramic view of the entire Ninemile Valley. The verdant spring delicacies nourish my soul with their varied green hues. I search for my favorite lichen-carpeted spot to spread my ground cover. The soft lichen is an unusual feature at this altitude, and it makes for a natural cushion.

Silently, I melt into the rapture of the moment. A cool breeze fondles my hair as I relax into quiet reverie. Nature has prepared a banquet for my senses and I could spend an entire day just relishing her fine delicacies. But the purpose for which I've come summons me to action.

Four medium-sized rocks beckon me to form the four directions—north, south, east and west. Deliberately, I pick them up and place them, finding smaller ones to fill in the spaces to create my Sacred Circle. I learned this from my years of study in the ways of the Native Americans. Also, from the instructions of my personal shaman, Speaking Wind, to whose spirit I now attune.

Standing outside the circle, I hesitate for a moment as another cool breeze prickles my skin. Regardless, my clothing falls gently to the ground before entering the Sacred Circle. It's an ancient metaphor for entering sacred space—naked, alone, vulnerable. No hidden secrets. No holding back. I'm completely open to my Creator to know me as I am known.

I was sent into this world seeking to join spirit with flesh, now in Vision Quest, I seek to join flesh with spirit. With my heart wide open, I surrender to the Great Mystery as I sit now in silent meditation. My eyes close to shut out the sensuous beauty surrounding me and to focus my thoughts. My thoughts, like water, begin to pour out of me in a passionate heartsong—a melody-drama filled with love, devotion, desire, and pain.

So many voices call to me…and I listen. Some beckon me to teach the wisdom that has become mine by learning to surrender to Spirit. Then there are those of my own flesh and blood needing my constant care and that I enjoy serving. Still there are cries of a desperate world seeking the healing wisdom I may offer. Which ones are the most important? Which ones should I follow? Always being pulled in different directions, I need to know which voices to listen to. I'm confused. The word says it—I'm "not together." So it's time I got an answer from God.

My mind drifts back to a previous Vision Quest years ago in Colorado. I'd spent two-weeks away from my family to get an answer concerning entering the principle of plural marriage. I was at a fork in my spiritual path—at the threshold of diving madly into the uncomfortable unknown. After fasting and praying for nearly two weeks in the Colorado wilderness, I was shaken to the core by a personal revelation. I questioned the revelation. Was I a prophetess of whom many sages had spoken that would come to heal the planet? Curiously, the world was waiting for the return of "a Savior" in male form. Yet the Native Americans spoke of a female prophet, naming her the White Buffalo Calf Woman. Their prophecies told of her return in skins of white during the "days of the long shadow." She would reclaim her sacred Peace Pipe and perform the final ceremony of joining all people together in a rainbow vortex. This dimension would then end, opening up the fifth dimension where peace, love, joy and bliss would reign throughout the earth.

These questions baffled me. Could I be this White Buffalo Calf Woman spoken of? Or perhaps I was just an archetype—a *wanabe* shaman? My ego could not wrap around the implications of such a significant revelation. So I denied it and stuck it hidden away from my mind's eye…and from the rest of the world. But now I was prepared for an answer. I reviewed the evidence in my mind as I meditated.

When I had first moved to Montana in 1984, I met a Mountain Man who fashioned willow furniture. We felt deeply connected, yet I couldn't recall his name it has been so many years ago. He said he was guided by the spirit to give me a book called *Mother Earth Spirituality* by Ed McGaa, "Eagle Man." It described the Native American paths to healing ourselves and our world. The first chapter was concerning the coming of the White Buffalo Calf Woman and her sacred Peace Pipe. I was fascinated at first and then became deeply intrigued by the story. It resonated with something deep inside me—something powerfully mystical and yet sublime. After reading the book, I was compelled to obtain my own personal peace pipe and become a "pipe-carrier." Unmistakably, I sent this intention to God and it wasn't long before the universe responded.

Kurt, at the time, was a traveling salesman selling food storage equipment in various cities in the Intermountain West. On one of his travels, he met a Native American vendor selling peace pipes made from authentic Catlinite. The "pipe stone" was blood red and mined in sacred stone quarries in southwestern Minnesota. Kurt thought a peace pipe might make a unique birthday gift since I'd always been fascinated with Native American lore.

According to his account, one of the pipes actually "spoke to him" through the spirit indicating that this particular pipe was for me. It had a buffalo embossed on beige leather wrapped around the stem, but Kurt had no idea it represented the White Buffalo Woman—the original pipe-carrier. The price for the pipe was more than Kurt had anticipated, and he couldn't justify the purchase with so many mouths to feed at home. As he walked away, again the pipe called to him. Curious, he turned to renegotiate with the vendor and explained his reasons for buying it. Caught up in the mystery, the seller softened, and he asked Kurt how much he could afford. It was nearly half the price, but he negotiated the sale anyway, placing the precious pipe into Kurt's hands.

Kurt put the pipe in the trunk of his car for safekeeping, but that evening, lying in bed in the motel room, the pipe spoke to him once more. It scolded him for leaving it in the trunk—a sign of disrespect. Kurt tried to ignore the promptings, but they persisted. He struggled with the pipe for several hours until he finally surrendered. He knew he wouldn't get any sleep until he went out to the car and brought it back inside. He slept with it next to his pillow and said it spoke to him and energized him throughout the night.

Kurt brought these stories and more home as he gifted the curious pipe to me for my birthday. It was then that I told him about my intentions to obtain a peace pipe after reading about the White Buffalo Woman. We were truly amazed. I felt its deep significance at the time, especially after we smoked it together in sacred ceremony and received blessings of peace and empowerment. But it wasn't until later that it all made sense—at least in the scheme of things.

It was nearly ten years later that I met Speaking Wind. My experience with this "Spirit Caller" from the Anasazi tradition shifted my entire consciousness. After he answered my first question, "What is it like to be spiritually one?" other questions kept surfacing. Who was I and what was my Indian name? He'd indicated that we'd shared a previous life together as Native Americans.

Yet *that* information was sacred and I needed to find out directly from God. But he did suggest that I was one of the Ancient Ones who'd come back to heal the planet. And he kept saying over and over again, "I can't believe you are here!"

I invited Patrick (which is what he preferred to be called) to come to Montana to perform sacred ceremony and bless our land, Higher Ground. When he petitioned Spirit concerning which ceremony he'd be allowed to perform, he was astonished when he was given permission to perform the most sacred of all ceremonies—the Seven Steps to Returning to Oneness. We then made preparations for me to go to Alabama to meet with many of the chiefs from numerous Native American tribes. Afterward, they would follow us to Montana to Higher Ground to perform the sacred ceremony that was destined to shift the planet.

But then everything came to a dramatic halt as Kurt went to war with Patrick over jealousies. When he threatened Patrick with his life, Patrick cancelled the trips—and the ceremony. The last words he spoke to me were "I'm sorry, Little One, but things are not in balance to perform this sacred ceremony right now. We must wait until things can come into balance." That was over two years ago and Patrick had not contacted me since.

And so now it was that I seek God for answers.

Hours pass as I sit in deep meditation, closing out the many voices that call to me so I can listen to the One True Voice. The sun beats down upon my naked body causing me to grow weary. Attention flagging, I curl up on the ground cover for a short nap and moments later slip into a deep sleep. I am startled awake when a black wasp stings my right foot, which has slipped beyond the boundaries of my Sacred Circle. I cry out in pain, knowing it's a message from the Creator. I have strayed from my purpose here.

I resume a seated position inside the circle and continue the meditation. My long golden hair, bleached from the sun and dampened from perspiration, cascades across my shoulders protecting them from the afternoon rays. Time passes slowly and I decide to open my eyes to gaze upon the wonderland surrounding me. Blue lupine, Indian paintbrush, and golden sunflowers are a delightful rainbow display.

I notice some unusual butterflies flitting about the wildflowers which I'd never seen before. Their tan wings contain markings resembling eyes opening and shutting as they flap. They look like real eyes. I laugh as my mind plays with the words. These butterflies see with real eyes—they "realize." Again the words come. They are like the children of Israel—they see what "is real." I enjoy the play on words and I laugh to myself.

Then I notice the black wasp, which had stung my foot, buzzing around the butterflies. A feeling of concern sweeps over me as I'm reminded of the sting on my foot which is starting to swell. The black wasp represents darkness and evil to me, and I'm concerned for the butterflies' safety. I intuitively call to them, beckoning them to come inside my sacred circle for safety. They continue to flutter about among the colorful flowers unaware, it seems, of my presence or the dark presence of the wasp.

With a touch of resignation, I return to my meditation. Silently I bring myself into harmony with the purpose for which I am here. Cleansing myself of my own desires, I focus on the desires of my Creator. And I just listen.

Suddenly, I feel a slight tickling in my cupped hands that are resting in my lap. I open my eyes and gaze down to see two "children of Is-real" butterflies resting gracefully in my hands. I smile in delight as I receive the sublime message from the Creator. So this is the gathering of Israel!

And just as if the Creator acknowledges that the message is received, the two amazing butterflies—now in hand—merge together in flight to form an energetic vortex spiraling them to heaven. I sit for a moment, awestruck, feeling profound divine messages my soul. My heart swells and my eyes overflow with the majesty and intimacy of God's love. I say a silent prayer of thanksgiving and know that my Vision Quest is complete.

I carefully return all of my stone sentries to their original positions. I dress and fold up my ground cover. These ordinary tasks seem illuminated by the radiance of my newfound knowledge. I now know that I must write my story and call it *Heartsong*.

When I get back to our log cabin, I am excited to tell Kurt about my experiences vision questing. He does not share in my enthusiasm as I disclose my own interpretations of the sacred meanings. In fact he mocks me with searing sarcasm, claiming my vision is a product of my own wild imagination. I retreat to my room and cry, again having allowed him to steal something precious from me. I pray to God for more answers and enlightenment—and perhaps another sign. And miraculously they come.

That week as I finish making a pair of boots for our neighbor, Andie McDowell (the actress), I notice something fascinating. As I am sewing on the last item—a buffalo-head nickel fashioned into a button—I get a strange feeling of de-ja-vu. I know I've seen this same image of a buffalo somewhere else. I then pick up my left foot to view the strange mark on its bottom. When I was young, it was a large black mole, but as I've grown older it's turned into a large, skin-colored tag. People would ask why I didn't have it removed, and I would tease them that I'd know my soul-mate because he would have a similar skin tag. My young children always tried to pull it off thinking it's a piece of gum. It also opens up my *kundalini* energies (my *chakras*) when I massage it. But now as I look down at it as if it is the first time, I notice something extraordinary. *It is the image of a white buffalo.* When I place the buffalo-head nickel next to it, the similarities are striking. I am nearly blown away by this new revelation. I dare not tell anyone about it, especially Kurt, who continues to mock me for my strange revelations.

During the course of the next few weeks, other remarkable coincidences occur. I receive two cards in the mail—one from my mother for my birthday and one from a dear friend, Shara, letting me know she's thinking of me. My mother's birthday card has the image of a Native American smoking a peace pipe. Shara's card contains a picture of three buffalo in an open field. Coincidence? I believe not. But again I am careful not to share these experiences with anyone, thinking they would believe I'm crazy! And perhaps I am a bit crazy as the mind has a strange way of creating extraordinary manifestations. I realize that my entire life has been a series of incredible coincidences, and it's time I write them all down in a book—at least it would make a good story for my posterity. And so I begin the journey into *Heartsong.*

Chapter One

Gathering

God stretches forth his hand in springtime passion. His warm, caressing fingers beckon those who would come to celebrate sacred communion with him atop Marriage Mountain. It's Memorial Day, 2027, a day to remember "all our relations" and also a day to celebrate Grandma Jesse's 70th Birthday.

Lupine, shooting stars, and sunflowers decorate the hillside as the birthday party climbs the steep incline to the summit. Grandma Jesse, dressed in her white leather ceremonial dress, beaded with yellow roses, butterflies and buffalo, leads the procession—her sacred staff in hand. Like Moses, the staff gives her strength to climb the sacred mountain. Her moccasined steps are steady, perhaps a bit brisk with anticipation. Her long, flowing hair dances in the breeze blending with the white of her leather dress contrasted by her characterized tanned face.

The large procession of family and friends follow, numbering over a hundred, arms loaded with gaily wrapped gifts, plates of food, and ground covers. Ashley, Jesse's firstborn daughter (her beauty untouched by over five decades of life) carries a hand-decorated cake complete with seventy candles.

Everyone gathers at the summit to watch Grandpa Karl spread the well-worn buffalo robe upon the ground. Grandchildren scramble to find a spot to sit. Grandpa Vincent tucks a gift under his arm while he unfolds Grandma Jesse's favorite wooden stool.

Others busy themselves setting up a large folding table, spreading it with lacy tablecloths before placing the cake and plates of food on. Colorful quilts and blankets are spread on the ground surrounding Grandma Jesse as she gracefully sits on her wooden stool. Family and friends sprawl out on the patchwork tapestry, practically covering the entire summit. Spring breezes playfully frolic with hair, skin and clothing of parents who quiet their rambunctious children.

Now is the time of celebration—of unwrapping gifts, feasting on goodies, telling stories, making music, and dancing. It has become nearly a 30-year tradition for the tribal community at Higher Ground—but it is much older than that. For centuries, tribes have gathered to celebrate passages of time, a tradition that spans generations linking past, present, and future into one great circle... the circle of life. For the tribe at Higher Ground, it happens each Memorial Day, which happens to be Jesse's Birthday.

Grandpa Karl demands everyone's attention by clapping his hands and shouting, "quiet." The attractive, white-haired elder, a distinguished focal point even at 73, speaks and a respectful silence follows.

"It's time for Grandma Jesse to open her birthday gifts. Everyone sit still and pay attention." A stern look towards the wrestling children on the buffalo robe calls their mothers to take charge.

"I will begin by giving *my* gift first," Grandpa Karl declares and proudly hands Jesse a huge, carefully wrapped bundle of rose printed wrapping paper. She begins to unwrap it, but he interrupts by handing her a birthday card. She gently removes the card from the envelope and reads aloud:

> God said, "Let there be light,"
> And there was your smile.
> God said, "Let there be stars to brighten the night,"
> And there was the laughter in your eyes.
> God said, "Let there be warmth and gentleness,"
> And there was your touch.
> God said, "Let there be music,"
> And there was your voice.
> God said, "Let there be faith and trust and hope and joy and love,"
> And there was your heart.
> God said, "Let the world be beautiful and wonderful and good,"
> And there was you.

She opens the card and continues to read:

> Every beautiful part of our life as a family is a reflection of the wonderful
> Mother and wife you are.
> Happy Birthday.

Jesse's eyes mist with tears as she continues reading to herself the handwritten sentiments. She closes the card to embrace her lover of over 50 years. (In fact, it was last August that they celebrated their Golden Wedding Anniversary together.)

Their lips linger in a kiss, and together they unwrap the bundle that fills her lap. The paper falls away to reveal an exquisite new buffalo robe—larger and plusher than the old one now occupied by precious grandchildren.

"Oh, sweetheart, how could you?" Jesse delights. "And you tanned it yourself, didn't you?"

Karl beams at her obvious pleasure.

"How wonderfully soft it will be for the little ones to sit on." She stands to find a spot on the ground for the beautiful fur.

"Oh, no, no, no!" exclaims Grandpa Karl, removing it from her arms. "This is not for grandchildren to sit on. They can use the old robe. This one's for *our own personal use*, my dear." He winks a mischievous smile.

"Oh, *I see*," she acknowledges with a reciprocal wink. Grandpa Karl refolds the buffalo robe and gently lifts her from her stool to place it underneath her. She settles on it comfortably to continue unwrapping gifts.

"Gram'ma Jesse." It's four-year-old Jessica, an adorable grandchild with absorbing eyes named after her Grandmother.

"Yes, Jessica," Grandma Jesse acknowledges.

"Why can't Gram'pa let us sit on your new buffalo robe?"

Jesse smiles. "Well, little angel, this buffalo robe is Grandpa Karl's *special* gift to me to remind us of our marriage. He wants me to save it for *special* times."

"But isn't this a *special* time, Gram'ma?" Jessica continues.

"Oh, yes, it is!" exclaims Grandma Jesse. "And that's why we've brought my *favorite* buffalo robe up here for you to sit on during the birthday party."

Jessica seems appeased by Grandma's reply—just long enough for her to formulate another question.

"Gram'ma Jesse."

"Yes, darlin'."

"Why do you like to come up here to Marriage Mountain for your birthday?"

Grandma pulses with joy at the curious, often comical, conversations she has with her grandchildren. After so many years of tutoring young children, Jesse never hesitates to give them the answers they seek.

"Well, this mountain is a *special* mountain—just like that buffalo robe you're sitting on. You might say...this is a *magic* mountain."

"Magic!" exclaims Jessica, bouncing up and down with delight.

Josiah, sitting next to her breaks in. "What kind of magic, grandma?"

"Well, you see over there?" Grandma points in the direction of a small rise framed by ancient pine trees overlooking the ardent valley below.

"That knoll is where lots of couples have come to be married. In fact," she reminisces, "your Aunt Ashley and Uncle Matt had one of the first marriages performed up here. Afterwards, it became sort of a tradition—something everyone liked to do. That's why we call it 'Marriage Mountain.'"

"And, little Jessica," interrupts Grandpa Karl, attempting to fill in gaps in her curious mind. "You see that spot over there."

He points to a small, shady hollow completely carpeted with a thick blanket of moss. "That is where the twinkle in your Grandmother's eye became your mother."

He laughs jubilantly, giving Grandma Jesse a wink of his eye and pretentious grin. Grandma Jesse laughs also. "You'll understand more in due time," she promises her curious grandchildren.

Now Granny Kissy, an exuberant woman with warm brown eyes and a bright smile, moves forward to give Jesse her beautifully wrapped gift. She kisses Jesse sweetly as she carefully slips the card from beneath the ribbon to be read:

A Special Birthday Wish

May you always have enough blessings
      to give a few away.
May you always see the good in others
      and the strength in yourself.
May you always feel good about the opportunities
      each new year holds.
May you always be a little happier
      than you were a year ago.
      HAPPY BIRTHDAY

Again Jesse's eyes fill with tears as she silently reads the personal sentiments her dear sister-wife, Kirstie, has written.

"Thank-you, my dear, Kirstie," she manages as Granny Kissy gives her a warm embrace.

"I hope you like the gift," murmurs Kirstie. "I've been working on it for quite some time."

"Oh, I'm sure I will, dear," replies Jesse sincerely. "If it's something you've made, how can I help but not treasure it?" She carefully unties the ribbon and opens the wrapping paper. A beautiful hand-spun, hand-crocheted shawl falls into her lap. "Oh, Kirstie, how divine!" Jesse exclaims. "How did you *ever* find time—and without me knowing?" What a magician you are!"

Kirstie's eyes sparkle gaily and her smile grows even brighter with pride. "Well, I know I'm not as good as you at spinning and weaving, even though I've been perfecting my skills for years. If it pleases you, it's only because you've been a good teacher."

"Oh, Kirstie, don't try the 'humble act' with me." Jesse mockingly scolds. "It's absolutely perfect, and I'll wear it on all special occasions."

Jesse gracefully wraps the elegant cream shawl around her shoulders, Kirstie lovingly pulling it into a cozy fold at her neck. "Oohs" and "ahs" arise from the circle of husbands, wives, children, grandchildren and friends, expressing their admiration of Granny Kissy's handiwork.

"Grandma Jesse." It's ten-year-old, Josiah.

"Yes, dear," Grandma acknowledges.

"How did you and Granny Kissy come to know each other?"

Both grandmas laugh like two old hens cackling. They have a long kept secret between them.

"Now that's an *amazing* story, Josiah, twinkles Jesse. But Granny Kissy can tell it better than me."

"Oh, no, no, no, not me! *You* are the story-teller, Jesse," exclaims Granny Kissy, removing herself from the "hot-seat." "Or better yet…perhaps you should start by telling the story of how you and Grandpa Karl met. That's a much better one."

"Oh, yes, Grandma… please tell us the story of how you and Grandpa Karl met. PLEASE!" chorus the young voices.

Grandma Jesse releases a sigh and settles herself comfortably on her buffalo robe to begin telling one of her true-life adventures.

Chapter Two

Serendipity

"Some words—like some people—come into your life and you immediately fall in love with them," begins Grandma Jesse as the grandchildren gather closer to hear.

"'Serendipity' is one of those wonderful words. It's so meaningful, so delightful, that you just can't help but fall in love with the word." Jesse shimmied with delight.

"But what does 'Sara-dip...sara-dip-a-dee' mean, Grandma?" queries little Adam, his eyes wide with curiosity.

"I know, I know!" exclaims his older brother, Jeremy. "It's like the story you used to tell us about the three princes from Serendip who discovered that even when they took what they thought was the wrong road, they found luck and treasures along the way.

"And those books you read to us at night, Grandma! They said 'serendipity' on the back. You told us that they had a special meaning that we might miss if we weren't looking for it," pipes in Jessica.

"Precisely, children!" exclaims Jesse approvingly. "I'm so glad you still remember. It's important for you young ones to remember to look for the hidden meanings because *that's* where the magic is. When you dip into the serenity of your heart, then God leads you on a path of serendipity that brings you back into his presence. You might say serendipity is the thread that binds us all together and spins us back to God. That's why it's so important to listen to your heart—so you won't get lost and confused along the way."

"But, Grandma, what does sara-dip-a-dee have to do with you meeting Grandpa?" This time it is six-year-old Karla anxious for the rest of the story.

Jesse's eyes twinkle as she begins again. "Well, as I was saying, some people, like some words, come into your life and you immediately fall in love with them. That is the way it was when I first laid eyes on your Grandfather Karl.

It was 1975, and I had just graduated from high school. My path of serendipity had led me to go to Utah State University. It wasn't my first choice of colleges to attend. I'd actually set my sights on Brigham Young University where my best high school friend, Charlene, and I had planned to go and to be roommates. But after visiting Utah State on an LDS Seminary conference, I felt drawn to attend there instead.

Not only that, but I had a boyfriend from my senior year in high school who was very persistent. I knew all the time I was dating Norman that he wasn't the one for me. But I felt sorry for him. His parents had been killed in a car accident a year before we met and he became extremely attached to me. He felt as if I was the only one in his life he could care about or love. He wanted to own me, as if that would secure the love for him that he had for me. I tried to break off the relationship with him after graduation, but I just didn't have the heart to tell him how I really felt. We really became attached during our senior year and it was difficult for us to just end things. I hoped that by moving to Utah State in Logan—some 90 miles away—that time and distance would naturally help drift us apart. But I found out it wasn't that easy.

After a month or so at Utah State, I was determined to make a new life with new friends and new experiences, regardless of Norman's feelings. I'd often sit in the Student Union Center between classes watching people walk by and wondering what they were thinking, where they were going...always moving in one direction or another. It was on one of those times when I was just sitting and watching students walk by, that suddenly the best-looking guy I'd ever seen walked through the door. My heart leaped and I got kinda dizzy with little butterflies dancing around in my stomach. Then I heard a voice whisper inside my head saying, "If I ever get married, it will have to be to someone just like you."

I don't know where the voice came from, but my eyes became fixed on this young man (who looked a lot like my favorite singer, John Denver) as he strode down the hallway and chose a seat on a bench *right across the hallway from me!* Three or four girls immediately surrounded him, obviously flirting with him and vying for his attention. I barely noticed them as all my attention was fixed on the expressions on his face, the easy way he threw back his head, his carefree attitude. Someone this good-looking had to have at least one steady girlfriend. And how could I compete with the flock of beauties around him?

But why did he keep looking at me, flashing me a friendly smile? It was as if he was encouraging me to come over and introduce myself. Well, I was far from being that bold, and the butterflies dancing around in my heart prevented me from doing anything but blushing warmly each time our eyes met.

The feelings were so intense that I finally got up and moved away, stopping down the hall where I could still observe him without being observed. Had disappointment shown on his face when I got up to leave? In any case, he made no effort to follow me—continuing to flirt with his adorers until I left for my next class.

For the rest of the day, I couldn't stop thinking about "the man of my dreams." How could I have let him go without meeting him? I scolded myself for not having enough courage to push through my fears and introduce myself. By the time I got home to my roommates at the "Morm Dorms" (what we nicknamed the Mormon Church-owned dormitories), I was really distressed.

"I can't believe I missed out on the opportunity of a lifetime to meet the man of my dreams!" I complained to my roommate, Bernie, as I flung my books on the bed. I told her about my chance encounter with the good-looking guy at the Student Union Center. "I just *know* I'll never get another chance to meet him."

"You don't *know* that, Jesse," consoled Bernie. "You never know...if it's meant to be, you'll run into him again."

"And how is *that* going to happen when you know I'm leaving to go to California at Thanksgiving and live with my sister?" I questioned.

Moving to California to live with Martha and Ben was my way of escaping Norman, who was still calling me every day and visiting me on weekends in spite of the strict dorm rules. I resented the fact that he didn't play by *any* rules but his own. I'd spent an entire weekend washing the dorm's huge picture windows because he'd been caught in my room without prior permission from the dorm parents.

"Oh, by the way, Norm's been calling you and wants you to call him back as soon as you get in," Bernie relayed.

"Oh, brother," I sighed, collapsing on top of the heap of books on the bed. "I wish I *never* had to *see* or *hear* about Norman again. He's just about ruined my life. I don't know how I'll ever get rid of him!"

Bernie understood my sentiments. She was truly disappointed I was leaving Utah State just as we'd become such good friends. We had a lot in common. Her real name was Bernice but everyone called her "Bernie." My given name was Jessica but was nicknamed Jesse when I was young. And we both loved to sing and were in choir together. She was convinced that I looked like her idol, Julie Andrews, and sang like her too. I was flattered by the comparison especially because singing was one of my greatest passions. I was the envy of my entire choir class when I was chosen by a student teacher to receive free voice lessons. The student teacher expressed that I had "real potential as a professional singer" after the first lesson. And now I would have to give it all up just to escape a frustrating relationship.

Norman was getting more and more persistent in his phone conversations. He insisted that if I didn't quit school and move to Salt Lake to live with him that he was going to kill himself. I was convinced that this was a *real* possibility, especially after his brother-in-law, a clinical psychologist, said that Norman definitely had "suicidal tendencies." He told me that he had been diagnosed as "manic-depressive" and I'd better be careful how I dealt with him emotionally.

Despite my feelings of sincere affection and concern for Norman, I knew we couldn't go on like this and think about completing our college education as planned. And so I felt like the only solution was to get as far away from him as possible before he completely destroyed both our lives.

My parents and I had come up with a strategy during the last weekend I'd visited with them in Salt Lake. They were going to visit my sister, Martha, and her husband, Ben, in Livermore, California for Thanksgiving, and they felt it was a perfect opportunity for me to get far enough away from Norman that he wouldn't pursue me anymore. And then, after he'd gotten over me, I could return back to Utah State to continue with my education. That was the plan.

Now here it was two and half weeks before Thanksgiving, and I'd just met the man of my dreams. I had no way of knowing whether or not I'd ever see him again, and I was desperate just to know his name. That night I knelt in prayer asking the Lord to help me meet this guy if, in fact, he was the man I was supposed to marry.

The whole next week dragged on, leaving me anxious about leaving college—abandoning my roommates, my 4.0 grade point average, my vocal career, and, last but not least, the handsome stranger. The passing days had not dimmed my memory of his image nor made that single encounter seem less significant. On the contrary, my desire to find him had become *insistent*. Each day I'd sit in the same place at the same time, hoping beyond hope, that I'd see him again. And then exactly one week from my first encounter, as I was hurrying around a corner not watching where I was going, I ran straight into a body traveling in the opposite direction.

Destiny was in the making (or perhaps it was she and a collection of other cupids wanting to get their turn on Earth). When I looked up (after watching all my books scatter across the floor), I was staring straight into the eyes of *the man of my dreams!* Dancing butterflies fluttered into my heart again. I couldn't express a single word. All I could do was stand there and stare speechless at the handsomest face I'd ever seen. A heat-wave washed from my heart right up into my face.

The spell was broken as the handsome figure leaned down to gather up the scattered books. We both apologized in embarrassed confusion and then out of nowhere he queried, "I know this may sound like a stupid line, but haven't I seen you somewhere before—but *not on this planet?*"

His question took me by surprise, yet I wanted to admit the possibility that was being confirmed in my *own* heart. As a Mormon, I'd been taught that we'd formed pre-existent relationships that play out on Earth. The familiar look in this stranger's eyes confirmed that what I believed was not only a possibility—but a reality. The here and now had collided with the distant past and possible future. I clamored for a rational response to his strange question.

"Well, I don't know about that—but I *do* remember seeing you across the hallway last week, talking with some of your...friends."

"Oh, yeah, now I remember," he replied, trying to dispel his own strange reaction. "I'm on my way to that little snack bar," he said, pointing down the hall. "Would you like to join me for a drink?"

I looked at my watch—twenty minutes before my last class of the day. "Sure, I have a few minutes," I replied. (But I was sure what my heart had in mind would take a lot longer than a few minutes!)

He found us a small table in a quiet corner and pulled out a chair for me. "He even has manners," I surmised as he went for the orange juice I'd requested. He brought back two and handed me one as he introduced himself as Karl Clark. "So what brings you to this planet?" he smiled wryly, seating himself.

For the next twenty minutes Karl listened intently, his warm eyes offering a safe haven to pour out my life's story. I related a brief history of how I came to attend Utah State and concluded in describing the current dilemma of Norman's pursuit and my escape scheduled for the day after tomorrow. Never before had I felt so comfortable disclosing personal details to a listening stranger. And never before had I desired, more than anything, to make this stranger...something more.

It soon became time for class and I resisted breaking off the communion we were sharing. The emotions in my heart coerced me to ignore anything that would interrupt the ultimate destiny that awaited us. But the fear of "too much, too fast" overwhelmed me and I sought reprieve from these intense emotions in the safety of Psychology 101. I abruptly stood up. So did he. "I've got to go to class," I stammered as I looked at my watch.

"Can I see you tonight?" inquired Karl.

Relief flooded me. "I'd like that," I replied, trying not to appear over-anxious.

"I've got a rehearsal with Orchesis at the dance studio tonight at 7:30. Would you like to come?"

"I'd love to!" I exclaimed. "I tried out for Orchesis but didn't make the cut. I'd love to see them rehearse!"

"Great. I'll pick you up at seven."

There were no disorders discussed in my Psychology 101 class that would account for the dizziness I felt from a heart full of dancing butterflies. I skipped all the way home as if on a platform of air eager to tell Bernie that she had been right—that I would "run into him" again if it was meant to be. How could she have possibly known that we were both on a collision course with destiny?

I burst into the dorm, ready to race upstairs to our room, when suddenly a pair of hands grabs me from behind, covering my eyes and stopping me in my tracks.

"Guess who?"

My heart sank. Norman. For a moment I tried to pretend I didn't know—hoping that my pretending would somehow make him disappear.

"Norman!" I finally blurted out in genuine surprise. "What are you doing here?"

I didn't pretend I was surprised to see him, but pretending I was *glad* to see him was a feat I wasn't capable of at that moment.

"Aren't you happy to see me?" inquired Norman, staring at me closely.

"Of course I am," I stammered. "It's just I wasn't expecting you...I mean, here it is...only Thursday...I mean, you usually come up on the weekends...I mean, what brings you up here today of all days?"

"Is there something *wrong* with surprising my Princess? Hey, if I didn't know you better, I'd think you weren't happy to see me." His dejected voice whined like a buzzsaw. "Or that I'd spoiled some great plans of yours for this evening. You *are* happy to see me aren't you, Princess?"

"Of course I am, Norman," I replied desperately, seeing his face turn stormy with indignation. "It's just that I did have plans to go somewhere with my...roommates this evening. But I'm sure they'll understand. Just wait here. I'll go tell them you're here and that I'll have to cancel my date with them."

"Wait...let me go with you," Norman insisted, still clinging suspiciously to my hand.

"No, you'd better not. Remember what happened last time you were caught up in my dorm room without permission? I can't see myself spending another weekend washing windows simply because you won't let me out of your sight. I'll only be a few minutes. Go wait in the rec room for me."

I pointed him in the direction of the recreation area as I fled for the safety of the stairs.

Bernie gazed at me baffled as I tried to explain in one breath everything that had just happened.

"Now just slow down, Jesse," she soothed, leading me to my bed and pushing me down on the edge. "You're making absolutely no sense at all when you're this hysterical."

"Bernie," I began again. "I just met him...the guy from last week. We ran into each other in the hallway—just like you said we would—and he asked me out on a date tonight!"

"You're kidding, Jesse!" Bernie interrupted excitedly. "That *really* happened? Oh, tell me all about *how* it happened!"

"BERNIE!" I shouted, "*Listen to me. I'm frantic! Norman's here *right now* and what am I going to tell him about my date with Karl?!"

"Wow!" breathed Bernie, "His name's Karl?"

Bernie obviously wasn't processing all of the information; but fortunately my mind was working overtime.

"Bernie," I instructed, "You're going to have to tell Karl the situation when he comes to pick me up at 7:00. I've got to keep Norman happy so he'll leave. Tell Karl I will try to meet him at the dance studio later—as soon as I can get rid of Norman."

Bernie was still firing questions at me about Karl as I changed clothes and freshened my make-up. I looked in the mirror. The second coat of make-up did little to hide the distress still left on my face.

The night was spent, appropriately enough, in the Logan cemetery located across the street from the dorms. Norman was in a desperate mood, reiterating endlessly his undying devotion, the agonies he suffered from his broken heart, and how he couldn't possibly live another moment without me.

He was so upset that he threw up twice. A bleeding ulcer he'd developed because our separation was making him sick—deathly sick, he kept saying. I was cold and hungry, and getting sick myself as the evening dragged on. Norman grilled me for almost four hours about why I didn't love him the way he loved me. He made me promise that I would transfer to the University of

Utah and live with him in Salt Lake. At my wit's end, I promised. Finally, Norman walked me back to the dorm. It was nearly 11:00 when I collapsed in my bed and sobbed uncontrollably into my pillow.

"So things went well," Bernie remarked, trying to lighten the mood.

"Why does he persist in trying to ruin my life?" I sobbed. "Why can't he just leave me alone?"

The next day was my last day at Utah State before leaving for California. I hadn't slept. I prayed all night that if God is a God of miracles, he would bring Karl and me together again so at least—if nothing else—I could apologize for the night before.

The hours dragged on until 3:00 which ended my classes. I then rushed to the Student Union Center to the snack bar where we'd talked the day before—fully expecting a miracle.

My heart leaped with joy as I spotted someone sitting at the same table, who looked a lot like Karl from the back. Dancing butterflies lifted me over to him.

"I can't believe you're actually here!" I exclaimed excitedly.

"I see you're not disappointed," he replied, trying to hide a smile but his eyes twinkled his own delight.

"Disappointed? Absolutely not! In fact, it's nothing less than a miracle to find you here. I *am* disappointed I missed our date last night, though."

"Not as disappointed as I was." he confessed sweetly. "Your roommate explained your situation," he confirmed.

I filled him in on the details, reassuring him that I'd never stood anyone up for a date before. He admitted that he'd never been "stood up" for a date and made me promise not do it again if I'd agree to another date that night.

I eagerly promised to be ready at 6:00 for our dinner date.

JB's was the local college-student hangout. Karl asked the waitress to seat us at a quiet booth where we could have a conversation. A corner booth secured, we sat down and ordered dinner.

It was Karl's turn to share his life's path. I listened spellbound as he talked about a difficult childhood, moving frequently, turning rebellious against his parents and religion, and being on his own since age 14. He wound up in the military where his independent spirit refused to be contained by rigid discipline. He was released from the military for its "breech of contract" in not putting him through flight training. After several years riding on the wild-side with friends, he began working to put himself through college so he could become a doctor.

After two years of college, his savings were spent, and he began working part-time at a sugar factory while continuing to go to school. But on the way home from work one evening, he was in a head-on collision with a drunk driver. He was thrown from his 1952 Oldsmobile and skidded several yards along the blacktop in the opposite lane of traffic. Fortunately no one hit him, and his heavy factory clothing protected him from serious injury although he was unable to walk for weeks. That had been only six months before, and he seemed fully recovered except for a small scar on his forehead. His miraculous escape from serious injury and his speedy recovery were also due to his well-conditioned body, being a dancer and a black-belt in karate.

"So the head-on collision with you was my second one this year." We both laughed simultaneously. "And if the first one hadn't happened, I never would have met you." He smiled as his hand reached across the table for mine. "Sometimes I feel like my life is being played out by forces beyond my control—like I'm an actor in some great drama." He then looked deeply into my eyes. "And all of it has been leading to this moment, Jesse…to meeting you."

JB's was getting too crowded for our conversation to continue. The evening had flown by. Soon it would be my curfew—11 o'clock—when the dorm doors would be locked.

We sat in the car outside my dorm noticing the twinkle of stars in the night sky. Lights began turning off inside. Our conversation dwindled as we looked at the sultry glow in each other's eyes. The glow ignited a flame in both of us, and our lips impulsively collided. We kissed as if the passion between us could never be satisfied. My heart raced and I could scarcely catch my breath between each sensuous explosion. I knew we were being consumed by our passions, and the "good girl" in me slowly pulled herself out of the arms I never wanted to leave…the lips I never wanted to stop kissing.

The last light on in the dorm was my dorm parents'. I looked down at my watch. It was just past 11. I cranked the car door open and exited the steamy compartment.

"I'll call you later!" I promised and ran up the entranceway just in time to squeeze inside before my dorm parent locked the door.

The next morning my parents arrived to help me pack my things and get ready for my escape to California. We drove the twelve-hour trip to Livermore in my dad's motor home where we spent a lovely Thanksgiving with Martha and Ben. My parents then went back to Salt Lake, leaving me there to make the adjustments of living in a new environment.

Martha and Ben helped me unpack my things in their spare bedroom. Ben made suggestions about finding work in Livermore the following week. After a few days, my younger sister, Rosalie, called and insisted that I call Norman as he'd been calling her incessantly, trying to find out where I was. She said he even came to her school and threatened to commit suicide if she didn't tell him where I was. My heart was torn because there was still a lingering love for Norman, even though I was communicating by phone and letter with Karl nearly every day. I struggled with my decision to call Norman, but I finally conceded—for Rosalie's sake if nothing else.

"Where the hell are you?" came the voice at the other end of the phone.

"Well, I *really* can't tell you, Norman, 'cause I know you'll just try and come get me. I just need some time alone to sort out my feelings. I don't want to jump into anything without considering the feelings of everyone. I mean…I couldn't just shack up with you without considering my parents' feelings and…"

"Oh, just stop all of this nonsense and just tell me where you're at…so I can at least write you." His voice was becoming impatient.

"Well, I think it would be a nice idea to write each other," I considered. "But you promise if I tell you my address that you won't try to come out here and get me?"

"What? Do you think I'm *crazy?!* After what you've done to my heart, do you think I *ever* want to see you again?"

With that reassurance I told him my sister's address in Livermore. The connection at the other end of the phone went dead. My heart sank. Oh, my God. *He's on his way to come get me!*

That evening all of Livermore was fogged in. The fog was so thick you could barely see your hand stretched out in front of your face. My mind was in a dense fog, too. What would I do if by some miracle Norman was able to find his way in the fog? Would I stay here with my sister and force him to return to Salt Lake alone? Or would my emotional attachments to him come into play and again be pulled into his drama?

About 10:00 that evening the doorbell rang. It was Norman. He was pale and disheveled, showing signs of a long, exhausting trip. My brother-in-law, Ben, was firm. Norman was not to be allowed in the house. With every fiber in my body I tried to put up a strong resistance to his insistence that I come back with him. But when he pulled me close and I could feel the wetness of his tears on my face, all resistance melted. I knew my plot to runaway from Norman had failed…and failed miserably. The pain in his heart was more than I could bear. I packed up my bags, jumped into his white Pontiac and rode off into the dense fog—clueless as to what our lives together had in store.

Three months later, after struggling to live together in a small basement apartment with both of us going to school, I bolted. Or maybe I finally cleared the fog out of my head and realized that I didn't love Norman the way he loved me, and it just wasn't going to work. My heart was drawn to someone else and my heartstrings kept pulling me towards him.

It was Friday, February 13, the day before Valentine's Day. I wanted nothing more than to be with my *one true love* on the day set aside for lovers. I was in a desperate mood, and so when Norman stepped out of the apartment for a few moments, I grabbed the keys to the Pontiac and was out of there.

All reason had flown out of the window as I nearly flew up to Cache Valley to be with the love of my life. But still, there were some doubts that Karl would be around—let alone available. When I dialed the phone number to the Clark residence at a pay phone at JB's, to my surprise and delight, Karl answered. Yes, he was still around even though it had been nearly three months since we'd communicated either by phone or letter after I'd moved in with Norman. Yet neither of us had given up on each other.

That night we partied at one of Logan's popular dance clubs. After a few glasses of wine and a few slow dances, all guilty thoughts of Norman mysteriously disappeared. They were replaced with rapturous thoughts of Karl. At about midnight, Karl and I checked into a Ramada Inn.

My heart danced with butterflies as Karl slipped into the bathroom to fill the tub with a warm bubble bath. The effects of the wine had made me eager for Karl's touch on my bare skin. It was as if Karl had read my mind....

Grandma Jesse suddenly stops in mid-sentence, realizing the innocent ears of her audience. Her older children sigh with relief, hoping for a break to discharge their restless children. It was a good time for refreshments.

Chapter Three

Centered Living

The grandchildren race to the long folding table where they obediently line up and let their aunts dish up their plates, youngest first. The lacy buffet is spread with a myriad of delicious dishes made with food grown and prepared at Higher Ground.

The organic garden at Higher Ground produces an abundant variety of produce that create a decorative vegetable platter display. They are accented with tantalizing dips including guacamole made from avocados grown in the Garden of Eden biodome. This unique structure also produces exotic fruit such as kiwi, mangos and bananas since the hydro-thermal radiant heat provides three artificial climates—temperate, sub-tropical and tropical. Permaculture was introduced to the biodome at its inception and the tropical and sub-tropical plants thrive in spite of the harsh Montana climate.

A variety of berries such as blackberries and huckleberries grow wild all over the mountains at Higher Ground. Picking them is a favorite job for children while the adults preserve them in recyclable canning jars. They are mixed with other fruit and goat cream to make heavenly ambrosia; and are also used in bagels and ice-cream. Blackberry, huckleberry, herb, and onion bagels prepared in the bakery are spread with feta cream cheese made from goat's milk from the Higher Ground dairy.

Deviled eggs are a favorite for the children who gather the fresh eggs each morning from the chicken coop. Hens roam freely over an acre or so of uncultivated ground and lay their eggs in clean nesting boxes. The children learn to take only the eggs the hens leave behind, never disturbing a clutch the mothers decide to hatch. The dairy runs on the same philosophy. The kids nurse until satisfied and the milkers take whatever is left. With good feed and plenty of fresh water, the nanny goats always produce enough milk for everyone.

Smoked trout and jerkied buffalo meat are the mainstay at Higher Ground. Students from the Higher Ground Wilderness School learn to hunt and fish the traditional Native American way with hand-hewn weapons. The life of each animal hunted is sacred and is honored with prayers of thanksgiving—and every part of the animal is used. The hides are skillfully removed and brain-tanned to create leather for moccasins, clothing, and drumheads; the bones and antlers are saved for buttons and jewelry; the sinew is removed and split for sewing thread; hoofs are made into glue; and teeth are used for bangles for sacred rattles.

All creatures play a precious part in the great circle of life—where life begets life and death is only an illusion of the separation sprung forth from the belief that spirit cannot exist without the body.

"To be in good relation with all our relations" is the community intention at Higher Ground, which the White Buffalo Calf Woman taught her ancestors long ago. This means being in harmony with all things on Mother Earth, including the stone people, the plant people, the water people, the winged-ones, the four-leggeds, the two-leggeds and the standing people (trees). All kingdoms on the Earth are to be recognized and honored as part of God's kingdom—for each contains the spirit-that-moves-in-all-things. Each is sacred and holy and only through the right use or "righteousness" of human beings can they also be included in the sacred hoop of life.

The strong will of humans to dominate and control rather than to surrender to the great circle of life causes sin, a separation within oneself from all of life and the Great Spirit. This separation caused nearly the total annihilation of life upon Sacred Mother Earth. Grandma Jesse's vision in creating healing centers such as Higher Ground is to assist humankind in becoming aware of their great sins or separations within themselves and freely relinquish them to reconnect into the great circle of life.

At Higher Ground all things act and live in harmony because they act and live in harmony with the Great Spirit or "Holy Spirit." They thus become holy or wholesome because all things—all life—are considered part of the whole. Life becomes a celebration of gift-giving. Each recognizes the great gifts they have been given from the Creator and extends those gifts to one another.

The bakers and cooks extend their culinary gifts given them from Great Spirit in delicious foods and meals prepared for their beloved family of friends at Higher Ground. The gardeners utilize the precious gifts of Mother Earth in raising wholesome food to delight and satisfy the appetites. Carpenters, craftsmen, seamstresses, artists, teachers, etc., all have their own special talent given from their creator that they desire to share in order to help heal and build the community so that it will become a strong eco-village—a village ecologically and economically sustainable.

Healers, using all different modalities of healing, extend their healing gifts from Great Spirit to help heal the separations within the individuals and in community. The more loving energy that is generated and extended, the more it becomes everyone's vision of heaven on earth—the vision everyone's heart is anxious to manifest—an intentional community where soul-mates gather to live in perfect love, freedom, joy, and peace. That is the meaning behind the name "Higher Ground."

Grandma Jesse is filled with contentment as she sips a cup of her famous Higher Ground "Green Drink". This is another one of her visions made manifest as she desires to share the health benefits of her sacred herbal formula with others. Green Drink helped sustain her through thirteen pregnancies and fortified her milk to nurse thirteen strong, healthy babies. Now it helps keep her youthful and vibrant to do the work that Spirit has inspired her to do. At 70 she is still radiant.

She looks over the panoramic view of Fire Creek Valley where she has manifest her vision of Higher Ground for all to see and participate in. Fields of herbs are in the vigor of first growth—alfalfa, spearmint, peppermint, horsetail grass, stinging nettle, comfrey, catnip, yellow dock, dandelion, raspberry, plantain and St. John's Wort, each in its separate field awaiting the time of harvest to be extracted into different Green Drink formulas. Higher Ground spring water is then added to the extractions and bottled as Green Drink. Higher Ground ships millions of bottles a year to nearly every supermarket, health food store and convenience store throughout the nation, providing health benefits for each person purchasing and consuming the product. Green Drink is one of Higher Ground's many thriving businesses that not only provide a sound economic base for a thriving ecovillage, but also provide a valuable service to humankind.

Higher Ground also provides other valuable services. At the Heartsong Living Center, the latest in holistic health therapies are available such as massage, hot stone therapy, aromatherapy, Shiatsu, Ashiatsu, Thai yoga, Watsu, Nirvana, Reiki, Theta and others. Grandma Jesse's famous "Nu Yu Total Body Renewal System" has become legendary as thousands of people from all over the country come to participate in this life-changing rejuvenation process. This program is reinforced by the natural healing benefits of living at Higher Ground with its clean air, pure water, organic food, and wholesome companionship. And, of course, the Garden of Eden Biodome—inspired by Buckminster Fuller's tensegrity design—offers the finest in hydrotherapy and water recreation with its tropical atmosphere of waterfalls, hot-springs pools, natural slides, tropical plants and exotic fruit trees—not what one would expect in the mountains of Montana! How could any health therapy surpass a warm soak in the hot-springs pool; or a cold plunge after sliding down naturally-designed slippery slides? And how many faltering relationships have been revived under the midnight moon when the sense of being Adam and Eve before the "fall" revitalized both romantic sense and spiritual purpose?

Grandma Jesse smiles recalling the erotic nights spent with loved ones in the biodome's starlit gardens. She looks at it now as it glistens in the sunlight on the south hill atop the Heartsong Living Center—another one of her experiments in appropriate technology. The hexagon-shaped Light Center was modeled after the body's chakra system with each wing or section representing a chakra or energy center. It truly is a temple of light—just like the body is—to house the Holy Spirit.

The outside structure was made from shredded recycled tires. The shredded rubber material is mixed with an inert acrylic base and poured into forms to create the walls of the building. The plumbing and electrical inserts are built into the forms before the mixture is poured—providing for problem-free access. The rubber is self-insulating eliminating any need for added insulation. Rubber is also water-proof, sound-proof, UV ray-proof, wind-proof—making for an ideal recycled building material. A fire-retardant material is added to the mixture along with appropriate acrylic pigments for each section's coloration, according to the chakra color. The biodome on top of the donut-shaped hexagon infuses white light, representing the crown chakra, and diffuses it into the different incremental spectrums of light or color. It also acts as a passive solar collector along with the hydrotherapy pools, which help heat and cool the entire facility for energy efficiency.

The main level of the Light Center is the shared community space. Each area or section represents a different chakra or energy center; for example, chakra one—the conference room, chakra two—therapy rooms, chakra three—work-out area and retail center, chakra four—food-bar and informal dining area, chakra five—the entertainment center, chakra six—library and meditation room. The second level contains the private living area in which each individual or couple has their own bedroom/bath suite. This allows for personal "sacred space" and individual alone (all one) time for self-contemplation.

Other housing options at Higher Ground include a tribal lifestyle—a teepee village for those wishing to experience the benefits of Native American living. Instruction in living only from what the land affords includes classes from experts in fields of wilderness survival, wild-crafting, plant medicines, Native American folklore, crafts and ceremony. Gifts are exchanged freely for instruction rather than required fees.

And so it is for all services rendered at Higher Ground—each exchange is a gift offered in loving service to companions on the path of wholeness—as each recognizes from whence those gifts originate.

More conventional individual housing is also available in ecologically and economically sustainable domains. All add to the feeling of community or "together in oneness," which is what Jesse has taught "community" actually means. Individuals recognize that not everyone is on the same level of enlightenment and that there is room enough for everyone's individual uniqueness and growth.

The ideal Utopian community at Higher Ground is an example of "unity in diversity," God's harmonic kingdom. Government is simple—teach correct principle and they govern themselves. All decisions are made on the principles of equity and common consent, allowing for each person's voice to be accounted for.

Recycling is almost a religion for the communitarians as they recognize the great cycle of life, giving gratitude for the gifts given and then returning the excess or unused portions into the "re"-cycle of life. Therefore composting table scraps becomes a habit, using indigenous, recyclable products a must, and consuming only that which is required for joyful existence is a way of life at Higher Ground. Indulgence and waste are frowned upon, for when one person is in sin (separation within), the whole community is affected. Just as the whole is much greater than the sum of its parts, so does "dis-ease" or an out of harmony condition have an adverse effect upon the entire community. Only through living the Golden Rule could the disease of sin be healed and individuals returned to harmony and wholeness. Through this one great law—do unto others as you would have others do unto you—communitarians at Higher Ground maintain perfect harmony and balance.

"Grandma Jesse!" shout Justin and Josiah. Her eight and ten-year-old grandsons had been busy hand-churning the ice-cream. "The ice-cream's ready! Can we have the cake and ice-cream now?"

Grandma Jesse turns from the view across her beloved valley. "Oh blessed, what sweet boys you are!" she exclaims, coming to hug them. "To think you two boys have been churning that ice-cream while everyone else feasted. Have you youngins eaten anything yet?"

"Oh yes, Grandma, we ate," Justin assures her. "We each took turns churning while the other one ate. We're ready for the cake and ice-cream!"

"Oh bless your hearts, and so we shall. Ashley!" she calls loudly. "Light the candles. We're ready to cut the cake."

Ashley, a strikingly beautiful woman in her late forties, carefully lights all 70 candles on her mother's birthday cake. She carefully carries it to her mother and sets it on her lap, being careful not to let any of the candles blow out by the breezes on Marriage Mountain. Everyone gathers around Grandma Jesse to sing the traditional "Happy Birthday" song in a beautiful harmony concealing Grandpa Karl's off-key voice.

Grandma Jesse takes a long, deep breath, then blows softly and gently, extinguishing all of the candles except one. In an instant, a breeze catches the little flame and it flickers out.

"Wow, Grandma...did you see that!" exclaims Josiah, eyes wide open as everyone claps in delight. "You must have wished one powerful wish to have that magic happen!"

"Grandma Jesse, what did you wish for?" inquires young Karly.

"Don't ask Karly!" exclaims Josiah. "If you tell anyone your birthday wish, it won't come true!"

"Oh, Karly," interjects Jesse quickly. "It's okay to ask questions about things you're curious about. Never be afraid to ask questions—even the hard ones. Otherwise you will never get the answers, and then you may never know. As for my birthday wish—to tell you the truth, my dear ones, I didn't have a wish to make. All of my wishes have already come true."

Grandma Jesse spreads out her arms, taking them all into the circle of her love. In the background, the sun shines on Heartsong Living Center, reflecting golden light from the glass of the Garden of Eden Biodome.

Delaney, another one of Jesse's beautiful daughters, hands her mother a cake knife to cut her birthday cake. She holds plates already dipped with ice-cream as Jessie serves the cake.

As Delaney returns the platter to the table, Jesse savors the first bite of her own serving. "Mmm...spiced applesauce cake and huckleberry ice-cream... my favorite!"

Chapter Four

Near Death

Jesse finishes her last bite of cake as her six lovely daughters gather around her. Ashley is the first to speak, "Mom, we've all heard the 'children's version' of how you met Dad. We've all been curious to know the *rest of the story.*"

"Yea, Mom," Delaney pipes in. "We want to know the *good* stuff. The stuff you haven't told us before." The other four daughters nod in agreement.

"Well, I wouldn't exactly call it *good* stuff, Delaney," sighs Jesse. But I guess if you really want to know the rest of the story, it's about time you were told. Sit down on the buffalo robe and get comfortable—it's a dandy."

Her six daughters scoot their little ones off to play with Dads, Uncles and Grandfathers and then surround their mother in a private women's circle.

Your Dad and I had a glorious night in each other's passionate embraces that Valentine's eve. It was a bit of heaven on earth for both of us and we knew then, more than ever, that we belonged to each other. But there was one small glitch to the story…Norman. Karl was emphatic that it was my job to clear up that little glitch. As we parted that blessed Valentine's Day, I promised I would be returning soon with my full, unfettered heart to give him. As I drove down Logan canyon in Norman's white Pontiac, I became more and more apprehensive of how I would handle the situation—let alone how Norman would handle it. It was worse than I could have ever anticipated.

When I got back to the apartment, Norman was *absolutely livid!* He pulled on his coat and said he was going to kill himself after I told him where I'd been all night. I followed him as he headed for the car—convinced he was serious. I slipped in beside him in the passenger seat as he slammed the door shut. He revved up the engine and skidded out of the parking lot before I had a chance to think twice.

Norman drove recklessly at breakneck speed up Big Cottonwood Canyon. I saw my life flash before my eyes on several occasions as we nearly collided head-on with several cars. I didn't know if Norman was doing it just to terrorize me or if he was serious about killing himself, me, and anyone else that got in his way. Relief overcame me as Norman pulled over into a parking area half way up the canyon. He silently got out of the car and started up a hiking trail. I followed fast on his heels.

"Norman!" I screamed. "Are you *crazy?!* Please...let's try and be reasonable about this. Can't we just sit down and talk. We can figure this out together." By that time my voice had become breathless.

Norman stopped and turned around. "Why should I trust anything you say? You've betrayed me so many times I've lost count. You're nothing but a *whore!*"

His words struck deep. Perhaps he was right. Maybe I was a whore—or maybe I just didn't know what love was. All I knew, in that moment, was that I loved Norman...I loved him enough to do *anything* to stop him from killing himself.

Norman sat down on a large boulder a few yards ahead. I caught up to him and collapsed breathlessly beside him. We sat in silence for a moment. Cautiously, I broke the silence. "Norman, you know...maybe you're right. Maybe I am just a whore. I'm just so confused right now I don't know what I am. When I'm with you my heart tells me how much I love you—how much I love being with you. But then when I'm with Karl..."

"*I don't want to hear any more about Karl,*" Norman demanded with a hand gesture across his face. He then reached in his pocket and pulled out a small plastic bag filled with white powder. He fingered it in his hands. "You know what this is, Princess? It's a dime-bag full of the purest heroine there is. A pinch of this stuff will send you into a high that will last all day." He opened the bag, licked his little finger and covered it with white powder. "Yea, this is really good shit," he said licking the powder off. "Do you know what a whole dime-bag full of this shit will do? It will blast your head off!"

I looked at the bag and wondered if this was the way Norman was planning to kill himself—overdosing on heroine. "*Please*, don't do this to yourself," I begged. "I promise if you give me just one more chance, I'll be faithful to you. I'll forget about Karl and do *anything* you want. I promise."

"Will you get high with me, Princess?" Norman tested.

"Norman, you know how I feel about drugs. There are other ways to get high...if you know what I mean." I pressed my body close to his, wrapped my arms around him, and began nibbling on his ear. "You know we could be making love right now rather than fighting," I whispered softly. Norman's body softened and a tear began to fall.

"Princess…you really *do* love me, don't you?" he questioned, grabbing both my arms and forcing me to look into his intensity. His eyes were aflame with love as they pulled me into his heart. I melted into his arms as he relaxed his hold on me. Our lips collided and we kissed with the passion of two teenagers lost in a forbidden love. The previous events seemed to fade into oblivion as Norman unzipped his pants revealing his enormous erection. It throbbed in my hand as he eagerly stripped off my clothes. The rock beneath us was cool against our naked bodies as we made love in the February sun.

I really wanted to keep my promise to Norman and be faithful to him. For the next few months I focused all my love towards him and shoved any thoughts of Karl to the back of my mind. But my conscience was killing me. Until I met Norman, I had been a devout Mormon girl never dreaming I would get this far off the track. Here I was living with a guy in a dumpy basement apartment, struggling to make ends meet while we both went to school. Norman paid his tuition with grant money and Social Security. I was trying to pay my tuition by cleaning and doing odd jobs for Norman's grandmother. It was a far cry from the life I was used to. It was months since I'd spoken to my parents. I wondered if they were even concerned about me or had written me off as a black sheep. No matter how hard I tried, I couldn't come to peace with myself. Then one night I decided to do something I hadn't done for a long time. Pray. I prayed for some answers…answers to how I could straighten out my life that had become a total mess.

The next day there was a knock at the door. It was Charlene, my best friend from high school. Her arms were loaded with bags of groceries as I led her to the kitchen table.

"Whew, I can't believe I finally found you," she said as I simultaneously exclaimed, "How did you ever find me!"

"I stopped at your parents' house and they told me where you were living. They mentioned that you might need some help." She started unpacking the groceries—bread, cheese, fruit, vegetables, meat, canned goods—my eyes began filling with tears.

"Charlene, how could you? How can I *ever* possibly thank you?"

"Oh, don't thank me. Thank your dad. He paid for it. I'm simply the delivery person." Her arms free, she wrapped them around me in a warm embrace. My tears spilled over into rivulets. "Come on, Jesse," she said, leading me to the couch. "Let's talk."

In the next hour or so, I poured out my heart to Charlene, expressing how miserable I was. I didn't know what to do. I admitted I loved Norman, but not in the same way he loved me. I felt he was sucking the life out of me, and I needed a way out—without killing him.

"Have you talked to your parents lately, Jesse? They're really concerned about you."

"How can I talk to them—how could they possibly understand? All they ever do is lecture me about what a sinner I am and how I need to repent and go back to church. Well, I admit I'm a sinner and need to repent. But how can I do it without it killing Norman?"

Charlene thought for a moment. "Well, if it's okay with you, maybe I should go talk to your parents about how you feel. Together, maybe we can come up with a solution."

"Well, their last solution didn't work out so great. Running away from my problems is no solution. I suppose you heard the story about going to California to live with Martha." I recounted the story and we both laughed at how desperate Norman had been to drive clear out to California to rescue me.

"So what about Karl?" Charlene asked curiously. "Do you ever talk to him?"

"Are you kidding? Norman would kill me...not to mention himself, if I ever dared speak of him. Karl's just a lost chapter in 'what could have been.'"

"Well, if you and Karl are meant to be together, like it looks like to me you are, then God will find a way. Trust him."

Charlene got up to leave and I hugged her as my eyes filled with tears again. It felt so good to be connected again to the pleasant parts of my past. Charlene had always been a good friend to me, in spite of me.

A few hours later, as Norman and I were enjoying a fine dinner prepared with the food that Charlene had brought over, the phone rang. It was Dad.

"Hey, honey, how's it going?" he asked, concerned.

"Just fine, Dad. Norman and I are getting along just fine..." my voice started to falter with emotion. "Oh, by the way thanks for the...I mean, just thanks."

"Is Norman there?" he questioned.

"Yes," I replied blankly.

"Let me talk to him for a minute, will ya."

"Sure." I handed the phone to Norman. "It's my dad. He wants to talk to you."

They talked for a few moments and then Norman handed me back the phone. I said my "goodbyes" to Dad. He had talked Norman into going out with him for a "man-to-man" talk. He was on his way over. My spirits lifted. Maybe there was hope.

I greeted my dad with a generous hug as Norman grabbed his coat. A couple hours later Norman came to bed either drunk or exhausted. I questioned him on the results of the male-bonding encounter.

"I think your dad's gay," remarked Norman, nonchalantly. "I mean all he could talk about was our sex life. He even asked me how big my dick was."

"You must be joking!" I exclaimed outraged. "My dad would *never* talk to you about *that*…or to anyone for that matter! He doesn't even talk about sex to my *own* mother!"

"Maybe that's his problem," replied Norman numbly dozing off to sleep. I was still outraged! How could Norman say such things about my dad—even in jest? I pushed him out of bed and he crashed to the floor. This was one night Norman would be sleeping on the couch.

The next morning I was startled awake by Norman pounding on the locked bedroom door. "Jesse, come quick! You've got to see what's stuck in the front door!"

I reluctantly slipped out of bed and dragged myself to the living room to see what Norman was insistent about. *"Oh, my God!"* I screamed at the sight of a *twelve-inch butcher knife* stuck in the front door!

"*See*…what did I tell you? Your dad *is* crazy!" Norman exclaimed.

During the next few days, I could feel myself coming down with something dreadful. My body ached all over and I was running a fever. I could tell my tonsils were swollen as they often did when I became over-stressed. I knew I needed some medical help to get rid of the tonsillitis that had plagued me over the years. And neither Norman nor I could afford the medication. I was eighteen and still on my parents medical insurance. I begged Norman to take me home so that I could get the medical care I needed. Conceding to my suffering, he finally drove me home.

Home. What warm feelings that word evoked. My younger sister, Rosalie, was still living there and it was good to connect with her after so many months living on my own. It was also good to be under my mother's concerned care in spite of our strained relationship. And my dad, well, he was on the road during the week as a traveling salesman, and only home on weekends. And, to tell you the truth, the whole episode with the butcher knife I'd passed off as a bizarre incident. I knew my dad wasn't crazy…let alone gay. I was still angry at Norman for the things he'd said about my father.

First thing in the morning, Mom took me to the family doctor for an exam. Dr. Huntsman diagnosed me with severe tonsillitis and recommended a tonsillectomy as soon as they could contain the infection. He ordered a large injection of Penicillin. I waited nervously on the examination table for the nurse to arrive. I hated shots. I looked over at my mother sitting against the wall as the nurse pulled down my jeans for the injection. Boy, I hadn't done this since I was a kid, I thought as I felt the needle plunge through my skin. I felt a stinging sensation as the medicine entered my blood stream.

Then everything went black. The next thing I knew I was laying on the examination table with a strange ringing sound in my ears. Then the strangest thing happened. I could feel my body go numb from the bottoms of my feet upward to my head. It actually felt like my spirit was leaving my body from the bottom on up. Then I got real scared. I started to scream at my mother to help me, but I could see her just sitting against the wall, looking concerned. I screamed again at her even louder, "Help me Mom, HELP!" But still she didn't respond. What was wrong with her? Why couldn't she hear my cries? She acted as if I were dead. *Dead.* The word entered my soul with a chilling, frightening effect. Could it be that I was actually dying there on the examination table? The nurse was nowhere to be seen. How long had it been? No! This couldn't be happening to me! I had my whole life ahead of me and I was damned if I was going to be cheated out of it!

"Please, God!" I cried with the same fervor as before. *"Please* don't let me die! I know I've made a total mess of my life, but I just need some time to straighten it all out. Please give me another chance…PLEASE!" I pleaded with God, asking him for forgiveness for my many mistakes and blatant sins. I promised if he would let me live, I would change my ways.

Moments later the doctor emerged with a white-faced nurse. I was coming to as he checked my pulse. "It looks like she had a reaction to the Penicillin. We'll have to note that in her records and put her on another antibiotic. I'll write up a prescription for Amoxicillin." He returned with the prescription and advised me to take it easy during the next week in preparation for surgery. He had set up a tonsillectomy on May 15—two weeks before my nineteenth birthday—so my dad would be able to put it on his insurance.

The tonsillectomy was far worse than I ever imagined. My throat was so sore that I could barely swallow my own saliva. Attempting to eat anything was pure torture. I sipped warm broth and juice through a straw in sheer agony. And talking was impossible. When Norman called to see how I was doing, I could merely moan a reply. My parents refused to let Norman visit me because he was on their black list. Frankly, I didn't really care to see Norman—I was still bitter over his accusations about my dad.

One day when I was resting in my parents' bedroom, the phone rang. No one was available to answer it, so I made the attempt.

"Hello," I squeaked.

"Hello," came a male voice at the other end. "I'm calling to let you know about your dad. He's homosexual. He's tried to molest boys in the scout troop, and I wanted to let you know so that someone will do something about it. I think it's your responsibility to tell the bishop."

My strained voice was defiant. "Norman…if this is another one of your sick jokes, you've gone too far. You can go to hell as far as I'm concerned. Can't you see I'm in no condition to deal with this garbage?! If my dad were queer, then how come he has six kids?" I slammed the phone down. My throat ached. I swore I would never speak to Norman again.

By the following Friday, my throat felt much better and I was able to eat and talk. I decided to phone Karl.

"Hello," answered a female voice, which I assumed to be his mom's.

"Hi, is Karl there?" I inquired.

"No, he's gone right now. Can I take a message?"

"Sure…this is Jesse. Could you have him call me at my parents' house?" I gave her the number and hung up disappointed. I wondered if he'd call me—it had been over three months since I'd seen him.

That evening the phone rang. It was Karl.

"Hey, Jesse, what's up?" His voice sounded cheerful. "It's good to hear from you after such a long time."

I proceeded to update him on the current events since I'd seen him last. I apologized for not keeping in touch, but the situation was impossible. I told him I'd love to see him again—whenever possible.

"Why don't you come up tomorrow for a visit," he offered. "I'd come down but I'm still without wheels. I'm waiting for the insurance settlement from my accident to buy a new car."

"Well, I'd have to borrow my dad's car…but he's been pretty good about things since my surgery. Do you mind if I bring my sister, Rosalie. She's been anxious to meet you."

"Not at all," he replied. "How old is your sister?"

"Fifteen."

"Is she allowed to date?"

"Well, I guess so. Why, what do you have in mind?"

"Well, I have a friend, Bob, who's in town from California. He's a bodybuilder and maybe we can line him up with your sister."

"Sure, I think Rosalie might be interested. I'll ask her. If not, I'll call you back and we can make other arrangements."

Rosalie was thrilled at the idea of meeting a real body-builder from California. Not to mention Karl whom I'd told her so much about.

The drive up to Logan zoomed in my dad's silver Cordoba. My throat was feeling much better as I jabbered girl-talk with my sis. We were both anxious to meet Karl and Bob at the designated spot—JBs.

The familiar feeling of butterflies danced in my stomach as we entered the restaurant. I quickly scanned the tables to see if Karl and Bob were there. I couldn't see them, so Rosalie and I secured a booth close to the door. We sipped on ice water and chatted anxiously as two gorgeous guys walked through the door. My mouth dropped and my heart skipped a beat as I recognized the tanned blonde to be Karl. I couldn't believe it was him! His bleach blonde hair flowed down across his tan shoulders. His tank top rippled with muscles I hadn't seen before. He was an absolute Greek Adonis. And Bob—he was a brunette version of Karl only buffer!

Rosalie was star-struck as the two hunks strutted over to our table. "Jesse, how have you been?!" exclaimed Karl as he reached out for an affectionate hug. He slid in beside me and Bob slid in beside Rosalie. We both remained speechless as they ordered coffee—and remained in a dream-state during the entire lunch. Karl suggested we go to a friend's apartment to relax and catch up on things. His friend, Dave, wouldn't be there and Karl knew he wouldn't mind us dropping in. I was game and so were Rosalie and Bob.

Upon our arrival at the apartment, Karl led me to the back bedroom. "You guys will be okay if we talk privately in the bedroom," he remarked to Bob and Rosalie as they found a comfortable spot on the couch. I was a bit uncomfortable leaving Rosalie alone with Bob, but before I could say anything, Karl had closed the door. Immediately, he had his mouth all over me and his hands were undressing me at the same time. Any resistance to him fell to the floor along with my clothes. I began undressing my Greek God, anxious to see what lay beneath. His cock, excited by my touch, saluted me. Our naked bodies tumbled to the bed and we made passionate love without any regard or inhibition. Thoughts of Rosalie and Bob in the other room drifted from my mind like wisps of fog. A hungry fire of passion consumed us for over an hour. My only thoughts were—why in the world had I kept Karl waiting?

On our way back from Logan, Rosalie and I continued our girl-talk.

"Boy, you two were sure hot for each other!" she exclaimed. "I didn't realize you were so uninhibited."

"So how was it with you and Bob," I replied, changing the subject.

"Well, he really tried to make the moves on me until he found out how old I was. When I told him I was fifteen—that seemed to cool his jets. We had a good talk after that. He bet me that I couldn't put both hands around his biceps. I tried hard to stretch my hands around his flexed arm—but I lost the bet. Man, I can't believe how buff that guy is. He says he works out every day and is going to enter the Mr. Universe contest in California. I wouldn't be surprised if he wins."

I was glad that Bob hadn't forced himself on Rosalie while I was in the bedroom with Karl. I felt a bit guilty leaving her alone with a stranger. I also felt a tinge of guilt because of the promises I'd made to God. I wondered what God thought of Karl's and my passion towards each other. Was He angry... or even jealous? Was I wrong to feel the way I did towards Karl—and then act accordingly? I really didn't understand what God expected of me. He's the one who created me—with all the parts that made me feel so delightful. Could it be that He was playing a big cosmic joke on all of us, tempting us with sex and then having such strict rules regarding it? I made a mental note to take it up with God that night in my prayers.

During the next month I drove up to see Karl nearly every weekend. No matter how hard I tried to keep away from Karl sexually, the temptation always overcame me. He was my Greek God sent down from heaven and I was damned if I was going to reject the gift. But what I really wanted in my heart was to marry Karl.

For the Fourth of July, Karl invited me to go on a trip with him to Indiana to meet an old army buddy, Pete, and his wife, Nancy. He told me he'd take care of the trip expenses if we could use my dad's car. I knew my dad could loan me his car only on the weekends, but I was sure I could finagle something. Since the inevitable break-up with Norman (whom I refused to see or talk to since his last "prank" phone call to me) my dad and mom were more than willing to support my new relationship with Karl—even though they'd never met him.

After a long talk with my dad about Karl's plans to take me to Indiana, he suggested that we go down to the car dealership and look for a car for me—a Volkswagen perhaps. Dad had paid half on my other older brothers' and sisters' first cars, and he felt it was time for me to have a car of my own. He suggested that I pay him back for my half as soon as I got a job. We found a cute little 1969 green Volkswagen for a thousand dollars. He wrote the dealer a check and I spent the rest of the day learning to drive a stick shift.

I couldn't wait to show Karl my new prize. The next morning I drove up to Logan to show him what I'd newly named "the green machine." He was as ecstatic as I was and he couldn't wait to take it for a spin up the canyon.

We grabbed a blanket from his house, bought a couple of meals at Kentucky Fried, and then sped up Logan canyon. Karl had a secret place in mind that he wanted to show me. I closed my eyes as the wind from the sunroof (an added feature) caressed my face. I was as happy as a Jay bird. Karl pulled onto a grassy meadow and stopped the car. I opened my eyes to gaze over a magnificent panoramic view of Cache Valley—alive with brilliant green hues. Karl spread the blanket out on the grassy knoll overlooking the breathtaking view. He grabbed the chicken meals and set them aside. "We'll need those later."

He tackled me onto the blanket and began kissing behind my ear. "You're my precious angel and I've captured you for an entire day," he whispered. He then proceeded to tickle my fancy while kissing down my neck. I was wet for him and he knew it. Moments later we were naked, vying for our favorite position on top. As I straddled him on top, I felt like a bird with outstretched wings waiting for the wind to carry me to my next orgasm. Ecstasy exploded inside me and I screamed out loud knowing that only God could hear my cries. Orgasm after orgasm rushed through my body as Karl pumped me for more. He finally collapsed on top of me in his own grand finale. We lay side by side exhausted, allowing the orgasmic rushes to dissipate. We were both hungry now and Karl reached for the boxes of chicken. "I told you we'd be needing these later."

I convinced Karl that he needed to meet my parents before we left for Indiana. It was only right after all that my dad and mom had done for me. He agreed, and the next weekend Karl took the bus from Logan to Salt Lake. I met him at the bus station.

"Well, are you ready to meet your future in-laws?" I joked as I greeted Karl at the station. "We're moving a little fast, aren't we Jesse?" Karl remarked sharply. "I'm just kidding," I replied, feeling a bit dejected.

My parents and Rosalie were in the kitchen eating dinner when Karl and I arrived. By the looks on their faces they were quite impressed as I introduced Karl. We sat down and Mom served us up some roast beef, mashed potatoes and gravy—her eyes riveted on Karl. After dinner, Dad escorted Karl into the living room for a man to man talk. Rosalie and I helped Mom clean up the kitchen.

"So what do you think of Karl?" I asked Mom as I helped load the dishwasher.

"I can't get over how much he looks like the ballet dancer I just got through painting. I've got to call Mother—she needs to come over and meet your good-looking boyfriend."

Before long my grandmother, who lived three blocks away, joined us in the living room as Mom compared Karl to the ballet dancer in her new painting hanging over the fireplace mantel. I don't know who was more embarrassed—Karl or me. After Grandma left, I felt it was time to break the news to my parents about our weeklong trip to Indiana over the Fourth of July.

"Oh, Jesse, you can't go on a trip with a boy!" Mom exclaimed. I was prepared for her reaction.

"Oh, Mom, it'll be fine. Karl's friend, Dave, will be going with us and he'll be our chaperone," I lied.

She considered it for a moment. "Well, I guess it'll be all right—as long as you promise to sleep in separate beds."

"Oh, Dave and I will sleep together and we'll get Jesse her own room." Karl assured with a side wink to me.

A few days later we were off to Indiana in my Green Machine. Traveling the hundreds of miles of flatland got tedious as Karl and I ran out of things to say. In our moments of silence I admired the attractive scenery that sat beside me. I realized that Karl and I had little in common besides our passion for each other, but I was content to enjoy the view.

Each small town we came to, Karl would stop and get gas at a convenience store. I grew curious as to why we were stopping so often and when I questioned Karl, he brushed me off with a "never you mind, Sweetheart, it's just business." Finally, when my curiosity got the best of me, I followed Karl into the store to check on him. I stood behind Karl unnoticed as he was purchasing a pack of gum. He handed the cute, female clerk a twenty dollar bill and waited as she dealt him back the change. He pocketed the change and then stopped deliberately. "Hey, wait a minute, give me back that twenty. I think I have some change in my pocket." He then pulled out the exact change to pay for the gum. The teenaged girl's eyes were glazed over with infatuation as she held out her hand to receive the change. She never knew what hit her. I followed Karl out to the car.

"Karl, I can't believe what I just witnessed in there!" I exclaimed as I slammed the door. "So is that what you've been doing all this time—short-changing people?"

"Well, somebody's got to pay for the trip," he replied defensively.

We ended up in a heated discussion on the values of being honest. I was shocked to think I'd fallen in love with a two-bit con artist. I wondered how far and deep his deception ran. Had he conned me into thinking that he really loved me? I began to see Karl in a different light and that light became very revealing and unattractive. I sat in silence, staring at the view outside the car. It was dull and uninteresting—a metaphor for the company at hand.

When we arrived at Pete and Nancy's in Bloomington, Indiana, I was exhausted both physically and emotionally. Nancy, a perfect hostess, helped us carry our luggage into the spare bedroom.

"Pete will be home from work in about an hour or so. You're both welcome to take a little nap before he gets here. I'm going to fix dinner." Nancy's words were like a doctor's prescription—the bed like an oasis in a parched desert. I removed the bed-covers and stretched my tired body across the sheets. Karl took it as an invitation for intimacy. I surrendered myself to his advances—too exhausted to put up a fight. I must admit his nurturing hands and loving lips helped soothe the wretched feelings within. "I'll let him get away with it this one last time," I said to myself as we both dozed off to sleep.

Pete woke us up as he came through the front door. He knocked softly on our door—"Hey, buddy, you in there?" Karl sprang from the bed and quickly pulled on his shorts. I covered myself with the blankets as Karl opened the door. "Hey, Pete, how's it going?"

They hugged each other as old army pals do. "Get dressed and we'll talk over dinner, buddy. Nancy's got dinner ready."

Nancy's cooking was divine. Afterwards, we settled into the living room as Karl and Pete drank beer and reminisced about old times in the army while Nancy and I sipped on wine coolers. It was getting late and we all decided to turn in early and get rested up for the Fourth of July weekend.

The next day Pete and Nancy took us on a sightseeing tour of Bloomington. We stopped at a few quaint shops to peruse the souvenirs. I purchased a few postcards to send back to my family. Karl bought a pack of gum, winking at me slyly.

That night we sat on Pete and Nancy's back porch watching the fireworks explode across the sky. Karl and Pete were still drinking beers and catching up on the five years since army. Nancy brought out some expensive wine she'd saved for the occasion, and had Pete pop the cork. We all toasted to our friendship and the wonderful time spent in Bloomington, Indiana.

"So what are yours and Karl's plans when you get home?" inquired Nancy. We had moved to a quiet corner to exchange girl-talk.

"I have no idea," I replied. "Karl's so unpredictable."

"You can say that again," Nancy laughed, nodding in agreement. "Pete and I have been hoping that Karl would find a nice girl to settle down with. He really needs some grounding…and maybe you're the one."

"Hey, Jesse," Karl interrupted. Come on over here and show Pete your tits. I swear this girl's got the greatest looking boobs on earth, Pete." Karl's staggering speech did little to overshadow his obscenities. "And man, can this girl fuck—I swear I've never fucked a girl that could have so many orgasms."

"Hey Pete," Nancy interjected. "Don't you think it's about time you two turned in for the night?" Her voice was irritated.

"Oh, let them party. It's me who's had enough partying." I stood up to leave. "I think I'll go to bed."

I needed to get out of there and away from Karl. I walked out of the room and slipped out the front door. The cool night air did little to sober me up. I realized I'd drunk one too many glasses of wine. I walked down the sidewalk of the subdivision, thinking the night air would eventually sober me up. I must have walked a couple blocks or so when I noticed a comfortable patch of grass underneath a large tree. I sat down against the tree...the next thing I realized was someone shaking me, trying to wake me up.

"Jesse...Jesse, are you okay!" Karl's voice was frantic in my ear. "Hey, what happened? All the sudden we noticed you were gone. We couldn't find you anywhere. We've all three been out here looking for you for hours. You really had us worried. Pete! Nancy!" he called out. "She's over here!" Karl's shouts brought Pete and Nancy to the scene.

"I'm sorry everyone," I apologized, rubbing my eyes, trying to wake up. "I don't know what got into me."

"Don't apologize, Jesse. We all know what happened. It's Karl who needs to apologize."

Karl pulled me to my feet without any effort to apologize. He braced me as he walked the three blocks to the house. He led me to bed—this time without undressing me or showing any signs of affection. He then spent the rest of the night partying with Pete and Nancy.

The next morning was Sunday, and we'd planned to spend the day with Pete and Nancy. Instead, Karl hurriedly packed our bags, indicating an early departure. We said our "good-byes" to our gracious hosts, and I again apologized for my worrisome behavior. Nancy's eyes were sympathetic. Pete's were unsure. I fretted over what they must have thought of me. I certainly didn't make a good first impression.

Karl decided to be adventurous and take a different route home. He steered north until we came to the Rocky Mountains and decided to drive through Yellowstone Park. We toured some of the geyser areas and finally stopped at Old Faithful Inn for lunch. Karl had been unusually quiet most of the trip and I thought he was still holding a grudge. The rustic atmosphere of Old Faithful Inn created an ambiance for romance—but I wasn't expecting anything of that sort from Karl. As we waited for our lunch, Karl turned serious.

"Jesse, I want to talk seriously to you about something," his voice sounded tender but I braced myself for the break-up speech. "I really think I'm falling in love with you." He blushed and his voice trailed off into his water glass. I sat silently dumbfounded.

"I began to realize how strong my feelings were for you when I couldn't find you the other night. I was so worried about you. I even said a prayer that I could find you 'cause I thought something horrible had happened. I can't imagine what I'd do if something ever *did* happen to you. I just wouldn't want to live anymore without you." Then came a moment of silence. "Jesse, I don't want to take you back home. Why don't you come back to Logan with me and we'll find an apartment to move into together. We can both finish up our schooling at Utah State. That way we could really get to know each other before…I mean," he started to stammer.

"Karl, are you saying you want to live together first before we get married?"

"Yes, Jesse. That seems to be the next step for me."

I thought about if for a moment. "I'm sorry Karl. Living together doesn't work for me. If you want me—you're going to have to marry me." The boldness of the "m" word startled me as much as it did Karl. Did I realize what I had just proposed? Was I really prepared for a future married to Karl?

We both sat silently eating our lunch—thoughts spinning around in each of our heads. By the time we had finished desert, Karl was ready for a reply.

"Okay, Jesse—if marriage is what you want—marriage is what you'll get." He said it so matter-of-factly that again I was speechless. I watched as tears filled Karl's eyes. "I just know in my heart, I'll never find anyone I can love as much as you. I know you're the only one for me." Tears filled my eyes as I reached over to touch Karl's hand.

"You know, Karl, I feel the same way about you."

The rest of the trip home was filled with wedding plans. We set a date for late August so we could have an outside wedding. The mouth of Logan canyon had a perfect pastoral wedding spot, and we decided to have a Justice of the Peace marry us there. No pomp and circumstance, just a quiet wedding in the morning sun with the rabbits and ducks as our witnesses. Of course we would invite our closest relatives and friends, but the big reception would be in Salt Lake at my favorite reception center—the McEwen Mansion. It was always my dream to have my reception there, and my parents would tolerate no less.

The wedding ceremony took place at daybreak the morning of August 21, 1976. The wedding rings exchanged were that of our own design. Mine, a dancing butterfly resting upon two delicate flowers. Karl's, two fierce leopards with diamond eyes protecting a marquis ruby. Each represented the animal totems, which expressed our fervent love for each other.

Chapter Five

Total Surrender

Kandice and Jasmine get up from the buffalo robe to check on their little ones who are busy picking spring flowers on the hillside. Jesse's other four daughters, Ashley, Delaney, Amber, and Serenity sat dazed, trying to absorb the details of the story. Delaney's voice breaks the stillness, "Mom, I didn't realize your marriage started out so recklessly. You've told me about some of the struggles during the first part of your marriage. But you've never told me the story about how you finally found out about Grandpa Stone."

"Yea, Mom," continues Ashley. "And what ever happened to Norman?"

"Well," their mom begins, looking around to make sure she's out of hearing range of her grandchildren. "When Norman found out about my engagement to Karl, he tried to commit suicide by taking an overdose of drugs. Fortunately, his best friend found him and got him to the hospital just in the nick of time. Thank goodness I didn't find out about it until several years later. That would have been a hard cross to bear. As for the story about your Grandpa Stone—well, let me remember…"

After Karl and I were married, Karl decided he wanted to move to California to study professional kick-boxing instead of going back to college. He'd been corresponding with a famous kick-boxer, named "Benny the Jet," and Benny had invited him to his studio in the San Fernando Valley to train. Though my original intention was to stay in Logan and finish college, Karl was intent to study kick-boxing in California. Torn by my mixed feelings towards Karl and what our future would bring, I was still open for the new adventure.

We settled into a small apartment near Benny's studio. Karl worked part-time at Sears while studying kick-boxing in the evenings. After two employment disasters as a store clerk and secretary in North Hollywood, I finally landed a job as an editorial assistant for a nationwide publishing company called Jess Publishing. I was just getting my feet wet in the writing industry, when Karl decided he'd had enough of California—and kick-boxing—and desired the quieter lifestyle of Cache Valley. His insurance settlement had paid out and Karl was anxious to invest the money in a small house in Logan. I strongly objected, anticipating a successful career as an editor for Jess Publishing. I was enjoying my job as the only female employee in an otherwise all male editorial staff. I was being treated like gold; the atmosphere was mentally stimulating as well as sexually arousing. Perhaps Karl caught wind of my attraction to some of my colleagues and decided it was time to go. I tried to resist but finally caved into his demands to move back to Logan.

We put a down-payment on a small home in Logan and Karl got back his old job at the sugar factory, hoping to save up enough money to go back to school. Now that I was married, Dad figured I was responsible for my own schooling. I secured the only job I could find in Cache Valley—pre-staining pianos at the Wurlitzer piano factory.

Day after day, I felt God was punishing me for all my indiscretions as I laboriously applied oak and walnut stain to the keyboards of upright pianos as they passed by me in the assembly line. My only satisfaction was when I got to slam the pianos with metal-tipped whips to create the then popular rustic veneer. I fantasized about writing great novels laced with metaphors and hidden meaning. Each day I wondered how long I could endure burying my talent working at Wurlitzer's. My coffee breaks were spent with a kinky girl named Sally who reminisced about her "crack" episodes. Once in a while our boss, Randy, would join us and reminisce on how things "used to be" with his wife. He was a Stake President and he made it obvious that his prestigious position in the Church did not win him any points in the sex department. I felt sorry for Randy. In fact, the only thing Karl and I had going for us *was* our sex life. Everything else was non-substantial. We both came home exhausted from work—but still had enough energy to sex ourselves to sleep.

Months dragged on at the piano factory, but I learned to endure the fate God had decreed for me. As I got more and more acquainted with my boss and co-workers, our conversations steadily declined to the "dirty joke" syndrome. One morning my boss caught me off guard and alone. "Hey, Jesse. You know what would really look good on you?" he inquired with a serious expression.

"What?" I replied innocently.

"Me!" he exclaimed with a wink and a chuckle.

I knew I'd been set up, but I couldn't help laughing out loud with Randy. It was a good joke. Or perhaps it wasn't a joke at all. For the rest of the day I imagined the picture of Randy naked on top of me. The image sent warm, erotic shivers down my spine and I began to look at Randy in a different light. Had I ever noticed before how often he was staring at me? For once I didn't turn away as he offered a seductive smile.

Christmas was a time of holiday celebration at Wurlitzer's. We all got work off early to enjoy our Christmas Party in the break room. No one mentioned that the punch was strongly spiked as Randy, being a gentleman, offered me cup after cup. Sally, my ride to and from work, decided to go home early to be with her boyfriend. That left me to find a ride home with someone else. I knew Karl wouldn't be home until late and I was feeling in the party mood.

"Don't worry, Jesse, I'll give you a ride home," Randy generously offered. Then he offered me another cup of spiked punch. I felt the warmth of intoxication removing all rational thought, translating to any man as "horny."

"I think I'd better go home now," I said to Randy. "I'm really starting to feel the effects of the punch."

Randy seemed very accommodating as he opened the door on the driver's side of his station wagon to let me slip in. He scooted in beside me and pulled me close. This could be interesting, I thought to myself as we started down the road. A mile or two later, Randy pulled onto an obscure side road.

"Where are you taking me?" I asked with an intoxicated grin.

"Don't worry, Jesse, you're safe with me."

I liked Randy…and even more importantly, I trusted him. With him being married, a Stake President and my boss—what was there *not* to trust? Then the car pulled off the road and stopped.

"Hey, what happened? Did we run out of gas or something?" I inquired nonchalantly. I then looked into Randy's eyes. I couldn't avoid the passion staring back at me. He slid over next to me and lifted my chin with an adoring hand. He kissed me gently on the mouth, easing it open so that he could slide his tongue inside. Once inside, he knew he had breached me. His hand quickly slid up inside the back of my blouse. He expertly undid my bra and my large breasts escaped from beneath. His other hand immediately began fondling them, arousing the nipples to erection. He slipped off my blouse and his warm lips began sucking on them and I became wet and out of control. I climbed into the back seat where there was more room. Randy followed. I undid his pants and reached for his penis. It was flaccid. "I'm sorry," Randy muttered between kisses. "It's been a long time." That's okay—I'll work on it and I pumped it gently with my hand. No use, it just wasn't going to make it upright. I'd never experienced this problem before with Karl—or with any man for that matter. They were always ready way before I was.

"This just isn't going to work," we both expressed simultaneously as we sat up. "I'm sorry, Jesse, but I just couldn't resist you anymore. I hope you're not mad." I gave him a sweet, lingering kiss on the lips. "No, Randy...to tell you the truth I've been having fantasies about you for awhile, too. But I guess it's just not meant to be."

He drove me home in silence and I couldn't help feeling his guilt and shame. I wondered if I should tell Karl about the incident. I hoped he'd understand. I opted for "honesty in relationship" and when I told him instead of understanding, he flew into a violent rage.

"I can't believe you did this to me, Jesse! You're such a slut! I'm going to track this Randy guy down and cut off his balls! Better yet...I'm going to tell his wife and let her cut off his balls!"

There was no stopping Karl's rage and so I escaped in my Volkswagen to Salt Lake to avoid the fall-out. I needed some time away from Karl to think things through. I couldn't believe our relationship had deteriorated to this point. Was sex the only foundation for it? It seemed so.

While I was in Salt Lake, I visited Temple Square. I ran into my first boyfriend, Mike, who was working at the Visitor's Center. I had ditched Mike while he was on his mission and had gotten involved with Norman. Mike had never known the "rest of the story." It must have been fate or good timing when I finally sat down and shared it with him over lunch.

"Jesse, the most important question you need to ask yourself right now is, do you love Karl?" Mike's face was radiant and I determined it was because he had just gotten off his mission and was still a virgin.

"I just don't know, Mike. We really don't have that much in common. I really miss my connection with the Church or should I say...my connection with God. I mean you knew me. I was the captain of the scripture chase team in seminary. I was always talking about religion—it was important to me. I mean I don't know if Karl even believes in God. I never see him praying. He seems to think he can run his own life without God. And look at the mess it's got us into."

"Well, Jesse. These are some serious things you need to ask yourself. Maybe you need to sit down with Karl and talk about your feelings and your future together."

Perhaps Mike was right. Perhaps it was time to do some real soul-searching and figure out whether or not I even belonged with Karl. Except for one minor detail. I began to feel like I was pregnant. On my way home from Temple Square, I picked up an EPT kit. It tested positive.

I called Karl that evening to break the news to him. He was in a somber mood.

"Jesse, I'm sorry for the things I said. I really miss you and I want you to come home."

I broke into tears. "I'm sorry too, Karl. I'm sorry that I hurt you so bad. It really didn't mean anything...I was drunk..."

"Don't say another word about it. Just come home."

"Well, I do have one more thing to tell you. I hope it'll make you happy. I'm pregnant."

The silence at the end of the line was filled with mixed emotions.

"You are? Well, that *is* a surprise. Come home tonight and we'll talk about it. I promise."

We spent the next eight months trying to mend our broken relationship. Then Ashley was born, and when I held her in my arms for the first time, I knew she was the most extraordinary gift God had ever given me. Words could not describe the feelings of rapture I felt being a Mom. Yet being parents also brought on a serious tone. How were we going to raise this precious angel so she didn't make the same mistakes we'd made? Mom was ecstatic when she learned that Karl and I were going to church with plans to go through the temple. Dad didn't seem so enthusiastic when he heard the news. This meant he had to go for a bishop's interview to get his temple recommend updated. I confided to him that if they would let Karl and me through the temple gates, it would be a breeze for him.

A few weeks later, Rosalie called. She sounded distressed and I wondered if something had happened to Mom or Dad. I never anticipated what she would say.

"Jesse...I guess you heard what happened to Dad. I really need someone to talk to about it." Her voice wavered with emotion.

"No, Rosalie," I replied in alarm, assuming my dad's health had failed. "I haven't heard anything. Tell me what's going on."

She struggled to get her voice back. "Well, when Dad went to the bishop to get his temple recommend renewed, he broke down and told the bishop about his...homosexual activities." Silence. "I guess he's been a closet-case homosexual all of his life and no one ever knew about it...well, almost no one." Rosalie began to sob. "I guess he's been molesting Bryce and Kent since they were little kids and they haven't wanted to tell anyone about it. I talked to Bryce this morning and he was really upset. And Kent—well, he won't even talk to anyone about it because he's so embarrassed. I guess it happened while Dad was on business trips with them. It just sounds so awful…"

I was stunned as I listened to Rosalie sob. I couldn't believe what I was hearing. But then it all made sense. Norman's accusations. The mysterious phone call. Bryce and Kent's failed marriages. Even Dad's way of always trying to buy his love for us. And then there was Mom. Dad used to joke to people that they could count how many times they'd made love by the number of children they'd had. How could they even have sex with their bedroom arrangement? Mom had insisted on sleeping in twin beds separated by sheets and blankets and then pushed together to look like a king-sized bed with a king bedspread on top. And I'd never seen my mother naked. Dad used to joke that he never did either—that she always dressed in the closet.

I heard baby Ashley in the other room crying and I said my good-byes to Rosalie. My heart was in anguished turmoil as I picked Ashley up out of the crib. I sat down in the rocking chair and undid my blouse. My full breast brushed against her face and she immediately attached herself to the nipple. A feeling of contentment rushed through me as the milk started to flow. It was soon replaced with tears as I cried out to God.

"How could you do this to me God? How could you have placed me in a home that you knew was filled with such perversions? How could you have let it go on so long to have damaged my brothers so? Why didn't you stop this horrible atrocity?"

I sobbed uncontrollably, pouring my heart out to God. I wanted it all to disappear…to go away so I wouldn't have to deal with it. At least when I was in labor with Ashley there was something to look forward to—an end to the suffering—and then a reward. But how was I going to deal with this emotional heartache that nearly took my breath away. I just wanted to die!

Then I heard a still, small voice speak to me inside my head. "Jesse, don't be angry at me," it spoke. "These were *your* choices, not mine."

I tried to ignore the voice. I knew I was upset and it was probably my imagination running wild.

"Jesse," it began again. "It was your choice to come to this particular family at this particular time. You made the choice out of love. You loved them and you agreed to be part of their healing. And it would also be part of your healing."

Well, that was one thing for sure. I didn't know how I was going to make it through this trauma without some serious healing. I figured we'd *all* be in for years of professional counseling.

"Jesse, I'll help you. Trust me. I will help you learn to forgive."

My eyes welled up with tears again. How could I learn to forgive a father who had molested my own brothers? How could I learn to forgive a mother who lived all her life in a world of denial? How could I learn to forgive a religion that was responsible for creating such dysfunction? And last, but not least, how could I learn to forgive a God who had created a world full of so much pain? How could I learn to forgive all of this? It was just too much for me. I wasn't good enough to be that forgiving.

The voice came again. "You must learn to forgive yourself first, Jesse, and then the others will be easier to forgive. You are a beautiful daughter of God created in his image, and you must learn to forgive and love yourself. Then you can learn to love and forgive others."

I pondered this as I switched Ashley to the other breast. I knew I loved Ashley as I felt her suckling my tender breast. Love flowed out of me to her like the warm breast milk. But how could I learn to love others the way that I loved her? I didn't think it was possible.

"Just open your heart to love," whispered the still, small voice. "And I will fill it."

I agreed to try. I opened myself up to God's love—just as Ashley opened herself to my warm milk—and he poured his love inside my heart. I surrendered to it...and it warmed me...healed me from the heartache inside. I knew I could go on. I knew that with God's help all things were possible. I trusted him to see me through this life experience as he would see me through all life's experiences. And my tears flowed as I thanked him for the miracle that had just happened...the miracle of forgiveness.

Six months later on December 8, 1979, after my dad was reinstated into the Church and he got his temple recommend back, Karl and I were married in the Salt Lake temple—Mom and Dad acting as witnesses. A lot of forgiveness took place in the meantime for the entire family. But as I watched the temple attendants escort eighteen-month-old Ashley dressed in white to be sealed to us for time and all eternity, I thought to myself, *"Families are forever—and forgiveness is the key."*

Chapter Six

Zion —The Gathering of What is Real

"I thought I heard someone mention my name." A radiant Elder with glowing white hair came over to give Jesse an affectionate hug and hand her a gift. It was smartly wrapped with recycled brown paper and neatly tied with a yellow ribbon. Jesse smiled up at him affectionately.

"Michael, my arch-angel," she cooed. "What have you got for me?" Jesse carefully undid the yellow ribbon and unwrapped the book-sized gift. It fell into her lap. *Zion—the Gathering of What is Real* was the title of the book revealed.

"I spent many long twilight hours doing the last editing to have it ready for your birthday. Are you surprised?"

The look on Jesse's face was self-evident. "Oh, Michael, I can't believe you finally finished it after the many hours we spent on it together. I had nearly given up hope that it would ever be completed."

"Look at the dedication on the front cover," Grandfather Michael beamed.

To Jesse—my darling, my love—whose spirit will never be contained by mind or body.

"Oh, Michael, you are the sweetest man I've ever known. You have worked long and hard to gather so much information to share with the world about what Zion truly is—the pure in heart. I just hope that the world is ready for it."

"Well, the world wasn't ready for *your* book either, but you wrote it anyway—and published it. If it hadn't been for your diligence in publishing your book I never would have found you again and been part of your community. I was so glad that a copy of your book fell into *my* hands. I never would have known the rest of our story and how you truly felt about me unless you'd written it in your book. You must have been inspired."

"Inspired or foolhardy. I'm not sure which. I've been known to do crazy things, but writing our story down in my book was one of the craziest—but at least it got your attention."

"So tell us the story about how you met Grandpa Michael," encouraged Amber, who had just joined them after checking on her children.

Well, it was my sophomore year in High School and I was excited to get involved in everything possible. I auditioned for dance club, the school play and even Seminary Choir, but to no avail. I was beginning to wonder if anyone wanted me or if I had any talent at all.

"Hey, Jesse. Are you going to go to the meeting tonight about the Seminary Spook Alley?" Charlene and I were headed for the Seminary building where we had seminary together at the same time but not with the same teacher.

"I don't know Charlene. I've just about given up hope on trying out for anything anymore. Nobody seems to want me—or maybe I just don't have any talent," I replied dejectedly.

"Well, this isn't a tryout. Anyone who wants to be in the spook alley can. I thought it might be fun if you and I were in it together. Can you imagine how fun it would be dressing up in costumes and scaring all of our friends? Why don't you come with me tonight to the meeting?"

"Well, I guess it could be fun. I'll meet you at your locker after school."

Charlene was late getting out of her last class and I grew perturbed with her as I sat waiting by her locker. "Hurry up—we're going to be late for the meeting," I rallied as we sped across the street.

All eyes were on us as we walked through the door of the classroom… late. The student in charge was explaining more in gesture than in speech the designs of "his" spook alley as we passed by in front of him. He gave us both an obvious glare and continued. As he explained the layout of the spook-alley throughout the Seminary building—a mad-scientist's room, a mortuary, a graveyard and a torture chamber—I was quite charmed by his enthusiasm. I noticed his eyes fell upon me several times and I wondered if his smile was reserved for me.

As the sign-up sheet was passed around for our chosen rooms, the student in charge came over to "check-out" what Charlene and I had signed up for.

"If it was me, I'd sign up for the graveyard room. That's going to be the funnest." The student held out his hand. "Hi, my name's Mike and they've put me in charge of this whole gig. I've worked for three years at the Haunted Mill and I guess they think I know what I'm doing. I do a lot of the make-up for the characters there. I do a *mean* werewolf, which is what I'm going to be dressed as. I'm looking for some ghoulish girls to chase after. Are you two up for it?"

"Sure…" Charlene consented, taken in by Mike's charm. Mike wasn't exactly good-looking but he did have a certain attraction about him. He looked a bit like John Denver with his wire-rimmed glasses and straight blonde hair. I was curious if he could sing.

"Wait a minute, Charlene. Before you start signing us up for anything, I want to know exactly what's involved with him chasing us around. I don't want to spend all Halloween night running away from a werewolf."

"Oh, no—it's not going to be like that at all. Just when a group of people come into your room do you pretend I'm chasing after you. We're just going to give them a show. Most the time I'll be going from room to room to make sure everything's running smoothly. So are you game?"

"Sure." I agreed. "Sign us both up."

Halloween Day arrived and the spook-alley gang spent most of the afternoon decorating. We were all given room assignments and Charlene and I were given different ones.

"I think Mike really likes me," whispered Charlene as she entered the graveyard room I was busy decorating.

"So what makes you think that?" I questioned.

"Well, as he was helping me down off the ladder after I was done hanging cobwebs, he squeezed me around my waist. Then I caught him staring at me."

"Well, maybe he was staring at the cobweb stuck in your hair," I laughed, pulling the tangled cobweb from her hair. "I think he's kinda cute and you should go for him."

It was turning late and time for make-up and costumes. Charlene and I both donned our ragged white sheets and waited our turn for make-up. Mike first led Charlene into a teacher's office where he kept all his make-up. About fifteen minutes later she came out looking like a ghoul. It was my turn next. I sat on a stool across from Mike as he applied white grease paint to my face. His hands felt seductively warm on my face—a feeling I'd never experienced before. A feeling of sensual warmth started to radiate between my legs which

I'd never felt before. I wondered what was happening to me which made me a bit nervous and fidgety.

"Sit still while I squirt blood all over you," Mike stated emphatically.

"Aaaeeee…" I screamed as the cold, fake blood landed on my chest and sprayed all over my face. "Are you done yet?"

"Yea, I guess I'm done with you. Have a look in the mirror." He handed me a mirror and a white-faced, blood-splattered ghoul looked back.

"Nice job," I acknowledged.

"Here, now you can help me with my costume," he said handing me a brown chunk of hair. "Just tease it apart and hand it to me so I can glue it on my face."

I watched as Mike transformed himself from a John Denver look-alike to an impressive werewolf. I was astonished by the transformation.

"Turn around while I get the rest of my costume on please." I obeyed and stood for a moment listening to Mike undress and then dress. I screamed for the second time as two clawed hands came around my throat.

"Just practicing," chuckled the werewolf who led me out the door.

I'd never had so much fun in my life—sneaking up behind people and frightening them. All night long I crouched incognito behind my friends and students I'd met at school…and then scared the living daylights out of them! Mike was in rare form as a werewolf. He seemed to be everywhere at once. Each time he came into the graveyard room, Charlene and I would scatter to see which one of us he would chase. It was a riot!

Near the end of the night as things were winding down and fewer and fewer people were arriving, I decided to sit down for a break. But then in came Mike. It was too late to run from him so he took advantage of the moment to act out a grand finale. He grabbed me in his arms and went for my neck. His cape came around us and instead of cold fangs biting my neck, I felt warm, furry lips caressing it. Could I be mistaken or was Mike kissing my neck? The warmth exploded between my legs again and I could hardly stand as Mike's mouth went from my neck to my lips. Oh, my God! I'm being kissed by a werewolf! And then a moment later Mike lowered me to the floor and was gone.

I didn't dare tell Charlene about the incident in the graveyard. I wondered if she'd be jealous and I didn't want to hurt her feelings by bursting her bubble about Mike. But Mike kept showing up at my locker after school to talk. He seemed to have a lot to talk about and I found him quite interesting. His dad was a Dean at the University of Utah and his family lived in the Dean's Quarters. He was a junior and already had an impressive school record. He was on the debate team, president of the German club and in the Honor Society. I was impressed by his academics as it was something I also took pride in. I was a straight "A" student and worked hard to keep a 4.0 grade point average. Mike also taught Evelyn Wood speed-reading at night to earn extra money. He eventually wanted to put himself through law school—Harvard if possible.

One day I found a note in my locker: *Can I walk you home today?* It was from Mike. All day long my heart was filled with anticipation. At the end of my last class I rushed to get to my locker. Mike had already beaten me there.

"Did you get my note, Jesse?"

"What note?" I teased.

"So tell me, what's the route you take to walk home?" he asked as we exited the school.

"Up past the gully, past the triangle and then past my grandma's house." I described.

"Tell you what, why don't I carry your books and you can lead the way." He grabbed my books and then grabbed a hold of my hand. A warm, fuzzy feeling shot through me.

We walked hand in hand up the sidewalk and I wondered if anyone was watching us. Charlene had already left to walk home with another friend, and I wondered if she was keeping her distance because of Mike. I felt sort of bad. As we approached the triangle—a grass-covered island at the intersection of three roads—I bolted from Mike like a Jackrabbit. I heard him drop our books behind me and take off after me. I felt like a kid again on my own turf. This was where the neighborhood gang would come and play football and baseball. I was heading for a touchdown when I felt Mike's arms come around me in a perfect tackle. We both laughed outrageously in the damp grass. Then Mike slowly rolled me over to look into my face. I tried not to notice the passion in his eyes. I turned as his lips landed squarely on my cheek and I struggled to get away from him. Things were happening too fast and I was scared. I got up and ran to my grandmother's house across the street from the triangle. Mike went back for our books. I waited impatiently on the front porch wondering to myself why I had balked. I certainly had feelings for Mike but I couldn't understand what they meant. I was feeling out of control—yet I didn't want the feelings to end. I opened the door and called for my grandmother. No one answered—no one was home. I led Mike inside and then went into the kitchen to find something good to snack on.

"You sure your grandmother won't mind us barging in like this?"

"Not at all. I do it all the time. She loves me coming to visit."

I found some chocolate-covered graham crackers and led Mike into the living room. He sat down in an armchair and I positioned myself on his lap.

"Open." I said as I offered him a chocolate-covered graham.

"No thanks. I'm really not hungry Jesse," he said, sounding dejected.

"They're really good," I mumbled through a mouth full of cookie. "Here, you really need to try one," I continued shoving a cookie in Mike's mouth. He slowly took it out appearing annoyed.

"If you do that one more time, I'm going to have to kiss you," he stated matter-of-factly.

I took the cookie and broke it in half and put half of it in my mouth. The other half I again tried to shove in Mike's mouth. Again he took it out and before I could swallow my cookie his lips were on mine. The warm, fuzzy feeling exploded inside me and I became dizzy. I swallowed just in time to feel his tongue parting my lips to explore the regions within. I surrendered myself completely to his passions—feeling my own desires building steadily. Then the image of my grandmother coming through the door interrupted my thoughts and I pulled away.

"Mike…not so fast," I muttered breathlessly. "What if Grandma comes in and catches us in the act."

"So what? I don't care. I just want to make-out with you, Jesse."

"Not here, not now. You just don't know my grandma. She'd die if she caught me kissing a boy."

Mike pulled my off the chair and onto the floor and started tickling me.

"What would she do if she caught me tickling you?"

We rolled around on the aqua carpet—laughing as cookie crumbs flew everywhere. Thank goodness Grandma didn't walk in or she would have thought her house had been invaded by a couple of hoodlums. We carefully picked up the crumbs and rubbed out any indications in the carpet that we'd been there. Then Mike walked me the rest of the way home past Oneida and Berkeley Street.

There's nothing more precious than your first love. I never imagined I could feel this way—so alive, so vibrant. I looked forward to each time I could see Mike and spend time with him. It was the bud of infatuation blooming into the blossom of true love.

Christmas was a special time for both of us. I learned to crochet and crocheted Mike a beige scarf for Christmas. He, on the other hand, knowing of my love for guitar music, learned to play the guitar and played John Denver's *Late Winter, Early Spring* for me for Christmas. I was deeply touched and as I sat listening to him play, I knew I was falling hopelessly in love with him. I never wanted our love to end.

Then came my birthday. It fell on May 30, and we were in our last days of school before summer break. I woke up that morning wondering what Mike had in store for me that day. He was always full of surprises. Throughout the entire day at school, no one—not even Charlene—acknowledged that it was my birthday. Mike was nowhere to be found. I began thinking that everyone had forgotten about it in anticipation for summer vacation. As I was walking home with Charlene, I finally broke down and shared my feelings with her.

"Charlene, I don't mean to sound like a boob, but did you forget that it was my birthday today?"

Charlene's eyes were painful. "Jesse, I'm so sorry. I promised I would play along with Mike's…" Her voice trailed off as a car pulled up behind us and someone jumped out and yanked a pillowcase over my head. Someone else grabbed my ankles, and I was lifted into the air and then shoved into the back seat of the car. I could tell by the scent of *Elsha* that it was Mike's lap that my face was buried into. The car drove for an extended length of time veering in and out of parking lots attempting to confuse me. Boy's voices laughed and chattered merrily as they drove. Mike's voice was never heard. Finally, the car jolted to a stop and the car doors opened. I was relieved that we were finally getting out and putting an end to this silly game. Again I was lifted into the air by my arms and my ankles and brought to sit on a carpeted floor. Then the pillowcase was yanked from my head, and I was able to see for the first time the culprits behind this escapade. A room full of people screamed "Happy Birthday" at me and in the background I could hear the words to a Moody Blues song:

> My ship sails stormy seas
> Battles oceans filled with tears
> At last my port's in view
> Now that I discovered you
> I would give my life so lightly
> For my gentle lady
> Give it freely and completely
> For my lady…

It was *our* song playing in the background and I was flooded with emotion. Tears rolled down my cheeks over a ridiculous grin as I stared at a room full of friends. I burst into hysterical laughter and stumbled to my feet. I ran to vent all my pent-up emotions—combined anger and joy—on the one person responsible for all this…Mike. Mike was at the makeshift buffet table filling his plate with goodies, trying to play innocent. I rushed over—fists raised in the air—ready to kill. He set his plate down and reached out for an endearing embrace. How could I resist? I melted into his arms and my lips melted into his. Everyone cheered as we kissed for what seemed an endless moment.

My friends all agreed, this was the best surprise birthday party they'd ever been to. As the last person departed, Mike indicated that he still had another surprise for me. I didn't think anything could top this production. As the stillness of the U of U Dean's Center settled around us, I began to feel my heart pounding in my chest. What were Mike's intentions now that we were alone? Was I going to have to spoil a perfect evening by saying "no" to his advances?

"Jesse, I want to show you something…but I need you to close your eyes and come with me."

Again I played along grateful that he didn't insist on the pillowcase again. With his hands over my eyes, he led me into a dark room and closed the door. I was getting a little nervous when he turned me around and gave me a sultry kiss. He immediately turned on the lights to behold his final birthday gift—a painting of a beautiful sunset over the ocean.

"What do you think, Jesse? I painted it myself." I was speechless. It had all the makings of a professional artist and I was impressed by his talent.

"Mike, I can't believe you painted this. I never dreamed you were such a talented artist."

"Well, frankly, neither did I. But you seem to bring out the best in me. I was inspired to create something very special for your birthday. Do you like it?"

"Do I like? I absolutely love it! I still can't believe you painted it yourself. When did you ever find the time?"

"Well, I must admit it was a real feat…in fact parts of it are still drying as I stayed home from school today to paint. I even poked my finger trying to get it finished in time, so there's genuine blood in the paint. I think it added to the effect of the sunset."

We both looked at the painting and laughed. Gently I took his bandaged finger and kissed it. And, as usual, one kiss led to another and before you knew it we were making-out in the dark.

Summer arrived and Mike and I were together nearly every day. We enjoyed hiking in the mountains, riding bikes, and tubing down streams. One of our favorite places was Rotary Glen where we could swing from a rope across a pond and land in it or go sliding down the stream on tubes underneath the viaduct. Another favorite spot was a patch of mint we would hike up to and lay down in at the mouth of Immigration Canyon. That was our "dream spot" where we would share each other's dreams.

"So what are some of your dreams, Jesse?" Mike inquired as we lay staring at the blue sky scattered with billowy clouds. The scent of mint was refreshing to our noses.

"I don't know—haven't thought too much about it. I kind of would like to be a famous writer some day. I enjoy writing stories, and my English teacher, Mrs. Brimhall, thinks I have a natural talent for writing. So what about you? What are some of your dreams in life?"

"Well, my dad thinks I should go to law school. He thinks I definitely have the brains for it. But I don't want to be a criminal lawyer and defend criminals all day long. If anything I want to be a constitutional lawyer and defend the underdogs who stand by constitutional law. That really fascinates me—constitutional law." We both sat in silence enjoying the peacefulness of the moment.

"Promise me one thing, Jesse. That no matter where our lives take us we'll stay together. Promise me that."

"What Mike," I giggled. "Are you proposing marriage to me already? Aren't we a bit young for that?"

Mike didn't appreciate my humor and grew serious again. "Jesse...pinky swear with me. Pinky swear that you'll remember this moment forever and the love that we share together in this very moment. It is the greatest love that will ever be. Nothing can ever surpass this love that I feel for you right now. Pinky swear that you won't forget me even when I'm on my mission and off to school at Harvard. Pinky swear."

He held up his curved pinky on his right hand indicating for me to do the same. Without hesitation I held up my right pinky and entwined it with his. "I promise."

When school started again, we both tried out for seminary officers. Mike decided to try out for president and I tried out for secretary. The way seminary officers were chosen is by the teachers who interviewed all of the applicants for the office. They looked at each student's church records, school records, and participation in seminary events—and then came to a unanimous decision among them. Mike's and my records were impeccable. When it came time for my interview with the seminary teachers, I was confident they would choose me. I was already president of my own seminary class, captain of the scripture chase team and continuing to pull a 4.0 grade-point average at school. As I sat across from some of my favorite seminary teachers—Brother Quincy and Brother Woods, I smiled confidently. They quickly moved through all the basic questions and qualifications. They seemed quite impressed by all of my answers. There was some reluctance as Brother Woods breached the subject of dating between officers.

"You know, Jesse, we have a policy here of no dating between seminary officers. Are you and Mike aware of that?"

My heart sank. No, I wasn't. I drew a blank and didn't know what to say...I just sat there dumbfounded.

"Well, that sounds like a stupid policy to me," I finally stated matter-of-factly. "What's the purpose for that?"

Brother Woods went on to explain how the seminary officers must maintain an impeccable reputation among their peers—an example of absolute virtue and chastity. Dating among officers tends to demonstrate preferencing and oftentimes results in romantic alliances that may be distracting to the other officers. If I were to be elected an officer, would I be willing to adhere to this "no dating policy?"

I cringed. Brother Woods and Brother Quincy both knew my answer to that. They'd both seen Mike and I at seminary holding hands and being close. They clearly knew that we were already in a full-blown romantic relationship.

"No...I think your whole dating policy stinks and I guess you should withdraw my name as a seminary officer." With that statement, I got up and left the room brokenhearted.

I was happy for Mike when he got chosen as the Seminary President. He was also chosen for President of the entire seminary district. I was so proud of him, but his seminary officer duties took up a lot of his time as he attended numerous meetings after school to which our relationship came in second. But we still had some peak experiences. He invited me to Senior Prom and it was like a fairy tale come true. After a night filled with romance at the distinguished Capitol rotunda, Mike drove us up to Lookout Peak (or "Passion Flats" as it was popularly known) behind the Capitol Building.

We both sat in the front seat of his dad's Buick looking out over the entire Salt Lake Valley twinkling in lights. The view was breath taking and my heart was beating passionately. Mike put his arm around me and pulled me close. We sat silently enjoying the view. Mike then turned to me and gently lifted my chin. His lips ever so softly touched mine inviting them to join in a sweet kiss. The sweet kisses turned passionate as if an emotional damn had broken between us. I felt like I was on a raft nearing a dangerous waterfall and it was taking every ounce of self-control not to go over the falls. I knew Mike was nearing the falls too as his hand slid up the back of my dress and undid my zipper. Then he, ever so carefully, undid my bra and my breasts were released from their bondage. His hand then ventured underneath the front of my dress. The passion exploded inside me as I felt his hand caress my breast for the first time. Oh my God—was *this* what it was like to make love—I ventured as we began exploring our boundaries. I knew I was completely out-of-control as I fumbled for Mike's zipper. His pants were damp and his crotch hard. Suddenly Mike's hand came down on top of mine.

"No, Jesse, we just can't do this. We've got to get control of ourselves and stop this before it gets out of hand." I released a pent-up sigh. I knew he was right. If we let it go any further, both of our futures would be ruined. He'd be discharged as Seminary President and probably excommunicated from the church. I'd be strongly reprimanded and my entire reputation as a virtuous seminary student would be dashed. I did up my bra, and he zipped up my dress. He started the car and we drove to my house in silence. He didn't even get out of the car to walk me to the door to give me a goodnight kiss on the doorstep. He dropped me off, and then drove off into the night air leaving me wondering.

The next day was Sunday and I went to church with Charlene and my other friends from the ward. Everyone was firing questions at me wanting to know how my prom date went with Mike. I was abnormally quiet and felt a tinge of guilt pass through me as I partook of the sacrament and wondered if I should tell the bishop what I'd done the night before. I then decided against it as I really didn't want to open that can of worms. That afternoon Mike drove up in his dad's Buick. He looked unusually disheveled in his beige church suit. Normally, it made him look quite handsome.

"Jesse," he demanded, "Come with me. We've got to talk." He then opened the passenger door and invited me in. We drove up to Rotary Glen and stopped. The sun beat down through the car windows warming us as we sat in silence. Finally Mike spoke.

"Jesse, I'm not sure how to tell you this—but I'm going to have to try. This morning I called Brother Woods on the phone and told him what had happened last night. It was hard to tell him the truth about our relationship, but he was terribly aware and concerned. He said that our relationship was *way* more advanced than it should be at our age and if we keep on seeing each other we're going to end up in trouble. He suggested that we stop seeing each other and start dating other people. There's just too much at stake here to do anything else."

My heart sank. I couldn't believe what I was hearing. Mike was suggesting breaking up and my heart was breaking. How could he possibly suggest it after all that we felt for each other?

"It's just for a little while—until we can both get back on track and get our priorities straight. You know and I know that our love is strong enough to see us through this together."

"Well, Mike. If you think it's best. I just don't know how I can live with the thoughts of you dating another person. Please give me some time to adjust to it—promise?"

"I promise. I'm not even interested in dating anyone else. You're the only girl for me." And that was that. We were forced to break up according to the same passions that were forcing us together. How ironic.

The rest of the school year dragged by as I was lonely for Mike. I'd see him once in a while in the hallways and we'd wave and say "hi." But we never dated after that. I found out he was dating one of my schoolmates who really bugged me. Once in a while I'd see them holding hands and once I caught them kissing. My heart cringed with a sick feeling of jealousy that consumed me. The love that I held for Mike was slowly decaying into hatred and I wanted to strike back at him and everything that had torn me away from him. That was when Norman came into my life.

We were both in the school play "The Unsinkable Molly Brown." I played the part of a princess and he played the part of the boy in the lifeboat with Molly Brown as the Titanic sinks. When I first met Norman, I knew from the start that he was clearly radical and non-religious. We were both off-stage waiting for our scenes. A crowd of girls was surrounding him as he was showing something off to them. I thought it was his school ring and I pretended to be uninterested. Then he got up out of his chair and walked over to me and sat down.

"So don't you want to see what everyone's interested in?" I shrugged. "Not really." He then grabbed my hand and placed a gold ring in it. "Look at the inscription." I turned the ring over in my fingers until I could read it. *God Damn It!* was on one side. *Norman Neiderman* was on the other.

"So what makes you so mad at God?" I questioned.

"He killed my parents and I'll never forgive him for that."

The next year or so Norman and I journeyed together to get back at God what had been taken from us. I went to Mike's missionary farewell where he and Susan, his new girl friend, were all lovey-dovey. I resented him and how he'd embittered me towards him, love…and God. I mocked the church and all that it stood for as I let my life slide recklessly over the waterfall with Norman. It felt good to finally unleash the passion that I had held back so long for Mike. Unfortunately, Norman was a poor substitute for the true love that I had experienced with Mike. But then I started asking myself—what is *true love?*

The next time I saw Mike he was fresh off his mission working as a guide at Temple Square. I asked how things had gone with Susan, and like me, she'd gotten married while Mike was on his mission. After that he focused all of his energies into becoming the best missionary the church had ever seen. He became an assistant to the mission president climbing the Church's ladder of success. He'd been accepted to Harvard and was planning to leave the next school quarter. I left him my address in Logan and told him to keep in touch. About a year later I received a wedding invitation in the mail.

I went to the reception that was held in the McEwen Mansion—the place we both dreamed about having *our* reception. And we both did—except with other partners. Mike had met Chris at Harvard while they were both going to school. She wasn't a knockout but she seemed very sweet. Mike appeared happy and Chris was cordial as I introduced myself to her. "Mike's told me a lot about you," she said with a slight coolness. I gave Mike a kiss on the cheek and then left thinking I'd probably never see him again.

To my surprise, three years later there came a knock at the door. Karl and I had moved up to High Creek Canyon and were renting a run-down farmhouse on the banks of the canyon creek. I now had three children—Ashley, Jacob, and Delaney—and I was curious as to who would be knocking on my door in this "neck of the woods." When I opened the door and saw Mike standing there my curiosity was intensified.

"Mike!" I exclaimed with astonishment. "What brings you up to this God-forsaken place? And how in the world did you find me?"

Mike's face was grim. "I called your mom and she told me where you were living and how to find you. I hope you don't mind me dropping in on you like this?"

"No, not at all. Come on in and make yourself at home. Never mind the house. You know how kids are."

Ashley and Jacob dropped the toys they were playing with and came over to scrutinize the unexpected stranger. Baby Delaney started to cry so I picked her up and sat down across from Mike. "You don't mind if I nurse her?" He shook his head and I pulled out a breast to quiet Delaney's cries.

Mike then began to pour out his heart to me. Last month he'd taken off one night after work just to escape the prison he'd created for himself. Chris and he had just had a baby girl together. He pulled out a picture of her to let me take a peek.

"With Chris and the new baby, the church and my new job—it's become more than I could handle. Jesse, I just crashed. It was if everyone had conspired to create a beautiful, shining suit of armor for me and then stuck me inside it and locked me in. The only problem was—they had made the suit of armor *too small*. I was feeling extremely uncomfortable as I felt myself begin to rot inside. I didn't know what to do. Chris was great about listening to me, but she didn't have any answers. I finally did the only thing I could do. I breached the suit of armor and fled. I ended up in Evanston, Wyoming at a cowboy bar. I got totally drunk and found myself the next morning in bed with a gal from the bar. I couldn't believe what I'd done! I went home and confessed to Chris and the bishop. I was excommunicated, and Chris filed for a divorce. Jesse—I really don't know what to do next. I really screwed up my life royally and you're the only person I could think of who would understand. Help me make sense of all of this."

Delaney had fallen asleep in my arms so I took her and laid her down in her crib. I then came back and sat down next to Mike and wrapped my arms around him to give him the comfort he needed.

"Let me ask you something, Mike. Do you love Chris?" repeating to him the same question he'd asked me years ago about Karl.

"I don't know, Jesse…I just don't know. Maybe I just don't know *what love is*. I mean…how could I have done such a thing to someone I loved? It just doesn't make sense to me. Things have gotten way too complicated for me."

He laid his head back gently in my arms as tears began to fall. I wiped them with the sleeve of my blouse.

"I wish love could be easy like it was back when we were together in high school. Everything seemed so *real*, and it all made sense." He paused. "By the way Jesse—I'm sorry for what I did to hurt you. I never meant to hurt you, but I felt it was the best thing at the time. I *never* stopped loving you. When you saw me at Temple Square I wanted so badly to tell you to leave Karl and marry me. I was still so much in love with you, but I knew you and Karl had things to work out, so I chose to stay out of your way. But now that I'm here with you in this moment, I'm having second thoughts. Maybe if I'd said what was in my heart, I never would have married Chris and I'd have married you instead. Life seems to get so messed up…and so does love."

I held Mike in my arms as Ashley and Jacob looked on curiously. I invited Mike to stay for dinner as Karl would be coming home soon. He agreed. As I sat across the dinner table from Karl and Mike I was filled with mixed emotions I never thought possible. I was in love with both men at the same time. I loved Karl for the history that we shared together—of bearing children together, building a home and family, and surviving through all our struggles. Yet I couldn't deny the love that I still held in my heart for Mike—my first love.

When Mike left for home, I shared with Karl the feelings I was having towards Mike. Karl was outraged and flew into a jealous rage. I defended my feelings as being genuinely honest and simply wanting to share them with him. The argument escalated to the point where I threw the remaining plate of spaghetti across the room. It hit the wall creating a blood-like streak down it. Karl took the frightened children upstairs to bed with him, and I wrestled with my feelings as I slept alone on the couch. The next morning I got up early, nursed Delaney and left a bottle of breast milk in the fridge for her later. I wrote a note to Karl explaining my feelings and how I needed to work them out alone. I then drove down to Salt Lake to try and locate Mike.

Mike had left me an address of where he was presently living. I struggled to find it in the newly developed suburb. He was living in the basement of a friend's house and he'd mentioned that I needed to ring the doorbell next to the garage. I rang the doorbell and a few moments later the garage door screeched opened and Mike appeared in his bathrobe and slippers. He looked like he'd either been drinking or hadn't slept all night.

"Welcome to my parlor said the spider to the fly," he rehearsed as he escorted me through the garage and into his basement apartment. The apartment was in as much disarray as Mike. He sat down on a kitchen stool, picked up his guitar next to the wall, and began to play.

"You still like John Denver music don't you?" he asked as he began playing the first chords to "Lady."

I sat mesmerized, listening to the guitar strains. "You still don't sing a note do you?" I surmised as he finished the instrumental. "Nah...only in the shower. And you wouldn't want to hear *that*."

He then put the guitar down and led me to a comfortable couch. "So what are you here for, angel? You look like you've had a rough night, too."

I poured my heart out to Mike about the fight Karl and I had after he'd left. I was just trying to be honest about my feelings, but he'd been so unsympathetic. Mike put his arm around me and held me close. I cried against his terrycloth bathrobe. As the tears subsided Mike gently lifted my chin and kissed me tenderly. We both knew where this was headed and after a few passionate kisses, we got a hold of ourselves.

"Jesse. Go back to Karl. He loves you, and you love him. I have no idea where my life's headed. I'm in such a mess right now I can't offer you anything. Think of your children. They need you."

I knew Mike was right. I felt the pressure of my breast milk coming in again, and I wondered how Karl was handling taking care of the kids while I was gone. Had he panicked? Delaney was probably crying frantically for her mother and my heart went out to her. I loved them. That was real. The rest I wasn't so certain.

Chapter Seven

Berkeley Woman

As Grandma Jesse is served up another glass of her famous green drink by her daughter Amber, a handsome, bald gentleman with penetrating blue eyes embraces her warmly.

"Berkeley Woman," croons Grandpa Vincent, one of her companions of nearly thirty years, "my Berkeley Woman. May I offer my gift to you?" He picks up a long, knobbley parcel from the ground and lays it on her lap. She quickly finishes the last of her green drink as Vincent drops to his knees beside her. He helps her turn the package to find the spot where the tape is easiest to remove. Even wrapping paper is carefully folded for reuse in the community. As she removes the paper, the faintest reverberation comes from within, her eyes widen even before she lifts out...a beautifully hand-carved, rose-wood dulcimer. The musical instrument is an inspired work of art created by loving, adept hands. Wood inlays of roses, butterflies and vines decorate the sides and top of the dulcimer. The workmanship is divine.

"Oh, my stars!" exclaims Jesse, her eyes dancing with delight. "How gifted you are with your hands, my darling, to have created such a wonder!"

Her children and grandchildren gather around to get a closer look at the beautiful instrument. Some handle it with great appreciation for the work involved.

"Oh, the woodwork was the easy part, my dear. The real trick is to get it to produce music. And that is where the magic of your fingers comes in."

"Oh, Grandma, Grandma—*please* play us a tune on your new dulcimer. Oh, please," her grandchildren display their eagerness for her to play the newly gifted instrument.

"Well, if you insist...but just a short tune mind you," she replies, positioning the dulcimer on her lap.

"Wait a minute, Berkeley. I have one more gift."

Grandpa Vincent removes a beautiful white with black tipped eagle feather from his shirt pocket. "I found this on Marriage Mountain the other day when I was hiking. It told me it was for you—a birthday gift from one of the winged-ones who circle about here."

He places the sacred gift in her hair as Jesse smiles. Then her nimble fingers begin to dance upon the fine instrument in a lively Renaissance tune. At the completion of the song, everyone yells for an encore. Grandma Jesse pauses, trying to think of another song. "Oh, Grandma," interrupts six-year-old Angela. "Play my favorite song, 'Heartsong'."

"Yes, Grandma, yes," joins a chorus of voices. "Play Heartsong."

With a decided smile, Jesse begins again, and everyone, children and adults alike, join in lyrical harmonies:

Heaven wouldn't be heaven without you
No, it just wouldn't be the same
Not to see you, to touch you, to love you
No, I just couldn't handle the pain

So I sit and I sing you my heartsong
Hoping someday you'll find ears to hear
And I wait, and I watch, and I wonder
Hoping someday I will hold you near

It's my heartsong I sing in the morning
It's my heartsong I sing every night
It's the song of two lovers together
Two hearts beating as one...beating as one...take flight

Life isn't worth living without you
Your love makes everything worthwhile
To touch you, to hold you, to love you
To see you break out in a smile

So I listen to hear your heartsong
It plays a tune in my heart
And I still have the faith and the wonder
That someday we'll never be apart

I hear your heartsong in the morning
I hear your heartsong every night
It's the song of two lovers together
Two hearts beating as one... beating as one... take flight

Eyes fill with tears as the emotional language of the spirit touches their souls. The divine gifts of voice and music combine, courting those who listen into communion with the Holy Spirit. It is a mystical, magical moment. The oneness they feel is the oneness God desires for all who will listen to his voice through his gift of music.

"Berkeley, you can still play a mean dulcimer!" exclaims Grandpa Vincent interrupting the mood with his resounding enthusiasm. His face beams with pride at how well his dulcimer has performed.

"Grandma Jesse," inquires Karly. "Why does Grandpa Vincent always call you 'Berkeley?'"

Grandma Jesse laughs jubilantly and replies, "Oh, don't you ask the questions, Karly! It just goes to show you're on the right path, little darlin. Perhaps I should let Grandpa Vincent tell *that* story." She entwines her fingers with his and kisses his hand tenderly.

"Oh, no, no, no... not me, Berkeley," he says shaking his head defiantly. *"You are the storyteller* and this is *your* day to tell stories.

"Very well," begins Jesse.

It was another one of those paths of serendipity that led me to your Grandpa Vincent. It was in late August of 1991. I was eight months pregnant with my eighth child, Joshua, and feeling uneasy about the delivery. We were living in the Montana wilderness in a teepee with no phone, electricity or running water—working hard to get our log home finished before winter. I'd done natural deliveries with most of our children with Karl acting as midwife, but nothing this primitive. I decided to seek advice from a good midwife in Salt Lake and so I left Karl and the children on the mountain. Karl wasn't too keen on being left with all of our children, but I felt it was necessary for my health and the baby's. And by now I had learned to listen to my heart—or my inner voice—because it usually was correct.

Naomi, the midwife in Salt Lake, was concerned. My blood pressure was high and my iron count low indicating too much stress and an insufficiently healthy diet. When I explained our living conditions, she could understand why. She recommended that I take a week or so away from this challenging environment, so I could recuperate and assure a healthy delivery.

I couldn't remember the last time I'd had a week's vacation, and I knew exactly where I wanted to spend it—in Aspen Colorado at the Windstar Symposium. I'd been receiving invitations from Windstar every year since

I'd first attended their workshops over seven years ago. The brochures made it sound so appealing, with celebrities and authors speaking on the environment, spirituality, responsible action, and world community with the host being none other than my favorite singer—John Denver. But the idea of traveling alone, eight months pregnant, made me uneasy.

A little to my surprise my father encouraged me to go, offering the use of his Subaru Brat which he'd converted into a comfortable camper, calling it his "Brat-Mobile". My sister Martha, kindly offered me her emergency birthing kit—just in case. Now all I needed was a traveling companion.

I'd hoped that my younger sister, Rosalie, could accompany me—but she had a solid slate of massage clients booked for the week. She proposed an alternative. She mentioned my dilemma to a friend who had expressed interest in this kind of adventure. He said he was open to going as long as I wasn't opposed to having a "male" traveling companion. I laughed at the idea that anyone who saw my enormously advanced condition would consider that this might be a sexual adventure. However, I was concerned about how Karl might react when he found out I was traveling cross-country with a strange man—or should I say—a male stranger.

All my preparations were made to leave the next day—but that one. I wanted to spend some uninterrupted time in deep meditation, to clear out the busy chatter, to focus on the inner impulse that had brought me to Salt Lake and was now leading me to Colorado. I drove to Sugarhouse Park, a green refuge that I'd sought often during my years at Highland High School nearby. I parked my dad's Brat-Mobile in one of the parking terraces and walked across the open stretch of grass to one of my favorite spots—a bridge overlooking a bubbling brook. I stood on the bridge, listening to the music of the water rippling over the stony creek-bed. Through the meditative sounds, I was open to the voices in conflict. My inner voice was pushing me forward in a direction somehow connected with my spiritual journey, while my logical mind repeated cautions, warnings, and perceived fears. I pushed past both these present perceptions into a deeper quiet where I called upon a higher source to intercede.

I don't know how long I'd been standing there in deep contemplation, or whether I'd achieved the clarity I had come to seek, when I noticed a nice-looking man about my same age sitting on the bank of the creek in a full-lotus yoga position. His dark hair was thinning on top, although his trim body still held a youthful appearance. His eyes were closed and he seemed rapt in deep meditation.

"Curious," I thought observing him closely. I wondered if he was practicing one of the forms of yoga I'd been studying recently. I felt spiritually drawn to him and, heeding the impulse, I crossed the bridge and sat down near him on the bank. Without alarm, he opened his eyes and looked at me. His eyes were penetratingly crystal blue.

"Excuse me," I apologized. "I'm sorry to interrupt your meditation. But are you, by chance, into yoga?"

He smiled an irresistible welcoming smile without changing his position.

"Don't be sorry for interrupting," he said, his voice warm and inviting. "I just like to sit and relax in this spot and listen to the music of the creek. And to answer your question—yes, I've studied a bit of yoga, along with many other different religions. But I don't make a 'religion' out of it. And you?"

We were then off on the topic of religion and each religion's pros and cons in the pursuit of truth.

"I believe in just letting go of religion altogether and just following the path of Spirit. That always seems to work for me," he concluded. "How about you? What spiritual prompting led you here to meet me?" he inquired with his irresistible smile.

I then started to tell him about my plans to attend the Windstar Symposium in Colorado but, of course, not wanting to go alone in my obvious condition without a traveling companion.

"Wait a minute!" he interrupted in mid-sentence. "You wouldn't happen to be Jesse—Rosalie's sister, would you?"

"How could you possible know that?!" I exclaimed astonished.

"Well, *believe it or not,* I'm Vince, Rosalie's friend. The one she talked to you about going with you to Colorado!"

We both burst out laughing and spontaneously hugged each other. As he pulled me close, I felt a sense of security at how Spirit works when you're on the path of serendipity.

The next day we drove out of Salt Lake together headed for Aspen Colorado. The miles were filled with deep conversations on intriguing subjects such as religion, relationships, communication and, my own personal favorite—community. I'd never met anyone with a clearer concept of community, and I found myself agreeing with Vince over and over again—except when it came to the subjects of polygamy and vegetarianism.

Both Vince and I believed that because there was so much diversity in life, there was room for polygamy in community. I definitely believed that polygamy—or "polyfidelity," as I preferred to call it—was a more enlightened marriage system. But I felt there were strict laws pertaining to it which most practitioners weren't ready to follow. That people should be able to commit to "group marriage" and honor each other in committed marriage vows. Vince believed that the only "law" people needed to abide by was the law of the Spirit—for when Spirit directed, everything was appropriate.

I, too, believed everything was appropriate when directed by the "Holy Spirit," but how many of us were in-tune with the Holy Spirit? Most of us lived our lives by inherited dogmas or religious programs that influenced our very thoughts and actions. I used this same argument with Vince, who was a strict vegetarian. Granted, I could see Vince's point that vegetarianism was a more enlightened way of eating, as it didn't require the killing of higher life forms. But I argued that if one believed that everything had the Spirit of God—or life—then it was only a matter of choice of which life form you wished to deprive of its life. That we should use the "Holy Spirit" to guide us each time we ate.

He could see my argument and we both acknowledged that life—all life—was a gift of grace from the Creator and should be reverenced. We also both agreed that the most enlightened way to survive without depriving anything of life was to eat solely of the "gifts of life"—such as fruits, grains and vegetables harvested without depriving the plant of life. I insisted that eggs which went unattended, and milk taken from animals without depriving their young, were also by-products of life along with animals that had died naturally or accidentally should be consumed instead of wasted.

As our conversations continued to deepen and broaden, I shared with him some mystical experiences I'd experienced on the path of Spirit which I felt were quite significant to our conversation—and to our destination.

I told him how I'd been "born again" in the summer of my 26th year at a place called Windstar in the Colorado Rockies. Since then, my path had become increasingly synchronistic—as if life was a play and we were merely actors discovering the roles we had rehearsed for eons of time. I explained my belief that the whole purpose of the play was to bring us all to a remembrance of who we are and what it was like in heaven before we came—so that we could recreate it here. Collectively, we were like a big jigsaw puzzle, disassembled and flung down to this earth plane so that we could have the delightful experience of putting the puzzle back together again. But what I found so exciting and intriguing was that God, in his infinite grace and mercy, made the puzzle easier to fit together properly by magnetizing those pieces that fit directly into and next to each other. That is why certain people are so magnetically drawn to one another to form intimate relationships—as a gift of grace from God.

Unfortunately, we, as a human race, had collectively denied ourselves this gift of grace from God and had limited our relationships with arbitrary rules restricting us from using our full ability to fulfill or "fill in" more of the pieces to heaven's puzzle. I felt that it was a disservice to all humanity for men and women to deny themselves and their spouses this divine opportunity to grow. If we could just surrender to the Holy Spirit in all things, then we could truly find ourselves and how the human family fits together so perfectly.

"Here!" I exclaimed. "Listen to this song. It beautifully illustrates this concept." I plugged in a John Denver tape intriguingly named, *John Denver*. The first song I played for him was "Berkeley Woman," which he confessed was one of his favorite John Denver songs. I wasn't even surprised, and smiled as I sang along:

> I saw a Berkeley Woman
> Sittin' in her rockin' chair
> A dulcimer in her lap
> A feather in her hair
> Her breasts swayed freely
> To the rhythm of the rockin' chair
> She was a sittin' and a singin' and a swayin'
> Her cheeks were red, I declare
>
> 'Twas hard to believe
> What my eyes showed me then
> The color in her cheeks
> Was just her natural skin
> She wore no make-up
> To make her look that way
> She was a natural mama with her red cheeks
> What more can I say?
>
> Well, I fin'ly realized
> There was hunger in my stare
> In my mind I was swayin'
> With the woman in the rockin' chair
> But the lady I was livin' with
> Was standin' right by my side
> She saw my stare and she saw my hunger
> And Lord it made her cry
>
> So with anger on her face
> And hurt in her eyes
> She scratched me and she clawed me
> She screamed and she cried
> "Oh, you don't give me near

All the lovin' that you should
Yet you're ready to go and lay with her
You're just no damn good!

Oh, I guess she's prob'ly right
Oh, I guess I'm prob'ly wrong
I guess she's not too far away
She hasn't been gone very long
And I guess we could get together
And try it one more time
But I know that wanderlust would come again
She'd only wind up cry'n'

Well, now you've heard my story
As plain as the light of day
It's hard to feel guilty for lovin' the ladies
That's all I gotta say
Except a woman is the sweetest fruit
That God ever put on the vine
I'd no more love just one kind of woman
Than drink only one kind of wine

Vince joined me in the final chorus:

Well, a woman is the sweetest fruit
That God ever put on the vine
I'd no more love just one kinda woman
Than drink only one kinda wine
I'd no more love just one kinda woman
Than drink only one kinda wine

John's song definitely had the flavor of polygamy, but before we got into any more deep discussions about *that* subject, I flipped the tape over and asked him to listen to the amazing words of another John Denver song. It was entitled, "Joseph and Joe."

Joseph and Joe
The priest and the cowboy
The places they've been to
The spaces they're in
For a time between storms

At the side of a mountain
With another man's fam'ly
Fam'ly and friends

Joseph can give you
The keys to the kingdom
He'll put you in touch with
The spirit of man
Joe loves the desert
But lives in the mountains
His closest companion
A left-handed man
Where do you go?
If you've got no way to get there
Where do you go?
How do you know?
If you've never ever been there
How do you know?
Tell me how do you know?

Joseph I lost you
In some other city
Our paths are not crossing
We're way out of touch
Joe, how the seasons
Have drifted between us
Or is it your vision
Much greater than mine

Take heed of the darkness
Which gathers around us
A fire that consumes us
Forever to burn
Then look to the sun
For our father is with us
Our mother will teach us
What we need to learn

Where do you go?
If you've got no way to get there
Where do you go?

How do you know
If you've never ever been there
How do you know?
Tell me how do you know?

"Wow!" exclaimed Vince, his piercing blue eyes filled with obvious amazement. "That song is incredible! I've never heard it before and believe me I've listened to a lot of John Denver. Can you believe how prophetic it is? Especially if you weren't a Mormon—which I don't believe John Denver is."

"Yeah, that line about 'Joseph can give you the keys to the kingdom,' sends shivers up my spine every time. I wonder if John knew that Mormons believe Joseph Smith restored the 'keys to the kingdom' in order to set up the kingdom of God during this last dispensation of the fullness of times."

"Yeah," replied Vince his voice tinged with bitterness. "But my question is—what *are* those keys and what on earth happened to them? Joseph Smith obviously failed miserably in setting up the kingdom of God. The Mormon Church hasn't been able to set up any kingdom except perhaps the kingdom of Babylon. They not only steal money from the poor so they can build decadent churches and temples all over the world, but then they won't even let you in their 'sacred' temples unless you're a full tithe payer and obey all of their rules. To me it's just a crock of shit. I don't believe there's any truth—let alone any keys left in the Mormon Church."

Vince's experience with Mormonism had not been glamorous. His ancestors for generations had been Mormon and he had a testimony of Mormonism strong enough to get him through a two-year mission and married in the temple. But he'd expressed conscientious objections to the Viet Nam War; and when he voiced them publicly, he was excommunicated. His wife was placed in a difficult position—to stick with Vince, with whom she'd made sacred covenants in the temple, or divorce him and remain in good standing with the Church and her family. A devoted member of the church, she chose to divorce Vince.

Vince's resentment for anything that had to do with Mormonism showed up in his conversation and lifestyle. He married again, a divorced non-Mormon with a teenage daughter, and when Vince acted sexually inappropriate with his stepdaughter, it caused another divorce. His second wife, fuming over the incident after several years, was now seeking to throw Vince in prison for the violation. Vince was stuck between the proverbial rock and a hard place—choosing either to run-away from his moral infractions, or to let justice take its course.

I felt deep sorrow for Vince as I listened to his tragic story of broken vows, broken relationships, and broken homes. I felt he had, in a sense, "thrown the baby out with the bath-water" when he'd rejected *all* of Mormonism.

Granted, contemporary Mormonism held no resemblance to the original church that Joseph Smith set up. Just as water from a pure mountain stream has no resemblance to the polluted sludge it becomes after passing through a filthy city. But this was the history of all basic religion—it becomes more polluted the more man puts his dirty hands into it. But how could I deny the beautiful testimony of Christ, which the Book of Mormon contains—revealing how God is no respecter of persons and had come to visit the tribes over in the Americas after his resurrection and ascension? And how could I deny my own personal testimony of the redeeming power of Jesus Christ and how it had released me from my own prison of sin and suffering?

Whether Vince decided to shoulder his responsibilities and accept a prison sentence for his own sins, I felt he would never come to terms with himself and find a complete resolution until he allowed the atonement—the at-one-ment—to take place in his life. But part of my faith was that this very personal, powerful experience was waiting for him—waiting for the time and place when he could accept it.

As we entered Grand Junction, Colorado, my full bladder begged for relief under the enormous pressure of my pregnant belly. We stopped at a local drive-in and I escaped to the bathroom while Vince ordered me a chicken sandwich, fries and lemonade. I returned to find him in a booth munching on a dinner salad and some fries. His eyes glared at me as I unwrapped my chicken sandwich and began to gobble it down. I hadn't realized how passionate he was about vegetarianism until that moment. If only he was as passionate about other moral issues, I thought.

With our appetites satisfied, Vince offered to drive and helped me into the passenger side of the Subaru. The August heat and lunch made me drowsy and I dozed off, confident that my traveling companion would take us safely to our destination. A few hours later I awoke to a cool breeze blowing through Vince's open window. I looked out my window to a glorious view of the Rocky Mountains. We were nearing Glenwood Springs—the last leg of our journey.

Noticing that I was awake, Vince opened up the conversation again to polygamy, wanting to know my own personal views on the subject. I candidly told him I believed Joseph Smith had revealed a correct principle; but like any other truths revealed to humankind, it had become perverted. Joseph had asked God the question, "Why were Abraham, Isaac, and Jacob, as well as Moses, David and Solomon justified in having many wives and concubines?" And then he was revealed the marriage system of heaven by gazing into heaven. This system was based on perfect love and perfect freedom—a dual concept totally foreign to the neo-Puritanists of patriarchal monogamy. Difficult as it may have seemed to Joseph, he tried to teach the nature of celestial marriage by marrying Louisa Beaman as his secret plural wife in 1841, only after an angel with a drawn sword enforced the command. Because Emma, his first wife, resisted this foreign concept (she burned the first revelation), Joseph continued to marry other wives secretly without Emma's consent. Thus he violated a sacred law—the law of Sarah—which is the law of consent by the first wife. I believe this disharmony between wives was the beginning of Joseph's downfall. Because when the person to whom you are joined in sacred matrimony is vehemently resisting you, how can you possibly be successful? It's suicidal. Your marriage is a house divided against itself. It's like shooting yourself in the foot—your self-destruction is inevitable.

Not only that, but I believed that Joseph Smith, who is known to have married plural wives who were already married with their husbands' consent, probably took other men's wives without their consent. Such attacks on the male ego's territorialism and domination inevitably produced jealousy, rage and violence. Joseph Smith's assassination was inevitable.

"But I do believe the principle of polygamy is one of the 'keys of the kingdom' which Joseph Smith received through the veil and gave to humankind before his martyrdom," I concluded. "It's the only way we can get through our jealousies and the need to control. It definitely would put you through the refiner's fire."

I felt that I'd just completed an exhaustive discourse on one of my favorite subjects. Vince had listened without comment and I was afraid he might have lost interest in the subject. On the contrary, he fired another question at me.

"So, if you're so convinced that polygamy is a true principle revealed by God, then why aren't you personally living it?"

"That's a good question," I replied, a bit startled by his directness. "Again, it has a lot to do with the male-ego and its inherent instinct for dominion and control. Women have a relatively easy task of bonding if placed in a polygamous situation. Perhaps they can more readily comprehend the value of community and the real benefits it can provide."

I was prepared for a strong objection, but Vince continued to listen in silence.

"I believe that's why the principle of polygamy became so perverted in Brigham Young's time where he had *twenty-seven* wives all belonging exclusively to him. He became a modern-day King David or King Solomon. That's why there's such an inconsistency in the doctrines of Jacob 2, and

Doctrine and Covenants 132. The principle of polygamy is correct…if it is equitable and righteous. But when it is used to subjugate and dominate women, then it becomes an abomination. Jacob, in the Book of Mormon was issuing a manifesto. They needed it, just as the Saints needed it in 1890—when polygamy became so oppressive that women were crying out for equity and justice.

"But do you think that the kind of polygamy you're talking about can ever work given the history of the male ego?" Vince was more sincere than sarcastic.

"I believe it has potential…if and when men willingly choose to put their egos on the altar and get into the higher consciousness." I responded enthusiastically. It was a conversation Karl and I had had many times. "I mean, even the rational mind can comprehend the benefits of communal living—the more investment of male and female energy into a community results in a stronger, more integrated society. And we already have the results of what the out-of-control male ego has done to our modern-day society—wars, violence and bloodshed, not to mention adultery and divorce.

"Not only that but God, in his perfect wisdom, has biologically designed men and women to be polygamous creatures. Why do you think men become so frustrated when their wives become pregnant and lose their desire for sex? I've seen statistics showing that pregnancy and lactation is the most likely time in marriage for men to cheat on their wives. Some experts say that it's because their wife's attention is diverted to their offspring and not to the man. They naturally get jealous or sexually frustrated and find sex elsewhere.

"But nurturing their offspring is just as strongly inherent in women as the sex drive is in men. So what usually results is one or the other compromises their natural, God-given instincts. The wife either gives into her husband's sexual desires, thus channeling her energy away from her child, or the husband becomes sexually frustrated when his wife doesn't show any interest in him. If we would just surrender to our natural biological instincts—the ones God created in us—then we wouldn't have the frustrated, fragmented society that we have today."

Vince had another question. "So what about women—do you think they have a natural desire or instinct to be with more than one man?"

"All I can do is speak for myself and I can honestly say that when I'm in season—when I'm ovulating—*absolutely.* Not only that but a woman's capacity of achieving multiple orgasms during sex makes her far more capable of having more than one sex partner at a time. But I won't get into *that* fantasy."

"No really, I'd love to hear about your fantasies. This conversation is *really* interesting me." Vince's interest in the subject was turning to a more personal flavor.

"How do you feel about soul-mates?" I inquired, trying to steer the conversation to another subject.

"Haven't thought much about it, being pretty polygamous myself," he answered wryly.

"Well, I do believe in the ultimate reunion of soul-mates and how our ultimate path and destiny is to be reunited with our soul-mate. I believe that polygamy provides for that to happen. It also allows for the law of natural selection to operate so that a woman can select which man she wishes to father her offspring. And vice-versa for the man. He can select the woman he desires without the limitations of monogamy. If only men and women could overcome their need to control and possess each other, I believe a utopian community could exist.

"Have you ever thought of what it would be like to share your wife with another man?" I asked Vince curiously.

"Well, I know it wouldn't be easy," he acknowledged. "But I suppose if I loved her and the other man enough, I could. In fact, I think it would be quite erotic watching her make love to another man."

I heaved a sigh. "Well, *I've* had a little experience of what the male ego is capable of doing and it is *not* pleasant! Karl and I lived in a co-housing situation in Paradise, Utah for a year without even the added intensity of sex."

I then proceeded to tell Vince about how another of John Denver's songs had confirmed a decision to share a home with three other families in Paradise, Utah...and the nightmares it created. Conflicts had erupted into violence between Karl and another man until we were forced to leave. I'd hoped we could create a piece of heaven on earth in a place called Paradise. Instead, it had become hell.

I then shared with Vince my favorite song on the *John Denver* album still in the tape deck entitled, "You're So Beautiful."

> Born on a quiet morning
> Just a dream in someone's eyes
> A dream that's like a promise
>   meant to be...
> Giving rise to speculation
> On a place called paradise
> If I've ever been there
> It's when you were with me

You're so beautiful
I can't believe my eyes
Each time I see you again
You're so beautiful
That I'm in paradise
Each time I see you again

I remember some hidden valley
Where the skies are never still
And Alpine meadows burn in the
evening light
I remember the path to glory
And the way around the hill
And I remember true love's eyes
Shining in the night

You're so beautiful
That I can't believe my eyes
Each time I see you again
You're so beautiful
That I'm in paradise
Each time I see you again

And if Paradise is everything you see...
Then the place you must be coming from
          is ecstasy

You're so beautiful
That I can't believe my eyes
Each time I see you again
You're so beautiful
That I'm in paradise
Each time I see you again

Just wanna see you again
I wanna be with you again
I just need to love you again
I just wanna touch you again
I just need to love you again

"You're not going to the Windstar Symposium to listen to famous people lecture on ecology," concluded Vince. The stream of tears coursing down my face as the last musical strains echoed through the car's stereo system did not go unnoticed.

"You're going there to meet John Denver."

Chapter Eight

Rainbow Horizons

"Grandma Jesse," interrupts Karly. Grandma is tenderly lost, reminiscing past memories. "You never did tell us why Grandpa Vincent calls you 'Berkeley' all the time."

Grandma's laughter explodes the mist of tears. "Oh, mercy me...I guess I never did! Well, ever since that trip to Aspen, he's called me 'Berkeley' and the name just struck a chord with both of us and stuck ever since."

"So did you ever get to meet *John Denver?*" inquires anxious fifteen-year-old Amanda, who'd become quite a devoted fan of John Denver's—his inspired music becoming legendary after his death nearly 30 years ago.

Jesse's eyes grow misty again. "Well, I did meet him at the Windstar Symposium that year, but it wasn't much to talk about."

I was standing with a crowd of fans backstage after one of my friends, Tom Crum, had given an Aikido presentation. I'd met Tom at an Aikido workshop seven years earlier, and we'd kept in contact with each other ever since. Actually, I was anticipating talking with Tom, not John Denver, when John came through the backstage door, rushing through the crowd obviously in a hurry to get somewhere. He wasn't much for signing autographs and the sort of thing that goes along with being a celebrity. But you know, it was interesting—rather amazing actually—that when he saw me standing there, eight months pregnant and all, he stopped in his tracks and did a complete turn-around. He then came back to talk with me, as if I was the only one there in the crowd of fans.

"Hello, little Mother...when's your baby due?" he inquired with polite curiosity.

"Oh, in just a few weeks," I returned, unprepared for this chance meeting.

"How wonderful! Well, I hope everything goes all right for you," he encouraged as he turned to leave.

"Oh, I'm sure it will. Oh, by the way, John, if you have a moment. I've got an intriguing story I'd like to share with you," I suggested.

"Well, not now," he answered, still politely. "I'm in a hurry to get to the airport to pick up Whoopi Goldberg. Perhaps we can get together sometime later for a chat. See ya!"

And then he was off in his red Porsche convertible, his fans looking terribly disappointed at being ignored. "Later" never came for us at that particular Windstar Symposium.

"So, did you ever meet him again?" persists Amanda in her same line of questioning.

"Ah, now that's another story," twinkles Grandma Jesse, looking around at the ocean of eyes fixed on her awaiting the "rest of the story." "Well, perhaps we should start at the beginning when I met John Denver for the first time—another meeting along the path of serendipity."

Karl and I were living up High Creek Canyon in Cove, Utah, at the time, and we had just had our second child, Jacob. We were struggling to make ends meet financially and were still trying to make sense of married life.

After Ashley was born and we were sealed in the temple, we became passionate about religion. Karl and I both started on a spiritual path to discover more truth, so that we could become better parents to our precious daughter. I believe every one of us is a truth-seeker at heart, but for Karl and me, it almost became obsessive to find and follow the path of truth.

We discovered some real gems of truth in the roots of our Mormon religion. One of them was the Word of Wisdom found in section 89 of the Doctrine of Covenants. The value of a proper diet really struck a chord with both of us as we had been introduced to the health food movement in California. I figured if truth were truth it would speak for itself in any religion by its measurable positive results. And as we started to adhere to the laws of health contained in the Word of Wisdom we could see the results.

Jacob, our second child, was lovingly delivered at home by an experienced midwife, Joan. She was also an incredible herbalist who taught me the value of a proper diet and herbs during pregnancy and showed me how to make a vitality formula called "green drink" from the fresh herbs growing up our picturesque canyon. The drink really helped me throughout my pregnancy to keep my energy up; especially during my delivery, which was long and complicated due to the injuries to my cervix from my first delivery. But the Lord blesses us in spite of our ignorance—in this case, with a beautiful baby boy to add to our family.

By this time, Karl had become absorbed with the health field and we had used the equity in our home to put him through herbalogy and iridology school. And then came the opportunity to own and manage a health food store/restaurant—an opportunity we couldn't resist.

"Living Stream" became a metaphor for our search for truth and one of the finest health food store/restaurants in Cache Valley. It doubled at night as a lecture hall, where colleagues in the health food industry made presentations to our own clientele.

Because of the limited space at Living Stream, an idea started to develop in the form of Rainbow Horizon's Freedom Institute. It was a combined vision of a group of us living in the Cache Valley area to form a cooperative learning institute, not only for adults, but also for the home-schoolers of the valley who'd formed a coalition called the Cache Valley Home School Association.

Karl and I were also interested in the home-school movement and desired to create an institute where we could learn and teach correct principles for ourselves and our children. We felt that if we incorporated truths into our daily lives it would insure us our own personal integrity. The only hitch was that everyone involved was of the economic self-sustaining nature so extra income to pay rent or purchase a facility was hard to come by. I, as self-appointed spokesperson, tried a few different avenues to secure a facility or finances for a facility. I even wrote to the LDS Church headquarters to see if there were any old meeting houses in Cache Valley that we could use…but to no avail.

Then what I felt was the perfect opportunity for soliciting funds manifested. I'd heard about a World Hunger Symposium being sponsored by one of the senators running for re-election in Cache Valley. John Denver was going to be one of the main speakers and performers.

Now, you've got to understand my history regarding John Denver. Ever since I heard his famous "Annie's Song" and "Sunshine on My Shoulders," when I was in High School, I had been a devoted fan. But I wasn't what you called a "fanatical" fan. I never joined any fan clubs or stood in line to get his albums on the release date. The connection was more metaphysical. Each time I heard him sing it would open up something deep inside me that no one or nothing else could touch. It was as if he alone held the key to my soul—or at least the key to my heart. It was hard to understand or explain to people, but each time I would see him in concert or listen to him sing, it would reaffirm something deep inside me—that I knew him intimately in another existence.

But aside from all of that weirdness, how could I miss a perfect opportunity to see John Denver in person, in Cache Valley? But then the idea came to me. Why not sell him on my idea for sponsoring a Rainbow Horizons Freedom Institute in Cache Valley? I carefully prepared a letter describing my vision for Rainbow Horizons to give to him at the Hunger Symposium. The letter thickened as I stuffed it with information on some of the diverse classes we intended to teach at the Freedom Institute—nutrition and diet, herbalogy, organic gardening, yoga and meditation, martial arts, Cleon Skousen's Freeman Institute's political philosophy. I even included a brochure on the Joseph Smith story, which described Mormonism in a nutshell. I figured that some aspect would ignite his interest—or perhaps his compassion—and he would find it in his heart to donate a small offering of his wealth to further the cause.

As we entered Utah State's Sports Arena with hopes riding high and the letter in my coat pocket, I carried six-month-old, Jacob, in my arms. Ashley clung to the hand of a dear friend, Lindsey who was also a John Denver fan. Karl joined us in the lobby, still dressed in a suit from his job selling Living Scriptures. We selected a row of seats in a side section, just in case we needed to make a hasty exit with a fussy child. As the audience continued to file in, filling up the seats, I mentioned to Karl that *before* the concert might be a better time to give John the letter than *afterwards* when he was bombarded with fans.

Karl agreed and set off for the backstage, looking impressive dressed in his navy pin-stripe suit. I figured he'd have no problem getting past security. I waited anxiously for Karl's return, my eyes affixed to the door behind the stage. Suddenly, Karl emerged from the door and the audience broke out in applause, confusing Karl with John Denver. A few seconds later, John entered the stage and the audience continued to roar their applause. I couldn't help laughing as Karl sat down next to me, still holding the letter and red from embarrassment. He handed me the bulky letter and said a security guard had stopped him backstage—John was in meditation. Karl waited at the door until John Denver came out and tried to hand it to him then. John politely refused, saying he had no where to put it while he was onstage but he'd gladly accept it after the Symposium.

Disappointed but resigned, I settled back to wait through the World Hunger Symposium. It was a refreshing surprise to what I'd anticipated—a propaganda campaign encouraging support for political candidates actively engaged in the War on Hunger—and, of course, fund-raising. But John

Denver, an obvious non-politician, creatively described the hunger issue showing slides of different areas of the world impacted by drought, political oppression, and famine. The gaunt and distraught faces of men, women and children portrayed in the slides, told the story more powerfully than words, and I was moved to tears.

But still, I expected the same political agenda—reach deep into your personal pocketbooks and donate more CARE dollars to feed the starving victims. So absolutely ineffective, I felt, as I was reminded of a favorite poster I had on my wall as a teenager depicting a hunger victim opening up a box of Babe Ruth candy bars marked CARE.

Yet, John clearly articulated the age-old-adage that "if you give a man a fish, you feed him for a day—but if you teach him to fish, you feed him for a lifetime." He demonstrated through a progression of slides of how donated funds were being used to teach and implement farming techniques, which would effectively produce food in each unique locations.

I was impressed, but still skeptical. How could any program that the government was involved in be effective? Just look at their track record. The Forest Service with its clear-cutting of virgin forests with no appreciable profits, the Military with its outrageous expenditures building more bombs to blow up the planet, the welfare system, the public school system, the prison system—all have failed miserably to produce their intended results.

And so my own doubts overshadowed any hope in John Denver's vision for implementing his World Hunger program. The only hope, I felt, would be liberation from corrupt governments, which controlled and enslaved people in their diabolical systems. These systems created famine and starvation by politically controlling food and water supplies, preventing the free migration of nomadic tribes, and hampering the free distribution of goods in a free-enterprise system.

And the US Government was one of the worst. Look at its history of genocide and forced migration using food and water distribution for control. The US Military killed more than five million buffalo in order to subjugate a sovereign nation—the Native Americans. And they still control us through forced taxation, licensing, government mandates, and regulatory laws. Very few people realized that the only way out was out of the system. Taking this way out took true grit and "real education" which I felt the Rainbow Horizons Freedom Institute could offer.

When John Denver finished his presentation and the political candidate he was sponsoring came up to the podium to speak, I stopped listening partly because I abhor "canned political speeches," but especially because John Denver had selected a seat directly across from me. Our eyes had an unobstructed view of each other.

It's hard to describe the feelings that came over me as I looked directly into the eyes of the man who had so beautifully articulated some of my deepest feelings in his music lyrics and now in his political platform. The familiar dance of butterflies filled my entire being, courting me—no, compelling me to somehow meet this man. I felt our spirits communicating to each other as we looked into each other's eyes. I attempted to express to him, in spirit, my deep love and respect for him and his genuine efforts to better humankind. I, too, was committed to the cause of the planet, and I hoped that someday, somehow, our creative forces would be combined.

Then came the climax of the program, which everyone had been waiting for—John's time to sing. Everyone applauded their approval as John got up again and motioned for the entire Mormon Tabernacle Choir, seated behind the podium, to arise.

When the orchestra struck the first few notes, I immediately recognized one of my favorite songs, "I Want to Live." I sat spellbound as the words and music, the choir singing back-up to John, filled the entire Sport's Arena.

There are children raised in sorrow
On a scorched and barren plain
There are children raised beneath the golden sun
There are children of the water
Children of the sand
And they cry out through the universe
Their voices raised as one

I want to live
I want to grow
I want to see
I want to know
I want to share
What I can give
I want to be
I want to live

I couldn't help but join my voice along with other voices in the final verse—my eyes spilling over with tears:

We are standing all together
Face to face and arm in arm
We are standing on the threshold of a dream
No more hunger, no more killing

No more wasting life away
It is simply an idea
And I know its time has come

I want of live
I want to grow
I want to see
I want to know
I want to share
What I can give
I want to be
I want to live

The entire audience rose in a spontaneous standing ovation. Tears coursed down many faces in a passionate display of emotion. My own eyes were clouded with tears but not clouded enough to miss another heart-warming display of emotion as Ezra Taft Benson, a Mormon Church leader and former Secretary of Agriculture, reached over and embraced John Denver as he returned to his seat beside Benson. My two ideals—Ezra Taft Benson, whom I'd known and loved since childhood, growing up in the same neighborhood—and John Denver, who would always be my "soul-mate" were embracing each other, creating a powerful metaphor for me. It was a perfect blending together of religion and politics and I felt God's spirit moving through both men.

Elder Benson moved to the podium to give the closing prayer. It was powerfully appropriate. As he was speaking the words to his inspired prayer, I was silently praying, too, asking God to allow me an opportunity to give my letter to John.

No sooner had both prayers been offered, then I was propelled forward by a force beyond my control down the aisle towards John. And, as if he had anticipated my intentions, I was the very first one from the audience to shake John's hand and embrace him! After our heartfelt embrace—which sent butterflies dancing wildly—he continued to hold my hand as if he didn't want to let go.

"This is for you, John," I insisted, pressing the thick envelope into his hand. I looked deeply into his eyes. Holding his hand and looking into his eyes—that one moment in time became eternity. Time and space no longer existed between us. Everything became as one in a mystical, cosmic experience beyond any rational explanation. I had never felt like this before. My heart was so on fire with love that I wished that this moment would never end. And I wondered, "Is this the type of love I've been taught about all of my life? Celestial Love—a love destined to survive throughout the eternities?"

The jostling of other fans brought me back to reality and the present moment. But before John relinquished hold of my hand, he asked, "What's your name?"

My mind was reeled into the present moment in order to answer, "Jesse... Jesse Clark."

"Thank-you, Jesse Clark. I hope we meet again sometime," he responded sincerely. With that, he released my hand and allowed the inflow of the audience to take possession of him like a glimmering drop absorbed by the sea of humanity.

Elder Benson was also surrounded with admirers, and I noticed my friend, Lindsey, in line to shake his hand. I didn't attempt to join her, allowing others to meet Elder Benson for the first time. I'd heard him speak in my own ward many times and had visited with him and his family in his own home. My mother was a close friend of his, and they had traveled many a campaign trail together, trying to wake people up to the government conspiracy. Because of my mother's close connections with him, I knew I could visit with him any time.

But, oh, how I longed for that close connection with John.

During the next few weeks, I waited with eager anticipation for John to reply to my letter. After several months, I finally accepted the fact that none would come. But during that time my life was filled with the challenges of helping to run a thriving health-food business and caring for two active toddlers, while attempting to obtain all the "truth" possible to incorporate into Rainbow Horizons.

Then things became even more intense as Karl and I started to dig deeper into our Mormon roots, following an admonition in Karl's patriarchal blessing to "study the organization of the Church." We both took this counsel literally and began studying the history of the organization of the Church. We were startled to find blatant discrepancies in the organizational structure of the early and modern LDS Church. Was the present-day Church an advanced improvement over the newly-restored Church? Or was it like the proverbial stream running downhill from its primary source—picking up pollution and perversions along the way?

Karl and I made it our quest to find the answer to this question and many others. Thus, we became immersed in the doctrines of Mormon fundamentalism—or the fundamental principles that the Mormon Church was founded upon.

We discovered a group right under our very noses—friends who had been attending our weekly meetings at Living Stream. They were baptized Mormon fundamentalists, but kept a low profile, as excommunication was a real threat for fundamentalists. They introduced us to a group in Salt Lake who claimed to live the "fullness of the gospel."

After weeks of studying their doctrines with them, we decided to travel to Salt Lake to investigate the Mormon fundamentalists there, hoping to meet their leader, Brother Owen Allred, who supposedly "held the keys." Now this issue of "keys" was intensely controversial, the subject of debate among mainstream Mormons and fundamentalists for decades. Mainstream Mormons contend that all the keys of the kingdom Joseph Smith received through the veil had remained with the leadership of the Church from Brigham Young on down.

The fundamentalists, however, contend that because of the Church's willingness to relinquish one of the main "keys"—the doctrine of plural marriage—that Joseph Smith came back through the veil in a profound eight-hour visitation to John Taylor, instructing him to give sealing keys of plural marriage to others outside of the formal leadership structure of the Church. And these keys were authorized to be handed down to divinely appointed brethren so that the "fullness of the gospel" would remain intact and the doctrine of plural marriage would be propagated outside of the Church.

Merely believing in this doctrine known as the "eight-hour meeting" would threaten one's membership. And so it was with some apprehension that Karl and I traveled to Salt Lake to attend our first Sunday meeting of the fundamentalists.

We drove down with our fundamentalist friends from Cache Valley, who led the way as we excused ourselves into the middle of a row. I noticed the many women dressed in long dresses with long sleeves, their long hair cascading down their backs or pulled tightly back in a bun. Very few wore any make-up nor were there many smiles on their faces. The men also seemed to be a sullen lot as a result of holding tightly to a constantly challenged belief system. I noticed a few men sitting between two women holding tightly to each of their hands. The children beside them were strictly obedient, also dressed in pre-modern attire. The entire scene propelled me back a century in time.

"Fascinating," I thought as sat waiting for Brother Owen, their prophet of God to speak.

The meeting commenced with an opening song and prayer, announcements, and then the passing of the sacrament. The sacrament ceremony was also different than from a modern Mormon ward. Elders blessed and broke whole wheat bread and blessed water in a communal glass. I had no problem with the bread, but was a bit hesitant to drink from a communal cup rather than the individual disposable plastic cups I was used to. But the Spirit was directing me strongly to partake in spite of my internal reluctance. And so I followed Karl's lead, as he partook willingly. I was graciously rewarded with a warm burning in my bosom as I was filled with the Holy Spirit, eliminating any doubts that I was here for a divine purpose. So when the sermons began, I was opened to any light and knowledge that might be dispensed.

A fragile, white-haired man got up to the pulpit to speak. My friend whispered that this was Brother Owen who was purported to hold the keys of the fullness. The audience grew silent as their beloved prophet began to speak.

"Now, I want everyone in this audience to be aware of a product you need to get for the problem we're having in this group," he said holding up a small red box.

"Rid. R-I-D is the name of this product, and it's for all of you out there who are experiencing the problem of head lice, which has been running rampant in this group."

"Head lice!" I exclaimed to myself, looking around to see if anyone had noticed my startled expression. I also looked around to see if there was anyone around me scratching their heads indicating head lice. I immediately *wanted out* and so I charted my escape along the path of the row least occupied and closest to the door. Karl seized my hand, as if reading my thoughts, keeping me in place at least until Brother Owen was finished speaking.

"And I want to tell all of you who are sticking wet toilet paper all over the walls and ceilings of the bathrooms to *just stop!* And also, you young ladies who are flushing their sanitary napkins down the toilets to *stop also!* It's really making a mess of our bathrooms and is getting your Uncle Owen *very* upset!"

His face flushed, underscoring the anger in his voice. He became flustered and at a loss to continue. As Brother Owen returned to his seat, I quickly got up and excused myself to go to the bathroom.

"Be careful," Karl whispered as I moved passed him. "And watch out for falling toilet paper!"

Chapter Nine

Windstar

"So, Grandma, did John Denver ever answer your letter?" inquires Amanda, referring back to the John Denver episode. She was a fan of his and was hoping to add another artifact to her John Denver collection.

"Well, not exactly," Grandma Jesse replies. "Perhaps in his own way he did when I found out about Windstar."

"Windstar...what's a 'Windstar?'" inquires little Jessica, enjoying the way the name rolls off her tongue as she says it out loud.

"Well, Windstar is a magical place...just like Marriage Mountain is... and all of Higher Ground for that matter! It's the place you might say I was 'born again.'"

"Oh, tell us the story of Windstar, Grandma, please!" shouts a chorus of young voices.

Well, the first time I heard about Windstar was when I was working at our own *Living Stream* health food store. We carried a magazine called the *East/West Journal,* and one particular issue, August 1981, had a huge picture of John Denver on the cover with the caption: "John Denver's Dream—Healing the Earth with Country Love."

My heart was filled with anticipation as I leafed through the magazine to find the article about John Denver.

It was an impressive article—an eight-page spread with lots of pictures of John expressing himself out in nature. He talked to the interviewer about his latest album, his latest diet, and his latest dream that was being manifest in the form of Windstar.

EWJ: What are your future plans and goals?

DENVER: We're at a time now when it is necessary for us to take a real hard look at every aspect of our lives on this planet. It is necessary to know that we have the potential to destroy ourselves and are seemingly on the verge of doing so. We have to recognize that we can change that. We have to recognize that we can make a conscious choice in the matter.

Since I was twelve years old, I have had a dream of a place that could bring people together, people whose only thing in common was that they were friends of mine. A few years ago that dream began to develop. It's in Colorado, in the Roaring Fork Valley, about thirteen miles southwest of Aspen. It's called the Windstar Foundation or Windstar Project.

EWJ: Could you tell us about it?

DENVER: It's actually several things. First, it's a research and development center for alternative energy resources, organic gardening, and food production. Windstar is located on about one thousand acres in a beautiful little valley. We have several teepees up which serve as dormitories for the students who come there every summer.

We have a house that used to cost $800 every month to heat in the winter and which is now totally energy efficient. When we get our windmill up later this month, we will be an energy exporter in the valley. We have a new solar heating system, which we feel is the most effective heat storage system for water that has yet been developed. We do biodynamic gardening. People can come to us, from wherever they live in the country, and learn how to build or grow food for themselves.

We hope that Windstar will become a network for similar organizations and communities all over the world...

My heart raced with anticipation as I knew I was destined to visit Windstar and experience John Denver's dream for myself. I wrote to Windstar in the Roaring Fork Valley, Snowmass, Colorado asking for more information about classes at Windstar. Only time and distance came between me and the fulfillment of that destiny. Months passed without an answer, and Windstar was pushed to the back of my mind by more urgent issues.

Karl's membership in the Church was being threatened because of his associations with the fundamentalist group. The bishop told him if he didn't quit the path he was on he would be excommunicated. Even worse, a friend and employee at Living Stream was embezzling money from our business account. Karl was being threatened with arrest as check after check began to bounce.

I was eight months pregnant with our third child, Delaney, and in no condition to deal with all the added stress. To top it off, one night the police came to our home up High Creek at two o'clock in the morning to arrest Karl after charges were made of "theft by deception." But Karl had fled to the mountains to avoid being arrested and to make sense of what was going on.

I was left to handle the situation at the store and deal with my two small children myself. My emotional reserves were exhausted. One day, while trying to wait on a customer while the police were in the store going through Karl's records, my mind went completely blank. I experienced a nervous breakdown, which precipitated going into premature labor. At that point, Karl came out of hiding and turned himself in. He was put in jail for a few hours, then released on bail because of the extenuating circumstances.

It was a sweltering July afternoon and my contractions were about ten minutes apart and getting intense. I called Joan, my midwife, and she was concerned that I was going into labor three weeks early. She told me to relax in a warm ginger bath to see if the contractions would stop. About an hour later I called her again to let her know the contractions hadn't stopped. It looked like I would be delivering a baby that evening. Karl was getting everything ready for a home delivery when Joan walked through the door. She was visibly shaken and said that some kind of spiritual force had taken control of her car and nearly ran her into a ditch. She did not have a good feeling about delivering the baby at home and expressed, "I felt like it was a sign."

Karl, however, was confident that things would be all right and continued to set up a bed in the living room where the lighting was better. Joan checked my dilation and found me three centimeters dilated. She then asked me what I wanted to do. Did I want to have the baby at home or in the hospital? I looked at Karl's determined face and replied, "I guess we'll go ahead and have it at home."

At nine centimeters, my bag of waters started bulging in front of the baby's head. Joan asked if I wanted her to break the bag of waters to speed up the delivery. I was nearing transition and the labor pains were nearly unbearable. I readily agreed and during the next contraction, Joan broke my water. The force behind the water caused it to spray all over Joan and Karl and also sent the baby back up the birth canal. Joan checked my dilation and I was back to one centimeter.

The three of us were totally exhausted and discouraged—not knowing what to do next. I asked Karl to give me a priesthood blessing to see what God had in mind. Just as Karl finished the blessing, he immediately passed out onto the floor. When he came to, he blamed it on the space heater that Joan brought saying it had taken all of the oxygen out of the air. I felt differently.

I felt it was a message from God telling me I needed to go to the hospital to have this baby. Joan agreed.

They both carried me to the car and headed at break-neck speed to the hospital fifteen minutes away. We pulled into the emergency entrance at Logan Regional Hospital just as dawn was breaking. It had been a long night and the attending physician was warmly compassionate when we told him our story—which helped tremendously to ease my anxiety.

He quickly hooked me up to an IV and heart monitor and ordered an ultrasound. The ultrasound indicated that the baby was all right and still in a good position to deliver vaginally. By now I was hoping for a C-section just to get it all over with. The doctor recommended an epidural to assist me with my "second" labor and delivery. I agreed as I was totally exhausted and in pain. Karl came in as I was waiting for the anesthesiologist to arrive. He'd been keeping vigil, praying out in the waiting room.

"The doctor says the baby's fine and I'll be able to deliver normally," I sighed.

"Thank God!" Karl exclaimed with relief. A moment later the anesthesiologist arrived. "So what's all this?" he asked perplexed as the doctor prepared me for an epidural.

"The doctor recommended that I get an epidural to relax me and assist with the labor. I thought it was a good idea. I'm totally exhausted and I don't know how I'm going to make it through another labor."

"Are you crazy, Jesse?!" Karl exclaimed pushing the anesthesiologist aside. "No baby of mine is going to have drugs dumped into it before it's born. I can't believe you're even considering doing this."

"Hey, Mister!" the doctor interrupted, obviously irritated. "Do you even realize what your wife's going through right now? Just try to imagine what it would feel like to stretch your top lip over a bowling ball. That's the type of pain your wife experiences during childbirth. Let *her* decide what's best for *her!*"

Karl resisted the urge to punch the doctor and quietly made his retreat out the door. The doctor shook his head and murmured, "Some men are just plain assholes." He then administered the epidural.

A few hours later, Delaney was born. The doctor immediately placed her in ICU as she had Hyaline Membrane Disease—incomplete lung development. When she was stable enough, she was airlifted to Primary Children's Hospital for another ten days in the ICU. Each day as I watched her struggle to breathe in the ICU, I thanked God for his hand in all of it. If I'd delivered her at home, she would have died.

A month or so later, after Delaney was given a clean bill of health and we had both recovered somewhat from the ordeal, I found a schedule for the

Windstar classes. I was a bit upset that Karl had neglected to give it to me, but considering the distractions, he was easily forgiven. As I thumbed through the brochure, I discovered that most of the classes that summer were already over, except for an "Aiki Week" which was one week away.

Butterflies danced as I dialed the long-distance number to Windstar, thinking, "I really could use a vacation." A woman answered, introducing herself as Cathy Crum, Windstar's secretary. I told her I was interested in the Aiki workshop and asked if it was too late to register. She politely informed me that I was in luck—there was one space left. I told her I was nursing a newborn baby and would need to bring her along. She was hesitant at first, but then said she was sure arrangements could be made to accommodate me and my baby.

I was ecstatic when I hung up the phone—then reality hit. Karl had sold our Volkswagen to pay for hospital bills and we had no money. And the likelihood of Karl letting me travel that far on a bus with a newborn was next to zero. But as I'd learned a few times on the path of serendipity—never let doubts get in the way of fulfilling destiny—and always remember to *pray sincerely.*

I won't get into all the details of how I got Karl to drive me out to Windstar in his parents' borrowed car using my parents' borrowed money, but miracles do happen. Also, Karl's mom volunteered to tend Ashley and Jacob while we were gone, as she, too, realized we *both* needed a vacation.

I was feeling road-weary when we got to the turn-off at Snowmass and stopped at the filling station to pick up cold drinks and some snacks. I nearly gasped when I glanced at my reflection in the rear-view mirror. My eyes were tired and bloodshot, my face pale and gaunt, my hair a tangled mess. I looked horrid!

"Boy, I hope I don't run into John Denver looking like this," I said to myself as I slapped my cheeks to get some color in them and pulled a brush through my hair. I turned to look at Delaney in the back, sleeping contently in her car seat. I smiled. At least she had enjoyed the trip.

After a few more miles on a long winding road, we reached the turn-off marked "Windstar." A feeling of *de`ja`vu* passed through me as I looked at the artistically carved wooden sign. Butterflies danced and spiraled within me.

We parked Grandpa Clark's Oldsmobile with other vehicles in a parking area just below a large, gray building which looked as if it was built from recycled barn wood. It wasn't quite what I had expected. I looked around to find the utopian community I'd envisioned as being part of John Denver's Windstar dream. But all I could see was a circle of teepees, a few outbuildings, and a thriving garden in view.

"Interesting," I said out loud, as Karl helped me out of the car as I held Delaney. I'm glad he had his arm around me, because as soon as I set foot on the Windstar land, a powerful surge of energy went through me, nearly knocking me off of my feet. Karl grabbed the baby from my arms as I attempted to steady myself.

"What's wrong?" asked Karl concerned. "Are you okay enough to walk?"

"I think so," I said. The electrical jolt had traveled up through my legs and was now penetrating my heart. "It must be from sitting in the car for so many hours," I reassured Karl. "I just need to stretch my legs a bit."

We entered the Windstar complex through a corridor of glass and columns of water, which acted as a passive solar heating system. We had arrived too late for the orientation, and a crowd of people were eating dinner. I asked the first person we met where we could find Cathy Crum.

Cathy, an exuberant gal, greeted us warmly and listened compassionately as I explained that Karl had come as father and baby-sitter, but not as a student. We didn't have the money to pay for the Aiki classes for him, but we'd be happy to pay for his food and shelter.

As she looked into Karl's attractive countenance, I could see any resistance to the proposition melt. She said it wouldn't be any problem putting up a pup-tent for the three of us. As for the meals, we'd work it out later. She encouraged us to make ourselves at home and get something to eat as we must be exhausted from our trip.

Any weariness from the trip had vanished, replaced with indescribable warmth radiating from my heart. I had no way of explaining the feeling except I had never in my life felt so connected with a divine source. I knew it had to be something supernatural, because the more I tried to discount it the stronger it grew. It was as if the moment I stepped foot on Windstar, I had plugged myself into a power outlet I never knew existed. Thoughts and feelings of a divine nature were filling my soul so quickly that it was hard to stay connected with the here and now. I felt as if I were wading through a syrupy veil, trying to get to the other side of everything—attempting to get from the edge of enlightenment to the place of knowing.

As I was entertaining these thoughts, I caught a glimpse of an attractive man with an electric smile and penetrating eyes. My spirit leaped and I was magnetically drawn towards him.

"Hi, I'm Tom Crum," he introduced himself. "I'll be your instructor for the Aiki Week."

"I'm glad to meet you, Tom. I'm Jesse, and I guess I'm a little late and missed your orientation. Could you fill me in on a few of the details?"

"I'd be glad to."

Karl was still conversing with Tom's wife, Cathy, and so he offered to take me on my own personal guided tour of Windstar. He showed me where the bathrooms and indoor showers were located and then we walked past a row of offices and into the large kitchen area where the cooks were busy cleaning up. The main area contained a buffet bar with long tables and chairs along side. For the most part, people were sitting on the steps surrounding a huge hardwood dance floor, balancing plates of food on their laps and conversing casually.

Tom shared a bit of his background—how he'd become John Denver's bodyguard because of his Martial Arts background; and how they had founded Windstar together to teach people a "better way."

I asked Tom if John Denver ever attended any of the classes there at Windstar. Sensing my feelings of anticipation, he gently replied, "Occasionally, but I wouldn't expect him to show up this week. I believe he's on a road tour."

Just then Karl came over, carrying the baby, to meet Tom. They launched into a very male conversation about the Martial Arts—discussing which martial art was more effective, powerful, offensive, defensive, appropriate, instructive, etc.—leaving me an opportunity for my own unguided tour of Windstar. I lifted Delaney from Karl's oblivious arms and wandered around looking for a quiet place to nurse her. In my wanderings, I noticed a wall full of beautiful photographs depicting scenes in nature and real-life drama, which drew my attention. I looked for the artist's name—John Denver.

"I never knew he was a still-life photographer, too," I murmured amazed. I found a comfortable bentwood rocker and pulled it into a quiet corner to nurse. "I wonder where he ever finds the time."

The next morning at the crack of dawn, a bell rang drawing me out of my sleeping bag in the pup-tent that Karl and Tom had set up especially for us. I knew it signaled the invitation to meditate for a half an hour before breakfast. Since Karl and Delaney were still sleeping contentedly, I quickly dressed and joined the group gathering in a small conference room upstairs. Many of the students were already sitting on the floor in the lotus position. I comfortably joined in because of my prior training in TM and Yoga. After people stopped filing through the door, Tom closed it and began a simple orientation on the value of meditation. Already an enthusiastic believer in meditation, I listened contently.

"It's important to get into a daily routine of meditation, shutting out the outside distractions in life and tuning into your own inner voice," he instructed. "This is a time when much wisdom and clarity can come to us so that we can better handle the issues which arise in our lives. This is also a time when we can ask our higher selves or God for answers to our deepest questions."

Well, I could certainly use some answers to a lot of questions running through my head. But the most pressing question in my mind was "Why am I here? It didn't make sense. Why did I feel so compelled to be here at Windstar at this time—with a brand-new baby?"

With these questions running through my mind, I closed my eyes to meditate. To my delight and surprise, a divine source began flooding me with insights.

I had been on a spiritual quest for truth, seeking answers in the roots of religion and especially in my own tradition of Mormonism. This was good as it had grounded me in the "letter of the law" which was an essential part of the formula for integrity. But God was showing me now that integrity consisted not only of universal law, or truth, but also unity based on love. Love is a divine gift of grace from God. The feeling of warmth in my heart intensified as God poured out his spirit of love into me, healing me, bathing me in rapture, transforming me into the divine self he intended for me to be. All I had to do was open up my heart to receive it, and this boundless gift would be poured in. This was the "spirit of the law" or the gift of grace that complemented the letter of the law. God was showing me that both were essential for the "fullness of the gospel"—his good word—to be manifest in me.

All during the rest of the week, as the workshop participants ate together, worked-out together, played together, and sang together, God poured out his "good word" of grace into my heart. I learned to love the strangers who became my family of friends. They came from all walks of life, from all parts of the country—some old, some young, some beautiful, some not so beautiful. But the spirit of unity and harmony among us far transcended any outward appearances. Was it the magic of Windstar itself? Was it Tom's intuitive instructions, teaching us the art of centering and the martial art of love—or the Aiki Way? Was I the only one tuned into this mystical, magical experience? Or was everyone feeling the same love, which radiated through my heart and extended out to everyone, inviting them into a unity of heart and spirit. I felt as if I'd "left yesterday behind me and had come home to a place I'd never been before." And I never wanted this feeling in my heart to leave.

On Wednesday of that week, Tom invited us to spend an entire day in silence, communicating with each other in forms other than words. Tom instructed us in Aikido that morning using hand signals; and although there was much laughter, no words were spoken. After our delightful workout, we were encouraged to seek a quiet place of refuge where we could silently commune with the Spirit. Karl volunteered to tend Delaney while I sought solitude on a small bluff overlooking Windstar.

God's spirit was serenely shining down upon me as I sat silently feeling the warmth of the sun upon my face. But the sun's warmth couldn't compare with the warmth in my heart as I expressed heartfelt gratitude for the gift of love God had generously given me. Thanksgiving and gratitude poured out from me as if I was a fountain of living water forever flowing unencumbered to God. And he, in turn, was a fountain of living waters pouring his love into me and through me to all who thirsted and were in need of refreshment. I prayed with all of my soul that this feeling of divine love would never leave me and that I could help others to discover this exquisite gift of grace. As I sat in silent prayer of heartfelt gratitude, a still, small voice came into my mind overwhelming me with a sense of vision.

It was a very holistic experience involving awareness on all levels. It was revealed to me that soon a great cleansing of the earth would occur as Mother Earth rid herself of all the disease (out of ease conditions) humankind had inflicted upon her throughout the generations of time. Many would not understand this cleansing for what it was, seeing it as a great punishment from God. But in reality it was a blessing, for it would rid the earth of her sin (separation within) and awaken humankind to realize (with real eyes) the imbalance we had created within ourselves and in all of nature. Through this cleansing process, we would discover the truth of who we are and our relationship with God. That we are, and always will be, a part of that oneness that is God. But due to our own sin (separation within) we had created an illusion of separation. Because of this illusion of separation, we have felt justified in disrupting the balance of nature by selfishly taking more than is necessary to sustain life, and by thinking we can rob others in order to sustain our own existence.

But we would eventually come to realize (real eyes) through this process of awakening and cleansing (or cleansing and awakening—I saw that some would awaken by choice, some by force) that the only way we can continue to survive on Mother Earth, after her cleansing begins, is to be in oneness with God, each other, and all of creation. Anyone who willingly chose the illusion of separation would not survive into the next millennium—which would be the millennium of peace, balance and beauty.

I was filled with rapture as I experienced this vision. I saw the new heaven descending upon the earth as if in a brilliant spiral rainbow to greet the remaining inhabitants of the earth after her cleansing process had transpired. I then asked the Great Spirit—the Holy Spirit of God—what I could do to help my family and others survive this period of dramatic change. I was shown that it was like the process of labor and delivery I had experienced a few short weeks ago, and I must prepare for this intense experience.

I was shown that there were safe havens or places of refuge along the Rocky Mountain corridor, which acted as the spinal chord or chakra system of Mother Earth. I would be guided to help prepare these places or energy centers—not only for me and my family—but for others who believed in God's words. I would act as an instrument in God's hands in preparing these places of refuge and also give voice to God's words, which he would reveal inside my heart from time to time. By heeding his voice in all ways and at all times, I would be able to help many, including my own loved ones, survive through these dramatic earth changes. By living in communities of love or energy centers, we would help Mother Earth transform the negative energy that we had all helped create. I would be given the principles by which these energy centers would be established if I would continually surrender to the inspiration of the Spirit. And I would know when everything necessary for the community energy center was complete when I experienced the same burning in my bosom as I felt now.

I was overwhelmed at the magnitude of the mission which I felt the Spirit had given me. Here I was—a woman, mother of three, with no money, no land, and no idea of how this all could be possible in the few short years before the millennium 2000.

As if God heard these doubts rise within my heart and soul, he spoke again in his still, small voice to reassure me that he expected me to walk only one step at a time and that he would give me direction each step of the way. If I would follow the still, small voice within me in the future as I'd done in the past, I would be continually reassured of his guidance. I felt as if I was being held in the arms of his love as my fears were comforted. If I would just look forward with faith, as I had done in the difficult delivery of Delaney, everything would be provided for the magnificent delivery of his Kingdom on Earth.

My thoughts turned to my tiny infant, Delaney, whom I knew would be hungry as my breasts had become full. I walked in rapturous reverence from my spot atop the hillside filled with the Holy Spirit of divine love.

The rest of the Aiki week was mystically magical as our hearts continued to be knit together with divine, unconditional love. We spent one night singing songs around a campfire and watching a breathtaking display of shooting stars.

"Why hasn't there been a community developed here at Windstar so that people could stay and live off the land, incorporating the principles of sustainability taught here?" asked one student, echoing my own question to Tom.

"Because the land has been set up as a tax-exempt foundation, and the regulations pertaining to this particular foundation don't permit anyone to live full-time on the land," replied Tom.   "Besides that, we still haven't found any form of government that would sustain such a community as you envision," he continued, chuckling to himself.

I wanted to explain the Mormon concept of "United Order" or the "Law of Consecration" in which all things were held in common to use in building God's kingdom. But Karl pulled on my sleeve, indicating it was time to turn in for the evening and call it a night.   Delaney was getting cold and fussy in the night air and needed some "mommy-attention."

I slipped into our pup-tent and snuggled Delaney between Karl and me in our conjoined sleeping bags to nurse. I wished I could be in two places at once as fragments of the conversation floated by, punctuated by "oohs and ahs" evoked by a sky full of falling stars. But as my thoughts turned to my darling daughter nursing pleasantly at my breast, I drifted off to sleep thinking, "Life is so good."

We spent the next evening—our last evening together—in group healing and celebration. Many of us were experiencing the stress and strain of tired muscles from a whole week of Aikido workouts, using muscles we never thought existed. Tom invited us to draw numbers and divide into groups of five for a group massage.

Lights were turned low and candles lit, while we all stripped down to our swimming suits—some to their bare essentials. We rubbed fragrant oils on warmed hands while one person in each group lay down on the blanketed mats to become the "love subject." What a sensually relaxing and stimulating experience to have four pairs of loving hands caressing and massaging tired body parts! The feelings of joy and ecstasy radiating throughout the circle of friends could never be described, only experienced.

When it came time for my turn to be the "love subject," one person commented to the rest while massaging my heart area, "Wow, can you feel the warmth radiating from Jesse's heart chakra?" Everyone took a turn feeling my heart area, confirming that the warmth I had felt all week in my heart was not only spiritual, but physical as well.

After the massage, we felt so invigorated that we wanted to dance in a group celebration. Tom turned on the stereo and, to all of our delight, began playing one of my favorite John Denver albums. We all celebrated in joyous song and dance to the lyrics of "Dancing with the Mountains."

Everybody's got the dancing fever
Everybody loves to rock and roll
Play it louder, baby play it faster
Funky music's gotta stretch your soul
Just relax and let the rhythm take you
Don't you be afraid to lose control
If your heart has found some empty spaces
Dancing's just the thing to make you whole

I am one...
Who dances with the mountains
I am one...
Who dances with the wind
I am one...
Who dances on the ocean
My partners
More than pieces, more than friends

Were you there the night they lost the lightning?
Were you there the day the earth stood still?
Did you see the famous and the fighting?
Did you hear the prophet tell his tale?

We are one...
Dancing with the mountains
We are one...
Singing with the wind
We are one...
Thinking of each other
More than partners
More than pieces, more than friends

We all got the dancing fever and rock and rolled the night away. We didn't break off into partners, but all danced in a group, each separate and yet all together. It was an ecstatic celebration of life, freedom and oneness. Although each expressed himself or herself in a unique way, together we formed a symphony of movement.

The next day brought the time for passionate farewells. We exchanged tears, hugs, gifts and addresses, vowing to keep in touch. We posed for a group photo, me in the center holding baby Delaney. When my copy of the picture arrived from Tom, I laughed out loud as it was a joke on me. I was the only one smiling sweetly—everyone else had been told to pull a face or grimace. "This is a perfect illustration of centered living," read the caption on the back of the photo.

Jan Rensel, a friend who I connected with in a very big way, gave me a poem, which captured her own experience of Windstar.

> Throat ache
> as I try to think of words
> to give you, across distance
> to shake you
> with all ancient, deep, and
> human primal force
> I want to scream
> in the frenzy of a group,
> drum-driven chant
> and leap in bold, heavy-footed
> dance
> mimicking fire
> the inevitableness of waterfall
> the inexorable surf
> such is the necessity
> of our connection
> Let us give ourselves
> a blood ceremony
> such as the old-ones knew
> and children, now.
> Here we are
> for this day, this night only
> to feel the anguish
> of our separateness
> and fierce joy
> in the masquerade
> We are dazzling
> in our combinations
> the current flows
> because we have chosen
> opposites
> we have forgotten our unity
> on purpose to rediscover it
> in moments
> in pieces

Come let us find symbols
make music
wordless
let us make
let us be
love

And so, like seeds within a bright and shining star—we were cast into the wind like a Windstar.

Chapter Ten

Trials

"Grandma Jesse, how did you know it was God who spoke to you inside your heart, and not your own mind playing tricks on you?" It's teenaged Katrina, cornering her grandma with a difficult question.

"That's a *very good* question, Katrina, and one I ask myself over and over again whenever I feel the Spirit whispering inside my heart," reassures Jesse.

"God tells us that we should 'prove all things and hold fast to that which is good.' One of my favorite Book of Mormon stories tells where God instructs Alma on how he can prove *all* things. The truth is like a seed. If we make a place for that seed to be planted in our heart and it is a true seed, then it will swell within our breast and it will begin to enlarge our soul and enlighten our understanding. And the fruit of that seed will become delicious to us."

"I know all that, Grandma. But you said God would guide you on your path. What were some of the signs that God was guiding you?" presses Katrina.

"Oh, God is always showing us signs, dear, if we but have eyes to see and ears to hear. Our Native American brothers were very adept at seeing signs in nature and interpreting their meaning. Others look to the scriptures to find signs or confirmations. God speaks to us in many different ways depending upon what we are attuned to. And since God knew I was attuned to the music of John Denver, in his own mysterious way he would continually send me signs through John's music."

"But how, Grandma? Tell us how!" reverberated a chorus of curious voices.

Well, after Karl and I left Windstar, with the burning still strong in my heart, we decided to take a trip through Montana—down through the

Bitterroot Valley. Karl had been through that way before on a business trip and had fallen in love with the area. I could see why. It was the most picturesque valley with green meadows and quaint farmhouses surrounded by magnificent mountain ranges to the east and west.

But more than the sheer beauty of the valley drew us there, pulling us like a magnet. There was something else, something mysteriously spiritual. We even took a side road when we got to a place called Corvallis, looking for "For Sale" signs to a piece of the Bitterroot we could call our own. But even if we had found a perfect place to buy, we knew we were only two dreamers lost in the vision of building a piece of heaven on earth. We had barely enough borrowed money to get home on. And when we did, Karl was faced with three trials.

The first was a criminal trial where he was being accused of theft by deception. The bank had pressed charges for the bounced checks that had been drawn on our account by our dishonest business associate. Karl was found innocent, but the process was long and expensive. We had to close down *Living Stream* because of the unrecovered funds. That left us without an income and forced us into bankruptcy—the second court hearing. And then, to top it all off, in May of 1983, the bishop of our ward in Cove summoned Karl to church court. He was excommunicated for associating with polygamists.

Our life was like a freight train going downhill fast with no brakes. We wondered when we were going to hit bottom. I guess Karl really hit bottom when I decided to file for a divorce in July. I couldn't take the stress any longer, especially when Karl claimed to have a testimony of Mormon fundamentalism and was baptized into the Allred group. I never could get a spiritual witness that Brother Owen held any keys, let alone the keys to the fullness of the gospel. And I didn't feel that I could go forward with something I couldn't believe in.

Besides that, the magic of Windstar kept pulling me back over and over again like a magnet, reminding me of the mystical experience I'd had there. I came to the conclusion that I had a destiny to fulfill with John Denver— that our powerful energies combined could fulfill the vision I'd received at Windstar and perhaps change the course of human history. This conclusion was reinforced by the release of John's latest album, *Seasons of the Heart,* which sentimentalized his divorce from Annie.

Karl insisted that if I divorced him he would get custody of the three children. He tried to convince me of the polygamous doctrine—that if a wife leaves, the children stay with the husband, as they are *his* seed. After much heated arguments over this issue, I finally conceded as I figured the demanding lifestyle of a divorcee bent on fulfilling a divine vision to save the planet was no place for three youngsters. I tried to console myself with the thought that with polygamy on the menu, Karl would have no problem finding one or more wives to replace me. But leaving Ashley, Jacob, and Delaney was heart-wrenching to say the least.

I took a bus to Salt Lake to spend a few days with my family. They were unsympathetic with my decision to leave Karl and the children and offered me no support. I decided to call Norman for some emotional support. He gently informed me that he was happily married with two children. As I related to him the recent events of my marriage, he grew sympathetic and asked how he could help. I told him I had no money or a car, and perhaps he could loan me some money until I could get my feet under me. He offered me his '79 Opal GT and a hundred dollars and told me to pay me back when I could.

I headed to Snowmass, Colorada in a yellow Opal GT playing John Denver music on the stereo system the whole way. I moved into a small room in a co-housing project in Snowmass, hoping to find work at Windstar, a few miles away. But after a few days of fasting, praying and reading scriptures, the excitement about my bold adventure was replaced by a painful reality. I was depriving my children of their mother for what? To heal a troubled world torn apart by separation. What message would I be sending to the world—let alone my children—if I gave up on a relationship simply because it was difficult and painful? How could I heal a planet if I couldn't heal my own marriage? How could I bring peace to the world if I couldn't bring peace into my own heart?

The more I tried to justify my actions, the more my integrity, or lack of it, kept showing through. I knew I was being a hypocrite. My heart ached constantly from missing my three little ones and Karl. I began to feel another ache—the regret of those spirits who might not be able to fulfill their destiny of coming to earth if I were to turn away from the path of motherhood.

After a week of wretched agony, I called Karl to come and get me. Norman's car had died, a perfect metaphor of how little life was left in my quest. Karl was ecstatic. He had been fasting and praying for my return. The children were desperately missing their mother. We were willing to try anything to work things out. As Karl towed the Opal GT with me at the steering wheel behind, another metaphor occurred to me. This was the position I needed to take in our relationship for now.

What a joyous reunion we all experienced as I hugged my beloved children. I vowed to them and God that I would do everything in my power to make the relationship work—for the sake of love and integrity.

From our farmhouse up Highcreek Road, we moved into a co-housing situation in Paradise, Utah, where our fourth child, Amber, was born in June of 1984. John Denver sang a song I will forever think of as Amber's:

Born in the month of June
No silver spoon to help you out
Your mother had you naturally
And naturally was the way you came out

You know your own mind
And you show it to me
Give me the high sign
When you want to be free
And open up my eyes
To the wonders that you see

See the airplane fly
See the trees rush by
Be brave and strong when you
                hurt yourself
And don't you have a worry
                in the world

For the love that's been given you
Is the one thing time can't erase
And every day it's growin'
Like the knowin' smile upon your face

You're startin' out strong
You get a kick out of life
You like to sing songs
Be in the spotlight
And when everybody's watchin' you
You shine so bright

See the airplane fly
See the trees rush by
Be brave and strong when you
                hurt yourself
And don't you have a worry
                in the world

You know your own mind
And you show it to me
Give me the high sign
When you want to be free
And open up my eyes
Like your mother did for me...

Though it was another difficult delivery, I was able to deliver Amber naturally at home in Paradise, Utah. Our family was blessed with another angel from heaven.

Then disputes between the men living in the house, including Karl, made the situation impossible and we were forced to leave. We moved into a small apartment in Logan where we lived until the voice of the Bitterroot Valley beckoned us again.

We had discovered that a small group of Mormon Fundamentalists had formed a gathered community in the heart of the Bitterroot Valley—precisely where Karl and I had searched for land on our way back from Windstar! We visited with them and strongly felt the spirit to gather with them in community. Also, I heard on a Paul Harvey radio program that John Denver flew into the Bitterroot Valley every month to see a chiropractor. He had gained two inches in height since he had been seeing Dr. Binder. I figured this may be my way of meeting John Denver after all.

In May of 1985 we decided to give our best efforts to help create a piece of heaven on earth with the "saints" who were trying to live the "fullness of the gospel." A year later, I wrote this short story about our bitterest experience in the Bitterroot Valley. I was surprised when it won an award for second place in a short story contest.

He was Born in the Bitterroot Valley

"We need to come and spend a day fixing it up," observed Karl, his voice catching. I agreed silently. I had been waiting for Spring, so I could tend to the hastily prepared gravesite.

Spring had come, transforming the grove of pine trees, where we had buried our tiny son, into a beautiful sanctuary. A medley of birds were expressing themselves melodically from the pine boughs over-looking the lovingly tended graves of other Ranch members who, like our Jadon, had been taken back to their heavenly home.

Karl and the children had wandered off to investigate the intriguing wonderland, leaving me alone to ponder by the pile of granite stones, which marked Jadon's grave.

The November morning had been frigid when I watched, through tear-strained eyes, as they lowered the small, handcrafted coffin into the cold earth. My arms ached to reach out and hold my tiny baby just one last time. Yet in my heart there was peace and comfort, perhaps from the reassuring messages of those who had spoken at the funeral, but more certainly from my own personal testimony that some day I would hold my precious infant son again.

The flood of "if onlys" filled my mind replaying mournfully as they had done during the three weeks Jadon was in the hospital. If only I had given him a superior home-birth instead of compromising and delivering him in the hospital. If only I hadn't exposed him to Mandy who had that terrible cough for three months. If only I hadn't panicked and taken him to the hospital where they could do so little for him. If only Karl had been there to help. Again the reassurance came that it was his time to pass on and that I too must move on, putting the "if onlys" aside to learn from the experience.

My mind turned to recall the happier times and the strong faith, which had brought us to the Bitterroot Valley.

It was May 30, my 29th birthday, when we had made the eight-hour trek from Logan to the Bitterroot. We had packed all that day, only to have the rental agency call to inform us that the house we intended on moving into may have been sold. Exhausted and discouraged, thinking we might have to move again as soon as we got up there, we knelt and prayed for guidance. After a brief deliberation, we concluded that it would be faithless to turn back now when our spirits were set on gathering with the Saints in Pinesdale—come what may.

We began the long journey at nightfall. Ashley, Jacob, and Delaney were asleep in the back of the U-haul with Shane, a friend who had come to help. Amber, nearly a year old, was asleep in my arms in what was left of my lap. I was five months pregnant and the possibility of having to move twice in rapid succession dampened my otherwise determined spirits as Karl and I drove through the darkness. I plugged in a favorite John Denver tape and listened to him sing "He was Born in the Bitterroot Valley."

My heart lifted. "It's a sign, you know," I smiled at Karl. He didn't respond to my humor but drove in silence, watching closely for deer crossing the road.

It was dawn when we arrived in the Bitterroot Valley, the scattered sunlight glistening in misty dew that covered the astonishingly green countryside. We had encountered frost in the mountain pass, but daybreak's warming rays brought in the promise of a new day...and a new life.

Bodies exhausted from the "moving marathon," we stumbled into our new home, bringing in only blankets to make quick beds on the floor. The children somewhat rested from their intermittent sleep were eager to explore their new surroundings. After a couple of restless hours, Karl and I gave up trying to get any real sleep. But we were still reluctant to realize that the marathon was not yet over—we must now unpack!

Karl and Shane hauled in the furniture while I unpacked items that were absolutely necessary, leaving the rest packed "just in case." The children weren't interested in helping unpack but were clamoring to take a swim in their new swimming pool—an added feature of the house. I suppose the pool was one of the determining factors in our decision to move. It wasn't often you could find a beautiful, four-bedroom home to rent complete with a pool—especially in Montana!

After Karl and Shane finished unloading, Karl went to buy groceries and get the utilities connected. By late afternoon, he and Shane were headed back to Utah to return the U-haul and tie up loose ends on his food storage business.

And the children and I were left to enjoy our new home—and new swimming pool.

One week later, Karl was back up and we were moving into a log duplex. With some extra boys from the community helping, the job was done in record time—two and a half hours. The duplex was a third the size of the house, but we would make it our home—at least until the baby came.

Spring blossomed into summer and ripened into fall—each season revealing the splendored secrets of the magnificent Bitterroot. October came—time for revealing the splendored secret, which had been growing within me for the past nine months.

I had wanted a home delivery, but I was so far from Joan, my trusted midwife in Logan. I always had difficult deliveries, and even though Ruth, the midwife in Pinesdale seemed sweet and competent, I didn't want to impose my difficult deliveries upon her. Besides, she would only deliver within "the Ranch" boundaries as Pinesdale was supposedly protected by the priesthood. With little support from Karl who was on the road a lot with his business, I opted for a hospital delivery.

The Marcus Daly Hospital in Hamilton was only ten miles away and Karl was home to drive me for my usual "trial runs." After eight long hours of intense labor, Jadon David was born October 9, shortly after 9:00 a.m.

No profound description or poetic metaphor could describe the feelings of sheer ecstasy I always feel after giving birth. But the added fulfillment of having my desired second son made me realize that perfect joy was not a promise, but attained in that first moment I held my newborn son. Every trial and hardship of the past few months disappeared, as my heaven-sent son suckled at my welcoming breast.

"Pain is only the carving away of a deeper chalice to receive more joy," I recalled.

Three days later, I unwrapped my precious bundle at home to the wide-eyed admiration of my four youngsters. They gathered round their new baby brother as I prepared to change his diaper. Jacob, my curious five-year-old, noticed the fragment of the umbilical cord and asked, "Why does he still have his tag on, Mom?" I laughed. It was so much like a child of this industrialized generation to conclude that all "brand-new" things come from department stores—complete with tags. As the other children bent over for a closer inspection, we all got a startling surprise as a golden arc cascaded magnificently into the air—measuring at least a foot. We all burst out laughing and were so astonished that it would have been a great deprivation to try and stop it. The children were all too thrilled with the new-found talents of their baby brother.

Unfortunately, Karl had missed out on all the excitement. And then he had to leave again on a business trip just two weeks after Jadon's birth. It was another one of the trials of living in the gorgeous, but remote Bitterroot Valley. It was hard to make a living there.

A few days after Karl had left, Jadon started to develop a cough at night. It didn't concern me much, since there was very little congestion, and he was fine during the day. But it grew progressively worse until by the night before Karl was due home, Jadon was coughing so hard he would lose his breath after a coughing spell.

About 1:30 a.m., Jadon awoke me from an anxious half doze with one of his coughing spells. I held Jadon up, patting his back gently, trying to dislodge what seemed to be something caught in this throat. My gentle pats turned into determined whacks as I noticed Jadon's color becoming blue. He had stopped breathing! I rushed him into the bathroom, picked up a suction bulb, and tried to suction his throat. It was no use—he still wasn't breathing. I took him into the living room where there was more light and held him upside-down on my lap, again trying to dislodge whatever was obstructing his throat. His breath or color had not returned, and so I raced back to the bed where I administered mouth to mouth resuscitation, pleading with God to bring him back to life.

He gasped at the breath I breathed into him, and then began breathing on his own. His color was returning as I thanked God and dialed the ambulance with trembling fingers. I managed to call the next door neighbor to ask her to send Mandy, her daughter, over to watch the children. They both stood at the doorway with concerned faces as I climbed into the ambulance with Jadon. We rushed through the night to Marcus Daly Hospital, sirens blazing.

Jadon appeared normal as the on-call nurse examined him and she tried to console me by telling me that sometimes newborns appear to stop breathing in their sleep. But I knew differently—I knew Jadon had stopped breathing and something was deathly wrong. Then Jadon started into a coughing spell and again stopped breathing. The nurse grew concerned and grabbed an aspirator that she shoved down his throat as he was turning blue.

The diagnosis was whooping cough. Jadon had been exposed to it practically the day he was born. I suspected the carrier—Mandy—the teenager who lived next door who had sustained a cough for the past three months. I didn't figure her cough was contagious, however, as she'd had it for so long. Also, she had been fully immunized for whooping cough. As for our children—Karl had become a firm believer against immunizations and so none of our children, besides Ashley, had been immunized.

One cannot comprehend the anxiety a mother goes through at having a critically-ill child in the hospital. Add to that having her other three youngsters threatened with the same disease at the same time was almost more than anyone could bear. Each day at the hospital I watched Jadon in the oxygen tent struggling for each breath, often choking and turning blue, panicking the nurses into artificially resuscitating him. At night I would go home to help Karl watch over my other three children struggling with the same ordeal. My only consolation was that someday this living nightmare would all be over with.

In a week, the three older children were out of danger though still coughing at night. After ten days in the hospital, our spirits lifted as the doctor expressed that Jadon had turned the corner and could go home soon. But then they came crashing down again the very next day as a secondary infection spread throughout his weakened body. He was rushed to Missoula Community Hospital 40 miles away where they had better facilities to deal with it. After a week punctuated with hideous seizures that left him brain damaged, his spirit slipped out of his exhausted body and returned to the heavenly home he had so recently left.

Karl returned with the children back to the graveside. We all knelt together holding hands in a circle around Jadon's small grave. We give thanks to a kind Father in Heaven who let us spend precious moments with one of his "angel children." My mind drifts off on the spring breeze recalling the cherished times I had rocked Jadon, singing to him the song that was his:

> He was born in the Bitterroot Valley
> In the early mornin' rain
> Wild geese over the water
> Headin' north and home again
> Bringin' a warm wind from the south
> Bringin' the first taste of the spring
> His mother took him to her breast
> Softly she did sing
>
> Oh…ah oh, Montana, give this child a home
> Give him the love of a good family
> And a woman of his own
> Give him a fire in his heart
> Give him a light in his eyes
> Give him the wild wind for a brother
> And the wild Montana skies

Chapter Eleven

Pinesdale

Our five-year journey on the path of Mormon fundamentalism and especially our residency in Pinesdale, Montana or "the Ranch" can be perfectly described by another John Denver song. Please excuse my obsession, but it was *truly amazing*.

It Amazes Me

He came looking for some answers
To some questions on his mind
Seeking truth and understanding
In the hope that he would find a way
To better serve his brothers
And sisters in the sun
Sharing all that he was given
Giving all to everyone

Come and listen to the story
Of a journey once begun
Of a people and their plenty
And their season in the sun
And how they gave themselves to symbols
And things that they could hold
Living lives in desperation
In the fear of letting go

It amazes me
And I know the wind will surely someday
Blow it all away

It amazes me
And I'm so very grateful that you
Made the world this way

Though our paths they come together now
Where do we go from here?
Will our differences divide us?
Must we always live in fear?
For there are things that we must move through
Some things to cast aside
But our Father watches over us
Our Mother will provide

It amazes me
And I know the wind will someday
Surely blow it all away
It amazes me
And I'm so very grateful
That you made the world this way
It amazes me
It amazes me
It amazes me

It was March of 1997 and I was eight months pregnant with Serenity when we decided to move from our log duplex up to the Ranch. I think we made our first mistake by setting up a teepee for our residence on the tract of land the priesthood had designated for us. I'm afraid the teepee was my idea because I always dreamed about living like the Native Americans in a teepee in the mountains. But Pinesdale wasn't the place to live out my fantasy as Karl really got a reputation for being an oppressive husband and father. Members of the strictly religious community responded with curiosity, skepticism, and even criticism. Dozens of visitors dropped by that first week we moved in, wondering if we were "for real." Actually we weren't "for real" and you might call us your "modern-day Native Americans."

Power from a nearby power line ran our space-heater, TV and VCR inside the teepee, and a refrigerator outside it. A neighbor's back yard garden hose supplied us with unlimited water. We weren't exactly roughing it, but we were happy and having fun—that's all that counts. A month into our teepee adventure, heaven blessed us with Serenity, our darling papoose baby delivered at a nearby friend's home.

Even after we managed quite well in the teepee that summer, we continued to endure the verbal and non-verbal criticisms of the Pinesdale residents despite our best efforts to fit into their community. I even adopted the dress style of the Pinesdale women—long sleeves, high neckline, ankle-length dresses, designed to cover a long garment I'd never received as we hadn't qualified for their "sacred endowment." I tried to force myself to believe that Brother Owen held "the keys" and that "Adam was our God and the only one we should worship." But my strong testimony of Jesus Christ being our Savior and Redeemer of the world always got in the way of man-worship. I knew the Spirit had led us there for a purpose, so I tried not to openly dispute doctrines or resist their ways, but tried to support where I could. But I sensed strongly that our sojourn there was limited.

I became energetically involved in their school, becoming the sole PE teacher for all of the grades of their gathered elementary school. Despite my best efforts to enliven their bodies and enlighten their minds with John Denver aerobics, I was up against rigid traditions resisting anything unfamiliar. While the younger pupils seemed more open to change, strong family ties connected almost everyone with the Jessop heritage, which meant secured traditions and rigid principles. The leading brethren on the Ranch were three Jessop brothers who each had several wives and a multitude of children. We were not only non-Jessop outsiders, but we were doing things differently than they were used to, challenging some of their comfort zones. I grew increasingly uncomfortable with the elitism, man-worship, and judgements of anyone or anything that involved a different approach to life. Few were willing to open up their minds to change—especially if it involved changing their belief systems. And some of their belief systems, especially regarding the hierarchy of species, were absolutely intolerable.

The men on the Ranch were a proud lot—and why shouldn't they be? According to their belief in Doctrine and Covenants 132, if they lived celestial plural marriage (polygamy) in this life, they would be guaranteed to becoming gods in the next life—with dominion over everything. So instead of waiting for the next life, why not claim as much dominion in this life as they could over wives, children, animals, nature and weaker men?

Some of the most elite of the brethren had several wives living in depraved living conditions with ten or more children while they continued to pursue more wives to enhance their prestige and power. Mothers were forced to go on welfare or work long hours picking produce in the fields for less than minimum wages to try to support their large families. Their husbands were economically and emotionally unavailable and rarely put in an appearance except to get them pregnant with the next child.

The lucky wives were only neglected. The unlucky ones were physically and sexually abused along with many of their children. I heard several stories from trusted friends about incidences of incest on The Ranch. The sexual abuses became almost scandalous at one time to where outside authorities were brought in to investigate a group of older boys who had been sexually molesting some of the younger girls on the Ranch. But none of the boys from the elite families faced charges—only a young boy who lived off of the Ranch was charged, prosecuted and sentenced.

My heart went out to the women and children on the Ranch, living in such oppressive conditions, yet outwardly expressing support for a religious system of blatant injustice and tyranny. But inwardly I felt they were committing emotional suicide as chronic illness ran rampant throughout the women on the Ranch, indicating to me signs of suppressed anger and unresolved emotional conflicts. I could relate somewhat to the harsh life of living in a remote area and trying to make ends meet. Karl was gone constantly, his food-storage business taking him away on business trips outside of the state. I was left home to take care of the needs of my own five children. In spite of my own stressful situation, I thought I could help.

I had gained considerable knowledge of herbs, holistic health, and midwifery, and I wanted to share that knowledge with others. I had a few remarkable successes, helping some women through difficult labors and deliveries using herbs and pressure points. Yet very few husbands were willing to have me attend their births and care for their wives, and the women dutifully obeyed.

In the fall of 1987, I began a women's aerobics class three times a week, incorporating some yoga stretches for warm-ups; breathing and meditation for cool-downs. But when the news got out that I was teaching yoga, a mystical Eastern religion, it came to an end. A few die-hards kept coming for a while because they couldn't deny the benefits they were receiving. But I knew that they were under constant pressure from their husbands and other women. Rumors flew that I was trying to promote a new religion. If a "new religion" meant respect for other people and nature, they were right.

One morning in the spring of 1988, I was awakened from my sleep to the sounds of chain saws cutting down trees right next to our trailer. By that time we had given up the teepee life and had moved into a trailer close to our designated building lot. As daylight filtered through the musty air, I decided to take a walk down to my favorite sacred grove located a few hundred yards from our trailer.

To my absolute horror, my "sacred grove" was no longer there—replaced by the ravaged remains of a clear-cut. The trees lay toppled in the wreckage of their own limbs. My anguished cries joined the cries of forest creatures—birds, squirrels and chipmunks who had lost their homes due to the greediness of men. Without warning, without notice, Mother Earth was once again stripped and raped of another of her sacred places. And I became nauseated with disgust at the atrocity of man's unrighteous dominion. I fell to my knees and prayed out loud that God would deliver us out of this wretched place. Pinesdale—what an ironic name. (Years later some mischievous teenagers changed the letters in the town sign to the appropriate "Penisdale.") A calming influence came over me. God had led us there for a purpose and I knew he would lead us out when our purpose was fulfilled.

I made two resolutions. I would keep my attention focused on the positive aspects of Pinesdale, but instead of hiding my light under a bushel, I would let it shine brightly. No longer would I try to fit into the dogma of a corrupt system, but I would sing the songs of truth that burned within me. I became more outspoken about my beliefs in deep ecology, community-building, and spiritual awareness. I was willing to discuss them with anyone, and I didn't care who did or didn't agree with me.

In November of that same year, I became pregnant with my seventh child, Justin. I quit my aerobics, PE and children's ballet classes to ease the stress of such strenuous activities. Dee Jessop, the principle of the school, asked me to teach art to the older elementary grades. I taught classes in recycled arts and crafts teaching the ecological value of recycling things and making them into beautiful works of art. We made garbage pick-up art objects displayed for the entire school and crocheted rugs made out of throw-away socks or jeans. I taught the older girls how to weave willow baskets and press native wild-flowers into stained-glass wall hangings. They enjoyed the change of pace from the usual paper and paste art they were used to and I enjoyed sharing with them my love for the environment.

Oddly enough, I seemed to gain a new respect and acceptance in the community and began making friends with some of the more open-minded women on the Ranch. More boldly, I began sharing my vision I'd received at Windstar along with some of John Denver's amazing lyrics with those I trusted. One woman was Pam, who was also a teacher at Pines Academy. She had generously sewn Jadon's burial clothes—a baby blue satin suit complete with a bow-tie and pearl tie-pin—and had also made a matching baby blue satin sachet heart with a pearl pin as a keepsake for me. Her kindness touched me deeply and as our friendship developed, we found that I was exactly one day older and that we were both crazy about John Denver music. I was thrilled when she confided that John's songs had profound meaning for her, too. She had chosen "Annie's Song" to be played at her wedding to Gary and considered it "their" song. She felt utterly betrayed when he had it played at his wedding to his second wife, Teri.

One day Pam invited me to her small trailer to listen to some of John Denver's albums that I'd never heard before. She set the record player's needle down on the last song on an album called *Spirit.*

"You've got to listen to this song. It's my very favorite on this album. It's called 'On the Wings that Fly Us Home.'"

> There are many ways of being
> In this circle we call life
> A wise man seeks an answer
> Burns a candle through the night
> Is a jewel just a pebble
> That found a way to shine?
> Is a hero's blood more righteous
> Than a hobo's sip of wine?
>
> Did I speak to you one morning
> On some distant world away?
> Did you save me from an arrow
> Did you lay me in a grave?
> Were we brothers on a journey
> Did you teach me how to run?
> Were we broken by the waters
> Did I lie you in the sun?

The melody and lyrics were captivating, courting me into a mystical oneness experience again with John. As I listened I couldn't deny the deep connection I felt towards him. Then the song opened a floodgate of tears, laying an intimate hand on a precious part deep within my soul that had never been touched before...

> I dreamed...
> You were a prophet in a meadow
> I dreamed...
> I was a mountain in the wind
> I dreamed...
> You knelt and touched me with a flower
> I awoke with this
> A flower in my hand

I know that love is seeing
All the infinite in one
In the brotherhood of creatures
Through the Father, through the Son
The vision of your goodness
Will sustain me through the cold
Take my hand now to remember
When you find yourself alone
You're never alone…

And the Spirit fills the darkness of the heavens
It fills the endless yearnings of the soul
It lives within a star too far to dream of
It lives within each part and is the whole
It's the fire and the wings that fly us home
Fly us home…fly us home

I didn't try to hide the stream of tears coursing down my face as the last strains of the song faded into the ethers. Pam and I both sat in silence. I was absorbing the impact of divine truth so beautifully articulated in verse and music. No voice could reach so deeply into my soul and no words could express those deep inner feelings of knowing that John and I had a pre-existent life together and perhaps a joint destiny here on earth.

"Wow," I finally breathed in utter amazement. "What an incredible song!"

"Yeah, it really cuts right through you straight to your heart, doesn't it?" Pam whispered.

"You know it's really amazing." I surmised after recovering. "He uses the exact same metaphor I used in the last line of a poem I once wrote."

"You're a poet?" Pam queried. "Wow, I didn't know that! Share it with me."

I reached deep into my memory banks. I'd written it for Mike after our last encounter together. It seemed lifetimes ago. "It's called, "Metamorphosis."

Caterpillar, caterpillar,
Consuming all in thy path,
Nourishing body, mind, and spirit
With all that the world has.

Caterpillar, caterpillar,
Spinning the web of time,

Can't you see, the web you weave
Are memories gone by?

Caterpillar, caterpillar,
Trapped in your cocoon,
Struggling against the energy veil
Which you alone have spun.

Caterpillar, caterpillar,
Look within your heart,
And break the bonds, which hold you bound
To fly on wings of fire!

"Wow. I really like it. It's so...profound. Have you written any other poems?" inquired Pam.

I laughed a little embarrassed. "Sure, I've written some other poems... and a few songs, too."

"Songs! You mean to tell me you're a songwriter, too!"

"Well, I wouldn't exactly call me a songwriter, but I have written a song or two."

"Oh, I'd love to hear your poems and songs. Why don't I come over tomorrow and you can share your poems and songs with me, okay?"

"Sure, I'd love to."

I shared my poems and songs with Pam. She insisted that I share them with the entire Ranch at the monthly pot-luck dinner. I was a bit rusty on the guitar but I reluctantly agreed.

Pinesdale's pot-luck was one of the community traditions I thoroughly enjoyed. Every third Saturday evening of the month, everyone in the community would bring a dish of food for the dinner. Then would follow an evening of spontaneous entertainment as members of the community would volunteer to recite poetry, vocalize, or play tunes on various instruments. It was a lot of fun and cheap entertainment for the entire community.

So the next pot-luck Saturday, Dee Jessop invited me to play my guitar and sing some of my own songs. A bit nervous about performing in public for the first time, I began with my first and best-practiced song, "There is Time." Karl sat with the children, cheering me on.

Even now as I sit
Feel the sun shine on my face

Even now as I walk
Smell the flowers fill the space
Even now as I listen
I can hear the river hum
Today we must begin
Or tomorrow may never come

Even now as I watch
See my children smile in play
Even now as I touch
Feel the earth I see the day
When all of this is memory
There's no father to tell a son
Today we must begin
Or tomorrow may never come

Let our eyes turn towards the heavens
To seek the guidance of His light
Let our hands reach down to earth
To seek the goodness of Her might
Let our hearts feel for each other
With love and truth we can overcome
Each is our brother or our sister
We must learn to live as one
And there is time…a little time
So little time…let it be mine

Even now I feel the pain
My heart is broken with despair
Even now I see the tears
I cry for people to only care
Even now there still is hope
All the wrongs can be undone
If today we will begin…
Then tomorrow…we'll live as one

Let our eyes turn towards the heavens
To seek the guidance of His light
Let our hands reach down to Earth
To seek the goodness of Her might
Let our hearts feel for each other

With love and truth we can overcome
Each is our brother or our sister
We must learn to live as one
And there is time...a little time
So little time...let it be mine

For my next song I played, "Crazy Lady."

Some called the lady crazy
Got a dream caught in her eye
Some say she's full of fantasy
And they never could figure out why
And some who didn't know her
Say, "she's got the devil under her skin"
But if they'd ever got close enough
Would know the spirit that dwelt within

She dreamed about a place somewhere
The she could call her home
She imagined a people
That she could call her own
She talked about a process
Of livin' in harmony
Where hate and envy disappear
And love flows gentle and free

I see flowers bloomin' in sunlight
Rainbow dews from heaven above
Birds and butterflies wingin' in midflight
And the air is filled with love
I see you and me together
Livin' in perfect harmony
Let's imagine it all together
It's as simple as you and me
You and me—one, two, three

Perhaps the lady's crazy
But her dream is bound to come true
And if it's just a fantasy
I hope other folks have one too
And if she's full of the devil

Then he must be a pretty good guy
'Cause I know that lady's heart is true…
I'm that lady 'til the day I die

I see flowers bloomin' in sunlight
Rainbow dews from heaven above
Birds and butterflies wingin' in midflight
And the air is filled with love
I see you and me together
Livin' in perfect harmony
Let's imagine it all together
It's as simple as you and me
You and me—one, two, three

I continued with a love song I'd written, again for Mike, called, "Butterfly-Love."

Love is like a butterfly
Yearning to be free
You long to hold it in your hand
But this must never be
Just let it go and watch it fly
And someday soon you'll find
The butterfly has come again
To spend a little time

Beautiful butterfly, fluttering by
Won't you stop and stay awhile
And keep me company?
Beautiful butterfly, high in the sky
Let me catch you in my hand
And hold you close to me

Love is like a butterfly
So delicate and frail
You long to squeeze it in your palm
But instead just let it sail
Across the breeze, beyond the trees
And someday soon you'll find
The butterfly has come again
To spend a little time

Beautiful butterfly, fluttering by
Won't you stop and stay awhile
And keep me company?
Beautiful butterfly, high in the sky
Let me catch you in my hand
And hold you close to me

The audience seemed to be enjoying my songs, so I continued with a heart-warming, fun-loving song called, "Good Life Family."

I could have gone to Hollywood
And made myself a name
Or sung my songs on radio
And got myself some fame
But when I think about my life
As I lie with you in bed
I chose the good life instead

I could have gone to college
And earned my P.H.D.
Or flown around the world
Or sailed across the sea
But when you hold me in your arms
As we sit beside the fire
The good life is all that I desire

Singin' baby love songs
Playin' horsie on my knee
Lots of hugs and kisses
We're a good life family
Seein' Daddy smile
As he walks in through the door
Thank God I chose the good life
Why should I ask for more?

Perhaps some day you'll hear my name
As I sing my songs for you.
But don't forget this one thought
If by chance you ever do
If I ever had the option

To do it all again
I'd choose the good life just the same

Singin' baby love songs
Playin' horsie on my knee
Lots of hugs and kisses
We're a good life family
Seein' Daddy smile
As he walks in through the door
Thank God I chose the good life
Why should I ask for more?

And since the hour was getting late and folks were getting tired, I ended with "Perhaps Today."

How can I say I'm sorry
For the things that have been done
For the world's situation
And your future that may never come?
How can I help you understand?
Is there a reason in the wind?
For the conflict and confusion
And the awful state we're in

No, my mind can't find the answers
And my heart can't bear the pain
There's no obvious solution
And it's driving me insane
So I look to you for answers
And I look to you for love
For I know my generation
Doesn't know what life's made of

Little ones...
It's up to you
You're the ones...
Who'll see us through
Little ones…
It's for you I pray
You're the ones…
Who'll show us the way

Someday, some way...
Perhaps today

You know your mommy loves you
And your daddy's always there
Friends and relatives pray for you
Their hearts are filled with care
So I know it's hard to understand
Why the whole world isn't this way
It's just we've lost the child within us
That's why it's to you I say...

Little ones...
It's up to you
You're the ones...
Who'll see us through
Little ones...
It's for you I pray
You're the ones...
Who'll show us the way
Someday, some way
Perhaps today

I'd sung my heart out, but except for Karl and the children giving me a standing ovation, the polite applause afforded me was enough to make one weep. I packed up my guitar as the community center emptied, vowing that I would never play in public again. A few sweet old ladies smiled encouragingly and told me I had a "lovely voice." But the real clincher was a neighbor who commented helpfully, "You know, I think your songs would go over a lot better if you played them at the college campus."

Well, a few months later, Naomi Powell, one of the sweet little old ladies and president of the local chapter of *Women for the Constitution* asked me to sing for their 1990 Women's National Constitution Convention held in Missoula, Montana. With the wind back in my sails, I composed two brand-new songs, wondering if composition for John Denver had this same combination of mind-wracking labor and sheer creative joy. I struggled to put into musical form my tribute to two of our Nation's most famous symbols-- the newly refinished Statue of Liberty and the cracked Liberty Bell hanging in Constitution Hall.

I was nervous when I approached the stage, wondering if I'd get the same response I did in Pinesdale. Being eight months pregnant didn't help much either. I had to sit in a chair in order to play my guitar and sing. Karl and a hundred or so women were seated in the audience, their eyes warm and friendly, calming some of my nervousness. I began singing "Lady Liberty."

> We came to your bosom
> With visions of freedom
> To build a new life
> In the home of the brave
> But now they have taken
> The very best part of you
> And force us to live
> Not as free men but slaves
>
> Your skirts would encircle us
> With peace and prosperity
> We'd show the whole world
> That it could be done
> But now they have given
> Your strength to a stranger
> And force you to fight
> Without even a gun
>
> Oh, Lady Liberty
> What have they done
> To your red, white and blue?
> Your red is the blood
> Of unborn babies
> Your blue is the hearts
> Of the men who once knew
>
> They've raped and abused you
> With no thoughts of conscience
> And expect you to give them
> Love in return
> But now is the time
> You must stand on you honor
> For justice is one thing
> That they need to learn

Oh, Lady Liberty
What have they done
To your red, white and blue?
Your white has been soiled
By the hands of a tyrant
But we as your children
Can make it as new

Today you stand shining
In brand-new raiment
A sight to inspire
The hearts of us all
So let us begin to
Unite as your children
To bring back the virtue
That we allowed fall

The audience rose to their feet and was on fire with applause. It warmed my heart and melted the nervousness I'd felt earlier. With confidence I sang out my next song, "Sweet Liberty Bell."

A symbol of liberty
Herald by all free men
Proclaiming the cause of truth
As long as knees will bend
But will God hear the outcry
Of liberty once more
When the cause of justice we forsake
God's laws we ignore?

Oh Liberty Bell, oh, Liberty Bell
Ring out loud and long!
Oh, Liberty Bell, sweet Liberty Bell
Ring out freedom's song!

God heard the prayer of Washington
In Valley Forge's gloom
And healed the wounds of Gettysburg
Preventing freedom's doom
The cry of war was heard once more
In foreign nations' land

But still God heard the soldier's prayer
And showed his healing hand

And now a generation's passed
What will the future bring?
Peace or war—it is our choice
But let's let freedom ring!
Did Providence crack the Liberty Bell
When hearts of men grew cold?
He'll mend it as the wounds of war
When love of God we hold

Oh, Liberty Bell, oh, Liberty Bell
Ring out loud and long
Oh, Liberty Bell, sweet Liberty Bell
Ring out freedom's song
Ring out freedom's song

The audience jumped to their feet and exploded in a standing ovation. The words and music had touched their souls igniting the passion for liberty and justice that I felt as I sang the songs. In significant ways, I was singing to myself. Karl and I knew our days in Pinesdale were numbered as liberty and justice were foreign words to a people bent on following the dictates of corrupt men and a corrupt system. They tried to implement their own justice system, but the first jury trial showed us how far off the track they were.

By fall of 1989, we had moved from the trailer into a two-story English Tudor home in the heart of Pinesdale. All of the land on the Ranch was owned by the Priesthood corporation called AUB (Association for the United Brethren), which was owned and operated by a few authorities in Salt Lake and in Pinesdale. Even if these "authorities" allotted property to a family, they could reclaim it at will. Families could never "own" their own property but acted as "serfs" on someone else's property. This was one of the many injustices Karl and I protested about ever since we moved to Pinesdale. The Harris' were one of the few families who had joined us in our crusade against the oppression of "the Priesthood Authority." Both Karl and Ryan were hard-working men who took pride in their craftsmanship and wanted to enjoy the fruits of their own labors. Also, neither one had been authorized by the Priesthood to take new wives, which meant that they were not distracted from the needs of their current families by the delights and added pressure of a new wife.

One Saturday afternoon I was helping Karl do some finishing work on the staircase in the front entryway of the home. Suddenly the sound of a gunshot sent us leaping to the door just as nine-year-old Jacob tumbled in shrieking, "Dad, you'd better come up to Harris' fast! Gus Jessop caught the Harris' dog chasing the Ranch cattle. He's got his rifle and said he's going to shoot it!"

Karl dropped his hammer and untied his tool-belt. He grabbed Jacob's hand and ran for the Harris' house.

"Wait for me!" I called after them. I quickly told eleven-year-old Ashley to watch the little ones for a few minutes as I ran after Karl and Jacob. The Harris' lived only a few houses up the road from us and they had become our best friends since we'd moved into our new home. Our houses were two of the few "nice" homes on the Ranch; yet both needed some finishing work. But it was hard for a man to take pride in constructing a nice home on the Ranch, knowing that there wasn't any way he would ever own it.

When we arrived breathless at the Harris' home, I almost fainted with horror. Eight-year-old Rason, Jacob's best friend, sat in the front yard, crying hysterically as he clung to the dead body of his pet Basset Hound, Brandy. His face was splattered with blood. Gus Jessop was no where to be seen, but the story was gruesomely obvious. Jessop had lifted up one of the dog's long, floppy ears to put a contact shot through its head with a hunting rifle while the dog lay in Rason's lap.

I knew Ryan and Jody needed to be notified immediately at the battery shop where they worked—a short distance away. Should we call the police? Should we take Rason to the hospital to be treated for shock? I was put in charge of Jody's children while she worked but I wasn't sure what she would want Karl and me to do. Karl lifted the dog's body gently off Rason's lap, and I led him into the house where I could wash his face and comfort him until his parents arrived.

Ryan and Jody were outraged. They decided not to telephone the police as they knew the whole community of Jessops would come down on them. They would be expelled from the community—maybe worse. Instead they were convinced to try out the community's new justice system.

With Karl assigned as Harris' prosecuting attorney and another Ranch member assigned as Gus' attorney and a judge appointed, court was called into session a few weeks later. Most of the Ranch members attended this historic court trial—Pinesdale's first. I waited anxiously at home for the results, while tending Jody's and my children. When the verdict came in—we were stunned with disbelief. Not only was Gus found innocent of any wrongdoing, but the entire community applauded him for acting "in the line of duty" to protect the cattle on the Ranch.

We were appalled. Ryan and Jody were determined to appeal the case to the higher authorities—the "authorized police" in nearby Hamilton. But then they began to receive anonymous threats that they would be "burned out" or even killed if they let this incident get off the Ranch. Ryan decided to take out a large fire insurance policy on his house "just in case," fully aware what certain brethren on the Ranch were capable of.

And then one day it happened. Ryan and Jody returned home from work to find their beautiful home and all of their personal belongings burned to the ground. The insurance company, which conducted the investigation, couldn't prove that it was arson. Jody, who was an artist, had a lot of volatile materials stored in her home and so the insurance company claimed it may have been caused by "spontaneous combustion." It was mid-summer and I'd taken all the children swimming to the nearby pond so "thank God" nobody was injured.

Although it was a tremendous tragedy and loss; with the insurance money the Harris family was able to move into a beautiful finished home—off the Ranch and away from Pinesdale. And this time, they went to both the police and a lawyer to file a personal damage lawsuit against "the Priesthood."

The atmosphere was volatile on the Ranch, no doubt, and Karl and I knew we had to make our escape regardless of the fact we would be labeled "apostates." I was desperately concerned about our family's safety and welfare and a few other families in Pinesdale felt the same way. So the men got together and decided to look for a piece of land where they could start another United Order. Dutifully they went through the heirarchy of seeking permission from Brother Owen. Seeing the move as a quick way to defuse tensions in Pinesdale, he granted their request, and the men started looking for land within about a hundred-mile radius from Pinesdale.

Despite Karl's and my anxiousness to leave, the brethren spent months looking for just the right spot. To be self-sustainable, the community needed a fairly large stream with good gravity drop to generate its own hydro-power. Ideally, they wanted the land to pay for itself through selective logging and harvesting timber from home sites. The lumber industry was a big business in Montana despite environmentalists' efforts to shut it down. I felt that responsible resource management struck a balance between the environmentalist's hands-off approach and the irresponsible Ranch and Forest Service clear-cutting.

Karl with his diligent persistence found an ideal place, "Cedar Springs." It was a square mile (640 acres to be exact) smack in the middle of National Forest land. Fire Creek ran through it, promising adequate power. The only problem was there were no access roads into the property and we would have to create one through Forest Service property. Despite this obstacle, the group made a down payment and developed a plan on how to manage the purchase.

Then the Pinesdale brethren got wind of our plans to build a United Order 80 miles away. They didn't like the idea that a group of "conservatives" might succeed in living the United Order while they, themselves, had failed. Not to mention that we were taking away some of their biggest tithe-payers. They convinced Brother Owen to withdraw his approval for the Cedar Springs project because "it was causing too much division on the Ranch." Brother Owen rescinded his blessing. All the other men bailed out, leaving the former landowner holding the down payment and a mortgage contract. They were convinced that without Brother Owen's blessing, God would not be behind it and it would surely fail.

Karl and I were devastated. We had put everything we had—our time, talent and money—to building our highest visions and dreams at Cedar Springs. We were doomed thinking we had to live the rest of our lives in Pinesdale. At our lowest point, when the land was just about to go into foreclosure, I stopped in at a music store to see if John Denver had released a new album. I needed to lift my spirits a bit and to my delighted surprise, I was able to purchase his latest tape, *Higher Ground.*

I tingled all over as I peeled off the cellophane and plugged it into my tape deck. The first song began:

> There are those who can live
> With the things they don't believe in
> They are giving up their lives
> For something that is less than they can be
> Some have longed for a home
> In a place of inspiration
> They will fill the emptiness inside
> By giving it all to the things that they believe...
> They believe
>
> Maybe it's just the dream in me
> Maybe it's just my style
> Maybe it's just the freedom that I've found
> But given the possibility
> Of living up to the dream in me
> You know that I'll be reaching for
> Higher Ground

I will stand on my own
I will live up to this vision
I will trust in what I feel
And follow my heart
Until it brings me home

Maybe it's just a dream in me
Maybe it's just my style
Maybe it's just the freedom that I've found
Given the possibility
Of living up to the dream in me
You know that I'll be reaching for
Higher Ground

Keep me through the night
Lead me to the light
Teach me the magic of wonder
Give me the spirit to fly

Maybe it's just a dream in me
Maybe it's just my style
Maybe it's just the freedom that I've found
Given the possibility
Of living up to the dream in me
You know that I'll be reaching for
Higher Ground

Tears began to flow even before the first song ended. After listening to the entire tape three times without stopping, except to wipe my eyes and blow my nose ("For You" especially made me cry), I took it to Karl to listen to. He also wept as he listened to the song "Higher Ground," in spite of his well-justified resentment towards John (who was definitely the other man in my life).

I'm not sure if Karl will ever admit that this was a turning point in our decision to fight for Cedar Springs. But he, not I, decided to rename our property "Higher Ground."

Chapter Twelve

Higher Ground

"So Grandma, were you ever able to save Higher Ground?" questions eight-year-old Justin.

His grandma laughs, "My dear, Justin…if it wasn't for your Grandpa Karl's determined faith and effort, you wouldn't be sitting right here on top of Higher Ground asking me that question. But I'm sure Grandpa Karl can tell the story much better than I of how he—or should I say the Lord—was able to save Higher Ground."

Grandma Jesse motions to Grandpa Karl that she needs a break from her story-telling and gratefully surrenders the story-teller's stool to Grandpa Karl. She joins her grandchildren on the buffalo robe as the younger ones scramble to find a comfortable spot on her lap to listen to Grandpa Karl tell his story.

Well, the first battle for Higher Ground began when I had to get approval, or at least permission, to try and come up with two years back land payments plus interest, which amounted to $40,000. The ten families who were involved with the project could've easily come up with the yearly payments had they agreed to commit just $150 a month to the project. But no one was willing to make a personal investment, thinking that somehow God would mysteriously provide the resources. Some even thought that if they prayed hard enough and had enough faith, the entire land payment would mysteriously show up in someone's mailbox. Now, that may sound crazy, but I did get several hundred dollars anonymously a few times in the mail while I was working on the project—but only after I had done everything in my own power and had exhausted all of my own resources. That was just some of the miracles that happened once Jesse and I committed to saving Higher Ground.

Anyway, the first time I approached the brethren with my idea to let me save Higher Ground before it went into foreclosure, my idea was totally rejected. They felt that if Brother Owen wasn't behind the project it was dead in the water and I would be going against God to pursue it any further. But I made it perfectly clear to all of them that Brother Owen was not *my* God and that *my* God is a God of integrity that keeps to the contracts he makes. Besides that, I couldn't deny the strong spiritual witness I'd received while praying on top of this mountain—Marriage Mountain—that God wanted me and my family out of Pinesdale and on to Higher Ground.

But despite my pleadings, they kept insisting that it was better to let the land go to the Gentiles rather than to go against Brother Owen, their "prophet of God." But the more I prayed about it, the more I knew that God was behind the project, and if *he* was behind it, there was no stopping me.

And so I approached the brethren for the second time—this time begging them on bended knees with heartfelt tears in my eyes to let me try and save Higher Ground for me and my family, as we had invested our heart and soul into the project already. I guess something in my emotional sincerity melted their hearts of stone. They finally gave permission to let me go ahead to try and save it—since they had nothing to lose anyway.

With the way cleared, I knew it would take a miracle of God to come up with $40,000 before foreclosure—four months away. But I knew that with the Lord's help I could do it, because I'd been able to make that kind of money before—$15,000 in one day selling fire extinguishers.

I had a few ideas of how to make the land pay for itself. This had been our intention in the first place, only no one wanted to do the "dirty work." I was not only willing to get my hands dirty, but to make whatever sacrifices necessary for the cause of Higher Ground.

My first idea was to selectively cut timber for railroad ties. I felt that finished lumber was more cost productive than just sawing down trees and hauling them to the sawmill, as most people would do under the circumstances.

So I secured a contract for $300,000 with a company that bought railroad ties, and arranged with a friend to rent his sawmill for the summer. We hauled it up through a neighbor's backyard whom we thought had boundaries adjacent to the property. But it turned out that he didn't and that we were trespassing through Forest Service property. But there was another back road into the property, and so we went to the Forest Service to determine where our boundaries began and where the Forest Service boundaries ended. We found there was approximately a mile of undeveloped land between the end of their back road and a road on our land. This meant that to get equipment in and railroad ties out, we had to punch in a mile or so of road.

This was expensive work requiring a lot of heavy equipment. Since I was flat broke, I was praying for a miracle. And then one of the brethren on the Ranch said he'd do the roadwork on credit since I already had a contract for the railroad ties and he felt I was good for the money. He hauled his equipment clear from Pinesdale and put in the road in a few days. I was tremendously grateful to him and the Lord.

In the meantime, I was looking for a skidder to get the logs I cut down to the sawmill. I beat every bush, trying to find someone to loan me their skidder for a few months—but it seemed that every skidder around was being used. Lumber prices were sky-high that year and everyone was logging it seemed. But I finally came across an ad for a smaller, older skidder for sale. They wanted $10,000 for it. I didn't have the money, but someone told me about a lady who might loan me the money if I could sweet-talk her into it. And so I was able to get a loan from a very nice lady for $10,000 and I purchased the skidder.

By this time the cutting crew were getting a bit restless. It consisted of four boys from some friends of ours family and Reed, a guy whom we'd met in Southern Utah who believed in the project and had logged before. And Jacob, our eight-year-old, joined the crew, camping out on the land, eating nothing but serviceberry pancakes for breakfast, and potatoes and onions for dinner. He helped cut limbs off the trees the others had cut down to get them ready to put through the sawmill for railroad ties. Sometimes their faith would falter as obstacle after obstacle would get in the way of our progress. But I'd try to buoy up their spirits by telling them that "if you can move, you can win"—something I'd learned in the ring while kick-boxing professionally.

Then when they saw me getting discouraged, they all got together and inscribed on a log cut from the first tree going through the sawmill to make the first railroad tie—IF YOU CAN MOVE - YOU CAN WIN. This sign caught my attention as I drove my new skidder into camp along the six miles of Forest Service road and our mile of new road. It really choked me up to realize that others believed in me so strongly.

Spirits were soaring as we now had the means and enthusiasm to get our project off the ground. But then they came crashing down again as a Forest Service enforcement officer came into camp wanting to arrest me for trespassing and building a road on Forest Service property. I couldn't believe my eyes when I read the warrant. The Forest Service had given me the wrong information when they told me that their road had ended at my boundary line when actually, after a quick survey was done; it ended at the start of our old road. That meant I had built a mile or so of road on Forest Service property and was responsible for the damages. I was fit to be tied and fortunately, for the officer, he had the wrong middle name on the warrant so he couldn't haul me in.

The hearing date was set and the railroad tie project was kyboshed, all because the Forest Service had "made a mistake." All along I wondered if I was getting the real story from them or they were just trying to run interference. But their strategy seemed to be working and I couldn't prove anything according to their maps. They were in the driver's seat and I was getting more and more discouraged—but not discouraged enough to quit. Another idea came to me which I called "Plan B."

I knew the lumber companies in the area were anxious to log on private lands, as the prices of lumber that year were very competitive. (The ecologists were putting more and more restrictions on logging companies and I think that was the year Al Gore got into office with his own environmental impact statements.) So I decided to contact all of the lumber companies in the area (I think there were seven) to give me a bid for logging the entire 640 acres. I told them I wanted it "selectively logged" and I would mark the trees to be cut. I also said it was to be a "closed bid" meaning each logging company was to bid against each other in a sealed envelope. The conditions included $40,000 up-front money plus they would have to put in roads, including a two-and-a-half mile road through the Forest Service—this time with the necessary permits. It was too big of hassle for the smaller logging companies, but one bid did come in from Champion—the largest logging company in Montana and the only one able to afford the project. The bid was a lot more than I'd expected. After I'd signed the contracts, Champion's lawyers and managers asked me how I was able to pull off such a great deal so smoothly. Someone with some knowledge about the logging industry had to have helped me—someone with some clout. I just winked at them and told them that someone "big" had been behind the project—but no one they were familiar with.

I took the $40,000 check they handed me and drove to the bank. I paid the overdue mortgage note off the last day before it went into foreclosure.

Champion had the resources to handle the Forest Service's red tape. And red tape there was—miles and miles of it which included getting boundary surveys, putting in roads to *their* specifications, which meant putting in a foot of gravel where 6 inches would have been sufficient, and putting in a $15,000 bridge where a $2,000 culvert would have done. They even had Champion pay $1,000 for a survey to see if there were any remains of ancient Indian dwellings. After all of this and putting in over 12 miles of logging roads, Champion's venture wasn't as profitable as they'd figured. But I was totally satisfied as I now had a hundred or so acres paid off entirely and a little capital left over to start building our house. We had signed a deed-release contract with the owner of the land, which released forty-acre parcels out of mortgage after it was paid for which gave us a free title to build.

That summer we dug out a four-foot crawl space and poured a foundation. That winter we stayed in Pinesdale for half of the winter, then moved down to Salt Lake where Jesse and the six youngsters spent Christmas and the rest of the winter with her sister, Rosalie who had just gotten a divorce. I worked as a traveling salesman selling food storage to earn up enough money to continue building on the house. It was hard being on the road and away from my family; and I vowed that once I got our house finished and paid for, I'd never be gone away from my family again.

The next summer we hustled trying to get the house far enough along that we could move into it for the winter. We probably could have, had it not been for an early snowfall in October, which prevented us from getting the roof on. That, and the hundred or so visitors who came up to see what we were doing. It would've been nice if they'd grabbed a shovel or hammer and helped. But all they wanted to do was sit around our campfire, eat our Dutch-oven dinners and gab.

I guess it was hard on Jesse. She was pregnant with our eighth child, cooking over a campfire, cleaning up with no running water, and living in a teepee. I guess it really broke the camel's back when Kirstie came along that summer, telling everyone that she had gotten a witness that she belonged in our family. But I guess Kirstie should tell that part of the story.

Grandpa Karl surrenders the "story-teller's stool" to Kirstie, who reluctantly gets up and sits down on the "hot-seat."

"Well, I'm not much of a story-teller, but I guess I do have my story to tell. I suppose I should start at the very beginning when I first found out about the Clarks…and their adventure with Higher Ground.

My family first met the Clarks at the Women's National Constitution Convention. My mom, her sister-wife, Connie, and my younger sister, Lisa were also performing along with Jesse.

They all came home raving about this wonderful couple they'd met— talented, good-looking and, best of all, conservative. They told me how Karl and Jesse had six kids and were in the Allred group living in Pinesdale. Dad said he had a strong witness that I belonged in their family.

I think it may have been wishful thinking at the time, as he was very concerned about my physical and spiritual welfare. And he had a genuine right to be.

I was twenty-one, going to college and messing around with guys, including a Mexican named Carlos. I was rebelling against a lot of my family's beliefs including their religion, their politics and, in particular, their belief in plural marriage. I resented the pain it had caused my mom when my dad married Connie. Everyone in Lovell, Wyoming labeled us "weird." A few of our friends who were members of our local church were threatened with excommunication if they even associated with us. My whole social life went done the drain when they found out we were polygamists. I hated and resented every aspect of plural marriage, and so when Dad mentioned that I should consider being a plural wife to Karl Clark, I nearly threw up!

To tell you the truth, I actually did throw-up the first time I met Karl. He had flown over to Lovell with some of the brethren from Pinesdale. My parents didn't know it at the time, but I was pregnant with Carlos's baby and had morning sickness—bad! When my Dad came into my bedroom to introduce me to Karl, I rushed into the bathroom and vomited. That was our first meeting.

Karl said that he knew at the time what was wrong with me. The Spirit had witnessed to him that I was pregnant—that and he'd seen the symptoms so many times in Jesse.

I was afraid at the time to tell my parents I was pregnant. When it finally became quite obvious, they were terribly disappointed. It dashed any hopes that their daughter would be eligible to marry a righteous man—especially of Karl Clark's caliber.

I continued going to school and partying, living on Pepsi and Snack-ums. The reality of what I was doing to myself didn't hit home until I went into labor. I had toxemia and the doctors were concerned that it might turn into pre-eclampsia, which is life-threatening to the mother and baby. Well, after forty-eight hours of intense labor, with my mother by my side the whole time, Branson Joseph was born. Carlos, his dad, didn't even show up for the delivery, as he didn't want anything to do with the responsibilities of raising a child.

But Branson was well worth all the pain and suffering. When they laid the curly black-haired infant in my arms for the first time, I knew that he was a gift from God in spite of myself.

My life changed dramatically as the serious responsibility of being a parent now clicked in. No longer could I deny the reality of how I'd made a mess of my life. I was now willing to repent and be rebaptized to start a fresh, new life as a Christian mother.

I started attending the small gathered fundamentalist church in Lovell, which started me on a deep search into Mormon fundamentalism. My parents owned practically every book about fundamentalist doctrines, and

I read everything I could get my hands on. A few months after Branson was born, my parents invited me to go with them to the annual conference in Pinesdale. They were hoping that I might meet some eligible husbands there—including, perhaps, Karl Clark.

Karl spoke at a fireside, talking mostly about herbs and health. But then he got fired up about the gospel and how we really needed to live the "fullness of the gospel" in a "free" environment where the Spirit of the Lord could work through each individual. We didn't need to trust in any man or "arm of flesh" for personal revelation. That's why he said he was moving out of Pinesdale and beginning a new United Order at Higher Ground.

As I listened to him talk, I felt myself mesmerized, magnetized to this man—drawn deep into his very soul. I couldn't take my eyes off of him, and it wasn't just because he was the best-looking man I'd ever seen in my entire life! He had a spiritual depth and maturity that went well beyond his years. Of course, when I found out that he was thirty-seven, I nearly died. He looked only a few years older than me. But then I remembered that he had seven kids already, and Jesse was pregnant with their eighth. How could I have possibly mistaken him to be in his early twenties? The youthful spiritual glow, which radiated from his face told me he had to be doing something right—and I wanted to find out just what it was for myself!

The Clarks said they needed to get back home to Higher Ground, a two-hour drive from Pinesdale, but invited anyone who wanted to, to come visit the property. The next night my mom and I ventured up to Higher Ground. We were well rewarded.

We joined a few others from Pinesdale to enjoy a delicious Dutch-oven dinner and had a real "fireside" as we all sat around the campfire and talked about the gospel. The setting was so pristine, with pine and cedar trees all around and a musical creek running close by. It was so romantic!

Karl did most of the talking again that night, although Tod, a friend from Salt Lake, showed up a little later on and led a discussion on the deeper issues of Mormon fundamentalism. Tod's words flew over my head as I had other things on my mind and heart. I was falling in love with Karl Clark. Although the feelings in my heart were very clear indeed—the mere thoughts of him sent me swirling with ecstasy—my logical mind was telling me—no way. Here he was, a married man with a beautiful wife and seven, almost eight, darling children. And by the way Jesse was staring daggers at me, I knew there wasn't any chance *she* would be interested in enlarging the family with another wife. But I said a little prayer in my heart that night that if it were possible, and if it were right, that God would bring us all together in marriage.

Well, back in Lovell, my mom and dad tried to talk me out of any romantic notions towards Karl. They said that according to the sentiments expressed during the fireside, Karl and his group of followers were well on the road to apostasy from the Allred group. They said that Tod, his friend from Salt Lake, had spoken out against Brother Owen, saying that he didn't have any authority whatsoever to perform the sacred endowment ceremonies that they were performing in Salt Lake. Tod accused Brother Owen of stealing the endowment ceremony from the Church and then claiming that he had received it directly from God. That God had given him permission to perform this and other sacred ceremonies outside of the temple in their own endowment house. But Tod and Karl both believed that Brother Owen wasn't worthy of any revelations from God, according to the ways he conducted business with his so-called, "brethren."

My parents were shocked. They themselves had gone through Brother Owen's endowment house in Salt Lake and had received their own sacred endowments and the long garments. Anyone who attacked their belief system—that they were truly endowed with the priesthood or power of God simply by going through an endowment ceremony—was attacking the belief system of the entire fundamentalist group. Since Karl had refused the endowment, calling it nothing but a big farce, then he was part of the apostate camp.

Well, I didn't want anything to do with the political controversy, so I decided to put the whole matter on the shelf for awhile—including my feelings for Karl. I took Branson and moved to New York to help my sister, Cori, who had just had a baby. Cori and her husband, Jim, believed in Mormon fundamentalism and were, in fact, courting Summer Moore to be in their family. Her family lived in New York, and I could tell when I first met them that they were special people. They were all in the process of studying Mormon fundamentalism and selling their home so they could move to Utah or Montana to live the fullness of the gospel.

They had a son, Blaine, who was close to my age and it wasn't long before Blaine and I started dating. We shared a lot in common—the most obvious having weird parents who believed in polygamy. We were also studying Mormon fundamentalism, and although we both believed in the principles, we weren't sure whether or not we could handle the plural marriage part and all of its obvious implications. And so after several months when Blaine asked me to marry him (I think it was my way of escaping the ultimate destiny that God had in store for me), I said, "yes."

When the Moores sold their home in New York, Blaine and I joined the caravan headed to Montana to check out the saints living the fullness of the gospel in Pinesdale. It was conference time and Brother Owen would be up; and so at the same time Blaine and I could ask his permission to marry.

A year had passed since I'd been at Higher Ground and I encouraged the Moores to stop there before going to Pinesdale so they could meet Karl, Jesse and their beautiful children. I also wanted them to feel the spirit that was on the land. My parents and family weren't at all convinced that I should marry Blaine, especially after all of the witnesses they'd received that I should marry Karl in spite of their fears. The whole family decided to fast and pray for three solid days so I would get a special witness from God about whom I should marry. They also convinced me to fast all day the day I arrived at Higher Ground so that I would receive a special witness.

So when I arrived at Higher Ground and greeted Karl and his family, who were still roughing it in a teepee and trailer, I was open to anything. But I wasn't fully prepared for what *did* happen.

When Karl congratulated Blaine and I on our engagement, even Blaine sensed my feelings as I held Karl's hand. Blaine held onto my hand tightly and tried to shower me with affection, but I knew right away that I was still in love with Karl. The love for him was even stronger than before. But still, I needed a witness from the Lord that plural marriage was right—and that Karl was the right man for me.

That night I slept in the teepee with some of Blaine's family while Blaine slept in the van with his parents. Karl and his family were sleeping in their trailer next to the teepee.

That night I had a profound dream or vision. I dreamed I was sitting in the teepee talking with Cori, when Karl walked by outside of the teepee. Cori pointed at Karl and said, "That's the man you are supposed to marry, Kirstie!"

I awoke the next morning with a divine sense of destiny swirling through my soul—along with rapturous love towards Karl. But letting Blaine and his family know the truth about my feelings and my revelation wasn't going to be easy. They all took it pretty hard, especially Blaine who all this time thought I was the girl of *his* dreams.

After an awkward breakfast with the Clark's, we continued our journey to Pinesdale to attend conference. Some of my family, including my mom, had come from Lovell to join us for the conference. When I told them about my dream concerning Karl, they were filled with mixed emotions.

Although the dream confirmed their previous revelations about Karl, they were very concerned about Karl's "apostate" attitude towards Brother Owen and "the group." But their worries were somewhat alleviated when Karl and his family traveled two hours to Pinesdale to participate in the conference activities. My mother sat by Karl and his family during conference to feel of their spirits. She got a witness of her own that Karl was the man for me.

The next big hurdle came when I felt that I needed to tell Karl and Jesse about my feelings and recent revelation. I wasn't the most courageous person and expressing myself verbally was not an easy task. But Jesse made it easier on me. I sensed she already knew by the Spirit what was going on inside of me. The day after the conference, she telephoned me and invited me to come and help her with the children as Jonah, her eleven-month-old baby, was going in for a hernia operation the following morning.

I gladly consented, as I had decided to stay in Montana while the rest of my family and Blaine's family traveled back home to Lovell or to Salt Lake. I needed some time to sort everything out and this was a chance to really get to know the Clarks and see whether I could fit into their lifestyle.

Well, the rest of the story is just family history. Although there's been a lot of trials and struggles—more than I or anyone could ever imagine—my firm testimony and witness from God that I belonged here with the Clarks at Higher Ground has seen me through them all. That, and my deep love for all of them in spite of all their weaknesses.

With that, Kirstie surrenders the story-teller's stool back to Grandma Jesse. The two women embrace lovingly in a way that only sister-wives can understand after 35 long years of a very unconventional marriage.

Chapter Thirteen

Flower Power

"So Grandma Jesse—what was happening with you when all of this was going on between Grandpa Karl and Granny Kissy? Weren't you having jealous feelings about it all?" questions teenaged Katrina, digging deep into the root of the matter.

Grandma was somewhat reluctant to get off her "comfort zone" and return to the "hot-seat" to talk about the difficult experiences living the principle of plural marriage. But she's always an open book to her beloveds, sharing with them her personal experiences so they could learn from them rather than having to repeat the same mistakes. She returns to her stool and her story-telling, sharing "her side of the story."

"Well," she begins, "while Karl was busy trying to save Higher Ground, I was on my own personal crusade trying to save the world."

It was the summer of 1990 and the threat of war with Iraq was in every news headline. I was concerned that it might trigger a bigger war—perhaps even World War III—if it wasn't contained. Perhaps my initial response was selfish. I so wanted to complete our vision for Higher Ground, which was becoming more of a reality each day. I petitioned the Lord in mighty prayer, asking him if there was anything I could do to stay the war or prevent it from escalating into World War III. His answer came to me very powerfully and direct. If there were enough people in this country willing to sacrifice for the cause of peace, he would bare his arm in our behalf according to our desires and sacrifices.

A plan unfolded in my mind. I was to write up a petition for a unified prayer and fast day for peace in the Middle East. I should give this petition to a close friend of mine who was the leader of a nation-wide political group— the *Independent Americans*—and ask him to filter it through this organization. And I was also to distribute it to every other organization and politically-active person I could think of.

The next morning, I walked over to my friend's home and shared with him the revelation I'd received. To my delight, he wasn't the least bit surprised as he had received a similar revelation three nights in a row, prompting him to write a political petition against the war and call for a boycott on all foreign oil since control over oil was the real cause of the war.

Together we worked diligently to write up petitions and get them out to all the individuals and organizations we knew. He approached the conservative segment, while I addressed the more liberal segment, mailing them out to peace and environmental groups across the nation. I was even impressed to send one to Windstar through Tom Crum. Karl and I talked with Tom several times on the phone about the situation in the Middle East. We urged him to talk to John Denver about putting together a concert benefit and calling it "Desert Peace," a play on words in opposition to "Desert Storm"—the name of the war in Kuwait. He promised us he would if he ran into John.

One day on my way back to my car after mailing out several peace petitions, I received a strong spiritual prompting to stop in the music store to see if John's latest album was out. (He continued to produce one every year—I fantasized for my benefit if for nothing else.) The lady at the counter informed me that they were expecting his new album release "any day now," and it promised to be "a good one." Its title she thought was intriguing—*The Flower that Shattered the Stone*.

I mulled the title over in my mind, thinking what a beautiful metaphor it was. It reminded me of two of my favorite Mormon scriptures, which always went straight to my heart. Doctrine and Covenants 1:19-23, which reads:

> The weak things of the world shall come forth and break down the mighty and strong ones, that man should not counsel his fellow man, neither trust in the arm of flesh— but that every man might speak in the name of God the Lord, even the Savior of the world; that faith also might increase in the earth; that mine everlasting covenant might be established; that the fullness of my gospel might be proclaimed by the weak and the simple unto the ends of the world, and before kings and rulers.

And my other favorite, D&C 65:2, which reads:

> The keys of the kingdom of God are committed unto man on earth, and from thence shall the gospel roll forth unto the ends of the earth, as the stone which is cut out of the mountain without hands shall roll forth, until it has filled the whole earth.

I was filled with great anticipation the next few days, waiting for the new album to arrive. My patience was well rewarded with just a glimpse of the album cover. John's pictured sitting beside an oriental vase of flowers holding a single yellow rose. It was all done in black and white except for the yellow rose. A sense of divine revelation leaped within my heart. *A yellow rose was my favorite flower.* Then the words to an earlier John Denver song penetrated my soul with more impact than ever before:

> I dreamed…
> You were a prophet in a meadow.
> I dreamed…
> I was a mountain in the wind.
> I dreamed…
> You knelt and touched me with a flower.
> I awoke with this…
> A flower in my hand

I could hardly drive the few miles from Hamilton to Pinesdale, my sight was so blurred with tears. But then the flood of tears came as I began listening to the first song, "The Flower that Shattered the Stone."

> The Earth is our Mother
> Just turning around
> With her trees in the forest
> Roots underground
> Our Father above us
> Whose sigh is the wind
> Paint us a rainbow
> Without any end
>
> As the river runs freely
> The mountain does rise
> Let me touch with my fingers

See with my eyes
In the hearts of the children
A pure love still grows
Like a bright star in heaven
That lights our way home
Like the flower that shattered the stone

Sparrows find freedom
Beholding the sun
In the infinite wisdom
We're all joined in one
I reach out before me
And look to the sky.
Did I hear someone whisper?
Did something pass by?

As the river runs freely
The mountain does rise
Let me touch with my fingers
See with my eyes
In the hearts of the children
A pure love still grows
Like a bright star in heaven
That lights our way home
Like the flower that shattered the stone

I sobbed as I listened to John's prophetic words and I couldn't stop crying until the last song, "Stonehaven Sunset" was played. The song deeply moved me as it described scenes of destruction that would come if we will not soften our hearts and change. After listening to the tape over and over again several times, I kept pondering the meaning of "Stonehaven." Suddenly it hit me like a ton of rocks (excuse the pun). It was the world. The world was Stonehaven as the hearts of men had turned to stone—unfeeling, unloving, and uncommitted to any relationship that required a sacrifice of the heart. My spirit sorrowed as I thought of all the prophecies concerning the Last Days and the ultimate consequences of the hardening of people's hearts. John had depicted it so passionately in his final song, "Stonehaven Sunset" as if he, himself, had seen it in vision.

Stonehaven sunset
The water's on fire

My true love is singing
We kiss and conspire
Sing a song for the ocean
A song for the sky
Sing a song for tomorrow
Love's sweet by and by
For the child that is coming
And for dreams that come true
Sing a song for each other
For me and for you
Sing a song for all lovers
All the stars in the skies
Sing for Stonehaven water home
Stonehaven sunrise

Stonehaven sunset
The desert's on fire
Christ on the cross again
Burns with desire
They are shooting at random
Though they aim at us all
It's the children who'll rise up
And children who fall
All the angels are weeping
The sweetest of tears
Fall like rivers of mercy
To wash all our fears
Sing a song for Old Glory
And a future that dies
Sing of Stonehaven desert home
Stonehaven sunrise

Stonehaven sunset
The city's on fire
The soldier's just smile and say
"This gun's for hire"
Give into the beast boy
Give into the thrill
It's just human nature
To hunt and to kill
We all die together

And yet somehow alone
Cause together we have memories
And then they are gone
Singing songs for old soldiers
A chorus of sighs
Sing of Stonehaven's city home
Stonehaven sunrise

Stonehaven sunset
The mountain's on fire
My spirit is lifted
Rising higher and higher
All the prophets are laughing
Saying "We told you so"
It's one thing to play guessing games
Another to know
For the needs of the many
Are the sins of a few
The day is forthcoming
When accounting is due
Sing a song for sweet Justice
With a fire in her eyes
Sing for Stonhaven mountain home
Stonehaven sunrise

In spite of the terrible prognosis of Stonehaven—the world—I knew deep down inside that there was still hope (as John envisions) as he repeats the first verse for the last verse:

Stonehaven sunset
The water's on fire
My true love is singing
We kiss and conspire
Sing a song for the ocean
A song for the sky
Sing a song for tomorrow
Love's sweet by and by
For the child that is coming
And for dreams that come true
Sing a song for each other
For me and for you

Sing a song for all lovers
All the stars in the skies
Sing for Stonehaven water home
Stonehaven sunrise

For his final song, he included a reprise of "The Flower that Shattered the Stone" after "Stonehaven Sunset." It was beautiful duet with a Japanese artist—half sung in English and half in Japanese. Perhaps this was another of John's prophetic metaphors—that if men would come together in harmony and oneness, no matter what their differences, that love would eventually triumph. Just as the flower that shattered the stone, the gentle power of love spreading its roots abroad within the hearts of men would cause a shattering of their hearts of stone. I then got out the Bible and looked up a few more passages supporting this concept:

"And hope maketh not ashamed; because the love of God is shed abroad in our hearts by the Holy Ghost which is given unto us." (Romans 5:5)

"That Christ may dwell in your hearts by faith; that ye being rooted and grounded in love, may be able to comprehend with all saints what is the breadth and length and depth, and height; and to know the love of Christ, which passeth knowledge, that ye might be filled with all the fullness of God." (Ephesians 3:17-19)

"And again, Esaias saith, There shall be a root of Jesse, and he that shall rise to reign over the Gentiles; in him shall the Gentiles trust. Now the God of hope fill you with all joy and peace in believing, that ye may abound in hope through the power of the Holy Ghost." (Isaiah 11:1, 2)

"And I will give them one heart, and I will put a new spirit within you; and I will take the stony heart out of their flesh, and will give them an heart of flesh:
That they may walk in my statutes, and keep mine ordinances, and do them; and they shall be my people, and I will be their God." (Ezekiel 11:19, 20)

John's new album rekindled in me a desire to plant, grow and blossom the seed of love so that it could shatter what ever was in my own heart that had hardened. But more than anything I wanted to share this love with others to help soften their hearts. I wasn't sure about the full meaning of all of this, or how much impact our prayer petitions had. We still went to war, but thanks to an almighty God, it lasted only a short time with few casualties. But I was convinced more than ever that God had a special calling for me in this world. It wasn't until years later that the full meaning of all of this was revealed.

That summer I drove to Windstar with Vince, hoping to share my serendipitous story with John and perhaps to get some insights about how we may be connected in the mystical puzzle called life. But as I explained earlier, the opportunity never materialized.

But another miracle started to happen as my own heart opened to love— the love I knew God was pouring into my heart. It went against all of my previous concepts or expectations; but during that trip to Aspen, Vince treated me with such genuine respect and was such a gentleman, that I began to fall in love with him.

When we got back from Colorado, he continued to look after me in Salt Lake while Karl was still working on the house at Higher Ground. He'd sent Ashley and the three younger children to Salt Lake, while Delaney and Jacob were left to help him up there. Vince made sure every one of my needs was met. He would come over to Mom's and help me with the laundry, the dishes, and tending children so that I could get the rest that I desperately needed.

I also helped him with his daughter, Melanie's, labor and delivery. It was a miraculous story. She had started into labor 6 weeks premature and had been put on bed rest in the hospital. The doctors performed an ultrasound on the fetus and determined that it was so deformed (according to the ultrasound, it had no legs and its kidneys were on the outside) that they were hoping that she would miscarry it naturally rather than having to take it by C-section. I told Vince and Melanie that the doctors weren't always right and brewed up a gallon of herbal miscarriage tea for Melanie to drink in order to stop the bleeding. She drank it faithfully and the bleeding stopped so the doctors allowed her to go home.

But a few weeks later she went into labor again. At the hospital I asked if Vince would join me in giving her a father's blessing. We held hands over Melanie's pregnant belly as I gave the blessing (as Vince wasn't able to). I told her that everything would turn out just as God wanted. Miraculously Melanie delivered a healthy, normal baby boy a few days later with the only complication of the baby having a herniated navel which the surgeons were able to repair.

Shortly after that I started into labor and I was hoping Karl would let Vince attend my delivery since we had become such dear friends. But Karl's male ego dominated and Vince was brusquely sent on his way. Karl also refused to let my mom or Rosalie attend the birth, even though I'd already asked them to be there. Karl was totally against anyone but himself being there, and I was in no condition to argue. But part of me was heartbroken by Karl's controlling attitude.

Nevertheless, Joshua Heart was born September 18 on his grandmother's bed while the rest of my family was in the other room celebrating Gordon's (Rosalie's son) birthday. Joshua was a big baby, weighing nearly ten pounds—according to the fish scales we'd borrowed from my midwife, Naomi, to weigh him. His shoulders were so big that they got wedged on my pelvic bone in the birth canal, and Karl was inspired to use his hands to maneuver them out. Ashley and the other children came in after the delivery to help with the clean-up and care of their brand-new baby brother. I suppose everything turned out all right despite all the disappointed people at not being able to share in the delivery. I vowed that at my next delivery, I would insist on those I wanted there be welcomed (in spite of Karl's objections).

That winter we stayed in Salt Lake and house-tended for Mom and Dad while they went down to Yuma, Arizona for the winter as the cold weather was hard on my mom's asthma. Our plan was to save up enough money that winter to finish our log cabin at Higher Ground. Karl landed a good-paying job at Dr. Christopher's Herb Shop in Springville and I also helped him write and edit two books for their company—*Herbs to the Rescue* and *Thank-you, Mother Nature*. With the commission from the books and a loan from my dad for over $7,000 out of our family trust, we were able to get our roof on and our cabin enclosed with doors and windows. By the end of summer we were just about ready to move into our new log cabin when Kirstie came along with the revelation that she belonged in our family.

Of course after living in a polygamous community for nearly five years, I often wondered what it would be like to have a sister-wife. I thought it might be nice to have someone to help with house-hold duties, assist with childcare, share girl-talk, and, in general, have a best friend to love and trust like a sister—only more intimately. But I also wondered if it were possible to work out and overcome petty jealousies and the underlying need to control the relationship. Not to mention the sharing of a husband—our time and intimacy.

Most polygamous relationships I knew didn't seem to work very well. A lot of women instead of resolving their emotional issues, stuffed them deep down inside, causing "dis-ease" to erupt in their physical health. Most sister-wives chose to live in separate houses, distancing themselves from each other so they wouldn't have to be confronted daily with the reality of sharing a husband. I joked that this was God's approved system of "sleeping around," as a man went from house to house, wife to wife, only staying there long enough to "procreate." I thought this was a rather sick approach to a Divine principle that was supposed to refine people. I believed that transformation came from facing and dealing with issues, rather than sweeping them under the carpet—only to have them reappear uglier than ever.

Karl and I had talked about polygamy a lot. We'd decided that if anyone were to come into our family; that our family would remain together, with everyone living under the same roof, if possible. Not only had we witnessed the alienation which living separately produced in sister-wives, but we'd also witnessed the damage caused to children who had only a "part-time daddy".

But all of this was mere conjecture. Because of our so-called "apostasy" from the Pinesdale group, we never dreamed that we'd ever actually live polygamy. But when Kirstie shared her profound revelation things became more challenging for us. I needed to do some serious soul-searching to see if I was ready to take such a gigantic leap of faith.

So I called up Kirstie, who was staying with a family in Pinesdale, to come up for a week or so to help Karl and Ashley tend the children so I could go on my version of a "Vision Quest." It entailed going back to the Colorado Rockies where I'd first experienced my "born again" experience and journal all of my thoughts, feelings and experiences which happened to me since then. I wrote in a notebook the story of my synchronistic path, which had led me to my current point in time. Many of my experiences were so profound and sacred that I hadn't shared them with anyone. I didn't think anyone would believe me. I then felt impressed by the Spirit to type my story and deliver it to John Denver at that year's Windstar Symposium held the following weekend in August.

By the time I got back to Salt Lake, I felt physically and spiritually exhausted. I needed some added support to get me through this monumental task, as it seemed like I'd opened up a kind of Pandora's Box in the Spirit World. The Spirit told me to take Rosalie with me to the Windstar Symposium as she'd become somewhat clairvoyant, able to recognize and even identify different spiritual entities. It seemed as if everything on the dark side was using their power to stop me from completing my quest. Rosalie's keen intuitions would be an added protection.

When I explained to her my intentions of giving John my story, she agreed to go with me. As we prepared for the trip, Rosalie would sometimes perceive the faces of evil spirits surrounding us and be paralyzed to know what to do. I was sensitive to spirits, although I couldn't see them, so I would make the priesthood sign of the square and command them to leave in the name of Jesus Christ—and immediately they would. We had one experience where Rosalie's dog barked loudly at something in her bedroom which she perceived as an evil spirit. I commanded it to leave and we watched the dog chase after it as it left the room.

These kinds of experiences, too numerous to mention, punctuated our trip. It was as if all heaven and hell were testing our intentions and integrity to fulfill the destiny which I felt God had prepared for us. And so we went with serious fasting and praying to Colorado; and whenever we met an obstacle, instead of confronting it directly, we would simply maintain presence until we could pass through it or until it would pass.

For three days we kept vigil, maintaining presence outside of the conference tent where the Windstar Symposium was being held. I carried a brown paper sack containing my story bound in a yellow folder, waiting for an opportunity to give it to John. For three days the rain showered us, the hot sun baked us, and people asked us why we were outside of the tent rather than inside listening to the Symposium. The answer was simple: We hadn't come to the Symposium to listen to famous people speak on important subjects like the ecology and personal transformation. We were there to deliver a message to John. Rather than explaining such a bizarre story, we simply said we couldn't afford the $300 price of admission —which was also true.

On the second evening, a curious thing happened. We had traveled in our parents' minivan, which we slept in at night. We decided to spend that night in the parking lot adjacent to the Aspen Institute for Humanistic Studies.

An exceptionally attractive Native American artist with gorgeous, long, black hair (to whom we'd talked on several occasions during the past two days) followed us out to the minivan after the Symposium. His name was Sergio and Rosalie had struck a bargain with him. She would give him a full-body massage in exchange for one of his unique tribal paintings. That evening seemed an appropriate time to make the exchange.

As the three of us talked outside the van, the subject of polygamy came up. Surprisingly, Sergio had recently divorced an ex-Mormon who had believed in it. I shared with him my personal struggles of how I felt traditional polygamy was imbalanced and subjected women to male dominance even more so than monogamy. To my astonishment, Sergio actually agreed with me. He then shared his own concept of "just letting go of *all* religious structure and going with the *flow of the spirit.*"

We continued with the dialogue as he expressed, "I feel the spirit has been moving on all three of us together into this time and space so that we can share some profound intimacy between the three of us." Sergio then escorted us both into the van and before either of us could voice an objection, he began peeling off his loose-fitting clothes. His ebony hair cascaded down his rippling bronze back reaching down to touch a perfect buttocks. An uncontrollable gasp escaped my lips as he turned around to expose a fully erect penis measuring nearly the length of my forearm. He stretched his chocolate body the full length of the bed, inviting us both to partake.

"WOW," I heard Rosalie murmur, expressing both our thoughts. Silence followed as we considered the scene before us.

Here I was witnessing one of my greatest fantasies displayed in full view. Thoughts of Karl and Kirstie on the mountain—perhaps having sex with each other with me hundreds of miles away—began to cloud my judgment. I was about to give into my lusts when Rosalie spoke. "Hey look, Sergio. I'd be glad to give you a massage, but anything else—well, I just don't think so. We're really flattered, but we barely even know you. And we're both kind of stuck in other relationships right now—if you know what I mean."

Thank heaven for little sisters. My mind was still reeling at the thoughts of what it would be like to…yet how could I do that to Karl? I'd been faithful to him for sixteen years in spite of temptations. No, my heart just wouldn't let me go there no matter how much I thought my body would enjoy it. But why had Rosalie refused this outrageous fantasy? She was single, unattached, and attracted to Native Americans. Perhaps it was her way of protecting me from myself, but I still could have vicariously enjoyed the lovemaking. At least that would have fulfilled some of our fantasies.

"Aw, that's okay, I really don't feel like a massage tonight, anyway," Sergio replied a bit disgruntled. My eyes were riveted as he pulled his workout pants up over his luscious lingam. My fantasies soon disappeared along with it.

I was still recovering when Sergio asked if he could read the book I'd brought with me. I assumed he was talking about the book, *The Lamanite People* which I'd been obviously reading for the past two days. "Sure." I said, handing him the book by a Mormon author about what Mormon's believe to be his native ancestors—the Lamanites.

"No, I don't mean *that* one," he replied. "I'd like the *yellow notebook.*"

"How could you possibly know anything about my yellow notebook!?" I exclaimed, appalled by his trespass on my sacred ground. "I haven't shown that notebook to anyone!"

"Oh, the spirits told me about your 'yellow notebook' and said it was for *me* to read," he replied, undaunted by my reaction.

With that we both asked him to leave. My yellow notebook was personal, not to be shared with anyone except John. But Sergio continued to hang around, blowing puffs of cigarette smoke into our van. Finally, I *insisted* that he leave.

He departed with a shrug at his failure in obtaining what he really was after. After Sergio left, Rosalie panicked, envisioning a myriad of evil spirits surrounding the van. She was too paralyzed to do anything—except *anoint the inside of the van with consecrated olive oil!* I pronounced the priesthood command to leave, then took the wheel, driving at break-neck speed to Eagle County where Rosalie was convinced we would be safe.

The next day was the third and final day of the Symposium. Despite the provocative distractions from Sergio performing *Thai Chi* on the lawn outside the conference tent, we kept our vigil. Finally an opportunity arose to give my yellow notebook to John just as he was leaving. He accepted it a bit reluctantly with a polite "thanks" and then turned to Rosalie and asked, "Don't I know you from somewhere?"

"Actually, I've never met you before, John. Perhaps we have a spiritual connection being *her* sister," she replied, pointing at me.

John nodded in acknowledgement and then excused himself to leave. He then jumped into his cherry-red convertible and drove off in a blaze of celebrity glory. Rosalie and I were left wondering why we'd even made the effort to come. Nonetheless it did seem as if a heavy burden was lifted from my shoulders. Like an unpaid debt or some unknown contract I'd made with John perhaps in another lifetime. I knew I'd fulfilled my part of the contract. The rest was up to him.

With mixed feelings of disappointment and victory, Rosalie and I set off on our journey back home. We both agreed that we needed to stop in at the Grand Junction prison to visit Vince who had been sentenced and imprisoned there.

Vince looked rather disconcerting in his prison garb playing the role of a convicted felon. As we conversed through the glass barrier, he confided that they were treating him rather decent. They'd even agreed to give him the vegetarian diet he requested out of respect for his spiritual beliefs.

I expressed how I'd missed having him along as an escort for this year's Symposium—I'd so enjoyed his company the previous year. Rosalie and I then related all the extraordinary events surrounding this year's symposium concluding with our victory in giving John Denver the yellow notebook. Vince was more amused than amazed and we could have talked for hours. It wasn't long before the prison guard arrived to escort Vince back to his cell.

My heart winced as I watched him go. I probably wouldn't see him again for quite some time. What a terrible waste of human potential, I thought. But perhaps this was Vince's way of reconciliation with himself…and perhaps God.

Rosalie and I then stopped in Salt Lake to return the van to our parents. We thanked them and hugged our farewells. I hopped in my Toyota truck and headed back home to my precious family in Montana.

My head was racing and my heart soaring as I thought of being in Karl's arms and hugging my children, feeling that dazzling joy of being together again after four long weeks of separation. I never anticipated being gone so long. I knew it had to be as hard on them as it was on me, but I felt driven by my need to get my own spiritual witness before embarking on the path of plural marriage. I needed that reassurance, that certainty. I'd found it on my vision quest, and I hoped my children and Karl had understood the depth of that necessity.

And Kirstie? What kind of experience had she had? She'd gained her spiritual witness already, but did she understand the sacrifices, the complexities, and the sheer physical labor of living a close-to-nature lifestyle in a simple house filled with children? These four weeks had given her a taste of what being in the Clark family would be like before she made any final commitments to marriage. I couldn't guess whether she'd still be there when I got back. There was no phone service on the mountain, and Karl couldn't call me once I left Salt Lake. I wondered if he received the numerous letters I'd written, keeping him updated on my whereabouts. I was clueless what to expect as I rounded the last turn that led to our trailer/teepee compound.

My heart was filled with sweet anticipation, expecting to see a few of my children out playing. In the twilight of early evening all that greeted me was quiet emptiness. I parked the truck next to the trailer. As I entered the darkness, a cold chill engulfed me as I realized—no one was there! A trickle of twilight filtered through the trailer window to illuminate the note stuck to the refrigerator door: *I hope you had a nice trip. We decided to go on a trip of our own. See you later. Karl and the kids.*

My heart burst with sorrow and my eyes filled with tears. I suspected that Karl was seeking revenge for my being away so long. I was angered by his vindictiveness and remorseful for being gone so long. I felt consumed with uncertainty—had Kirstie gone with them? If not, where was she? I curled up in a cold bed and wept all night long in painful agony. The uncertainty of all of it was unbearable.

But that pain was nothing compared to the torture I would experience nearly a year later as I watched Karl and Kirstie walk off arm in arm to the car in which they would drive to the spot they had secretly chosen for their honeymoon.

It had been a beautiful wedding. I'd done my very best to help make it that way. Even though I was eight and a half months pregnant with our ninth child, Jasmine, I didn't spare any effort in preparing for Kirstie's and Karl's wedding.

Kirstie had moved up to the land in April, and we'd been busy for weeks sewing floral-printed dresses for all of my girls and bow ties and vests for the little boys—Justin, Joshua and her Branson. We'd gathered and dried Higher Ground wildflowers, then fashioned them into bouquets, wreaths and garlands for decorations. The older girls—fourteen-year-old Ashley and ten-year-old Delaney—helped with the refreshments creating rose and heart-shaped mints and huckleberry tarts to be served on floral paper plates and table-cloths which Kirstie and I had picked out together.

Kirstie and I had become fast friends. Her love for me and my children was unmistakable in the letters she'd written from Wyoming. I'd always been included in Karl's conversations over the phone to Kirstie and they never went anywhere without including me. They were both sensitive to my feelings of needing to feel included in the courtship. It wasn't just a courtship between two people, but the courtship of an entire family moving into a marriage relationship. Now came the final stages of preparation for the big event—their wedding day.

I helped Kirstie into her wedding dress—a beautiful, cream two-piece outfit that complimented her boyish figure. I watched her arrange her chestnut hair into an attractive bun in the mirror when suddenly I caught a glimpse of my own bulging floral figure. I flinched at the contrast between her radiant face and my distraught one. I'd hoped that being absorbed in all the busy-ness of wedding plans and preparations would consume the gnawing ache in my heart, the doubts and fears biting me each time I let my mind escape to the time I would finally have to let go…and wondering if I really could.

My mind reminisced over the past sixteen years of marriage, struggling through conflicts over money, family, sex, children, religion, politics, etc. You name it, Karl and I fought over it. And just as our fights were passionately fought, so was our lovemaking. In fact recently our lovemaking was more passionate than it had ever been in our entire life. We felt God's love pouring into our hearts and overflowing to others, healing them as it had healed us. Karl and I both felt that God was evolving us—that his direct influence had transformed us, making us ready for this gigantic leap into plural marriage. But was I *really* ready?

The ceremony was simple and beautiful. The three of us gathered in front of the newly finished stone fireplace while Kirstie's father conducted. He greeted the audience of family and friends and then said a few words of counsel to the three of us. He then went on to perform the marriage. During the part where he asked me to place Kirstie's hand into Karl's as a token of my consent to their marriage, I nearly broke. But somewhere deep within me, strength welled up to perform this sacrificial rite—of giving the hand of my beloved Karl to someone I'd come to love. And with that strength came a surge of pain, a warning that I would be tried and refined in ways I'd yet to learn. Karl then took Kirstie into his arms and kissed her for the first time I was witness to. They beamed as they looked into each other's eyes. I tried to smile, but the pains of jealousy for this fresh, new love turned my smile into a grimace.

When it was time for them to leave, my best friend, Jody, materialized at my side and took my hand. I squeezed her hand tightly in agony as I watched the two of them walk away hand in hand to the car. I truly wondered if I would survive. She sensed what I was feeling and her support gave me the necessary strength to bid farewell to all of the remaining wedding guests. With rigid composure I hugged Kirstie's family good-bye, trying to avoid eye contact. They cooperated—acting cheerful and departing quickly. Many of them had already been through "it" before as Kirstie's dad had recently married his third wife, Kirstie's two brothers had both taken second wives, and her sister's husband had just married his second wife. They were only too familiar with the telltale signs—the blank stares, the feigned smiles, the low-voiced remarks. Actually, the mood felt more like a funeral than a wedding—and I was the new "widow." They didn't try to hide their own eagerness to get away from the newest reminder of the hurt that plural weddings had caused them.

After the last guest had left and the last of the clean-up was finished, I asked the older girls to watch the younger ones, so I could go for a walk. Jody volunteered to go with me. From her concerned face, I could tell she didn't think this was a good time for me to be alone. I smiled wanly but reassured her that some things you just had to face alone.

And so I went alone to face and embrace the agonizing dragon that lurked within me. Thank God that *he* was the only one around to witness my heart shattering into a million fragments upon Marriage Mountain.

Chapter Fourteen

At-one-ment

"Grandma...how did you ever endure the pain and jealousy that living plural marriage caused?" questions Katrina, still wanting to get to the very heart of things.

"Well, Katrina, it was kind of like the time we lost our tiny Jadon. God seems to surround you with a warm blanket of love, letting you know that it is something you must walk through for you own good...and perhaps for the good of others who might learn from your experiences. But God *is always there* to comfort you while you go through it, no matter how difficult your path may be."

"Are you saying that God *wants* us to go through painful experiences for our *own good?*" insists Katrina.

"Well, I don't believe God really *wants* us to suffer, my dear," responds Jesse thoughtfully. "Sometimes our own illusions of our separateness causes us pain...and also our fears. Yes, God expects us to walk through these illusions and fears so that we can get through the darkness and into the light. Then we can realize, or with "real eyes" see our illusions and fears for what they truly are—sins or separations within us that prevent us from being one with each other and one with God. And that is where the *real* joy of love can be experienced."

Jesse looked intently at Katrina's face absorbed in what she was saying... then at the older children's blank stares. The little ones had broken away and were playing on the hillside with each other.

"Let me share with you how I discovered this sacred secret of the at-one-ment, or what others may term—the atonement."

Karl and Kirstie were on their honeymoon for three days. It was a heart-wrenching time for me, but afterwards I experienced a glorious reunion with Karl upon their return. He stunned me with his sensitivity. He gifted me with a beautiful bouquet of flowers and a card expressing his deep, heart-felt love because of my willing sacrifice. Privately, he shared with me that he felt like the last three days were like lying in the tomb after being nailed to the cross. Even though he had enjoyed his time with Kirstie, he'd experienced my pain although we were miles apart. That night we were joined together in tender lovemaking like we'd never experienced before and I knew that our relationship had truly transcended into higher realms.

I then shared with him my feelings that if God was truly part of this principle of plural marriage, then there must be a more sensitive way of consummating the marriage vows. I told him that I could've *never* put him through the pain that he'd just put me through. Karl didn't want to hear the agonizing details of my anguish, but recognized that he could never have endured it himself. I had a hard time believing that God was part of the principle of plural marriage—at least the way it was presently lived. It totally went against the Golden Rule—to do unto others as you would have others do unto you.

But with the birth of sweet Kandice two weeks later, those feelings of resentment towards God and Karl drifted to the back of my mind. I delivered her in the privacy and comfort of my own bedroom at Higher Ground with Kirstie, Ashley, and Delaney, all present. It was the easiest delivery thus far (perhaps the pains of childbirth were diminished in comparison to the pains of the heart suffered two weeks earlier). I was pampered for several weeks afterwards—a luxury I'd never experienced before Kirstie came into the family.

A few months after Kandice's birth, the Spirit brought us into a kinder place of marriage. We all three got a spiritual witness nearly simultaneously that we should reconsummate our marriage vows...all together. And so the three of us did the unthinkable in FLDS tradition—we all three made love all together. This experience allowed me to confront another one of my greatest fears—the fear of actually witnessing Karl and Kirstie making love. It was truly beautiful and it also made me feel married to Kirstie. It was a sacred and divine act of communion, which cannot be expressed in words. Words could never describe the sheer ecstasy we all felt making love together. It was truly liberating to the spirit and soul.

And so the three of us now united in love, began the journey of learning just what God was trying to teach us in plural marriage.

Some of the lessons were easy and positive as plural marriage had real benefits for us all. I now had a sister-wife to help with the difficult task of caring for this large household now numbering a dozen. And Karl had another "help-mate" to attend to all of his physical and emotional pleasures. As for Kirstie…well, her dreams were met each time she looked into Karl's eyes and welcomed him into her bedroom every other night. And believe it or not, Karl and I got to spend more intimate time together as we knew that the children would be cared for if we chose to sleep in. Someone was always available to make breakfast in the morning depending upon whose turn it was.

But then Kirstie became pregnant a few months later and things took a turn in a different direction. She was practically bedridden from the very start with morning sickness, sometimes refusing to get out of bed for the entire day. I struggled to take care of own my children, her toddler Branson, Karl, Kirstie—the entire household single-handed. Of course my older children were a big help as I cared for Kirstie with herbs and a good diet. I'd never experienced morning sickness like this before and I knew she needed to do a lot of physical and emotional healing from her past behavioral patterns. And though I loved her dearly and wanted to help her in any way possible, I knew it was a path she had to walk herself.

She gained a lot of weight during her pregnancy, which made her feel fat and unattractive. Her opinions about herself dampened the fire of passion between the two newlyweds, but worse was her depression. Finally, Karl didn't even want to sleep with her anymore because of her low self-esteem.

I was also becoming somewhat resentful towards the whole situation, as I felt overburdened with the added care of Branson and Kirstie. I didn't object to Karl's neglect towards Kirstie and his additional show of affection towards me. I almost felt justified that I deserved the added attention. I felt that Karl had finally gained the sensitivity he previously lacked in our relationship and was now considering my needs.

Unfortunately, Kirstie became so full of resentment and bitterness that she secretly prayed that neither of us would be at her delivery. Her prayers were partly answered. Due to complications of a tipped uterus, Ruth, the midwife from the Ranch, delivered her baby in Pinesdale. I was present, but Karl was left home to tend the children and didn't make it in time to witness Alma's birth.

But the blessings of a new life brought a refreshing, new awareness into our relationship. We committed to each other that we would try harder to be more sensitive to each other's feelings and needs. We also became more aware of God's hand in our lives as he began molding us into the kind of loving individuals he'd intended us to be. Our hearts became more open to his divine love, which enlightened and expanded our minds. God was leading us on a treasure hunt for the true meaning of "Zion" or the "pure in heart."

On our search for truth, we began studying various other religions, including Hinduism, Buddhism, Taoism, Native American spirituality, and even the Cosmic Mother religion, which had been labeled "paganism." We found that each religion contained similar seeds of truth cultivated around the mystical idea of our spiritual connection or "oneness"...and our ultimate return to that oneness through the path of enlightenment. Love was the ultimate master and teacher. If we simply followed this path—the path of our hearts and spirit—it would ultimately lead us back to God and who we truly are.

As I dove deeper into the roots of various religions, I became convinced that Joseph Smith had received many "keys of the kingdom" from a divine source. Faith, baptism, laying on of hands, herbs, holistic health, the gifts of the Holy Spirit—all were essential keys to turn the lock to God. But I became convinced that the "higher principles" of plural marriage and United Order were the *real* keys all the other religions lacked. How else could one experience first-hand the insights on how vast and expansive love can be? How else could one learn what it means to have unconditional, God-like love? The prophets of the Old Testament experienced oneness with God and received insights and revelations directly from God. The reason—they were living plural marriage. To deny this is to deny the very foundations of Judaism and Christianity. Islam is a religion founded from a plural marriage gone awry—Sarah and Hagaar's disagreement.

Perhaps the first century Gnostic Christians were living plural marriage with the concept of "all things common." Did "all things common" mean a common marriage? Was Christ himself in a common marriage to "the church" as is alluded to in the New Testament? Had this concept been destroyed by Constantine and the Christian Crusades, which eventually wiped out the Christian heretics who lived this way? Then it crept up again in the Renaissance Era to be wiped out again during the Inquisition. Had Joseph Smith attempted to recreate "the primitive church" in these, the last days? Had his death and the subsequent tyranny of Brigham Young—who perverted the truth about plural marriage, making it a male-dominated principle—thwarted his efforts? Was this why so few women in scriptural history were prophetesses receiving divine revelation? Were women also required to live plural marriage—the same as men?

These questions pricked my heart and I felt a longing to find people to share the concept of "all things common" or the true United Order. A people with a desire to build God's kingdom—or at least a prototype Zion community here at Higher Ground. Karl and I were led, at various times by the Spirit, to make connections with people from all over the country. We traveled to Salt Lake many times, and to Manti, where a group of people had gathered to live the "fullness of the gospel." A few of our old polygamous friends had ventured down there and had joined what they called a "United Brotherhood." Again, it was based on polygyny (favoring males) rather than true and equal polygamy.

And then in 1993, Karl and I traveled to Aspen, Colorado to attend, for the first time together, the Windstar Symposium. Of course I was hoping to finally connect with John Denver, not to mention my friend Tom Crum and their associates from around the world. But to everyone's disappointment this was the one year John was prevented from attending the Symposium because of a head injury sustained in a drunk-driving accident where he ran head-on into a tree.

We again attended the following year, but John Denver pretty much kept to himself due to a painful divorce with his second wife, Cassandra. (Isn't it funny how pain or perceived pain always keeps us in a state of separation?)

But who could deny the valuable learning afforded us at the Windstar Symposiums as we were able to make connections with influential people such as Whoppi Goldberg, Jerry Jampolosky, Frances Moore Lappe, Matthew Fox, Bro. David Stendl Rast, Lou Gold, John Michael Cousteau, Kenny Loggins, Carlos Nakai, John Robbins, Dennis Weaver, Joseph Cornell, and a long list of others who were authors and leaders of the world community movement. The inspiration and motivation from the various presenters was incredible and, in particular, John Denver's music. Always personally prophetic to me, it seemed to define in poetic metaphor how we must evolve in order to survive into the twenty-first century. And that evolution included the necessity of a world community based on love and integrity—or what I defined as "coming together in oneness."

One of my favorite songs capturing what this community metaphor meant was recorded on John's 1991 album, paradoxically entitled *Different Directions*—the album sentimentalizing his second divorce from Cassandra. He sang "Amazon" at a Wildlife Concert in Park City, Utah, which Karl and I attended for our eighteenth wedding anniversary.

Amazon

There is a river that runs from the mountain
That one river is all rivers
All rivers are that one

There is a tree that stands in the forest
That one tree is all forests
All trees are that one

There is a flower that blooms in the desert
That one blossom is all flowers
All flowers are that one

There is a bird that sings in the jungle
That one song is all music
All songs are that one

It is the song of life
It is the flower of faith
It is the tree of temptation
It is the river of no regrets

There is a child that cries in the ghetto
That one child is all children
All children are that one

There is a vision that shines in the darkness
That one vision is all of our dreams
All of our dreams are that one

It is the vision of heaven
It is the child of promise
It is the song of life
It is the river of no regrets

Let this be a voice for the mountain
Let this be a voice for the river
Let this be a voice for the forest
Let this be a voice for the flower
Let this be a voice for the desert
Let this be a voice for the ocean
Let this be a voice for the children
Let this be a voice for the dreamer
Let this be a voice of no regrets

I'd often wondered why someone who could write poetry and sing so brilliantly about love, unity, spirit and passion could have such tragedies in his own personal life as evidenced by John's drunkenness and divorces. But some insights into John Denver's personal life, which our mutual friend, Tom, shared, made me less quick to judge.

With added awareness, I noticed that our oneness relationship with Kirstie was again unraveling. She was left at home to tend the children and take care of the household chores; while Karl and I traveled around, expanding ourselves in new relationships and knowledge. She was, in essence, dying on the vine while we were growing and expanding. We all agreed it just wasn't fair! There had to be balance between expansion and maintenance or the integrity of relationship suffers.

And so Karl and I concentrated on strengthening our home-front and waited for God to move on individual's hearts to gather with us here at Higher Ground. I started developing a new curriculum for the children's home-school studies based on the principles of integrity that we were learning. And Karl worked on his relationship with Kirstie, helping her feel a part of our intricate circle. I began to compile my journey into a book called *Becoming One--a journey into relationship wholeness*. The initial inspiration for the book came from a passage in Doctrine and Covenants 38:27 regarding Zion or the United Order. It states:

"Behold, this I have given unto you as a parable, and it is even as I am. I say unto you, be one; and if ye are not one ye are not mine."

The book ended up being a 500-page volume defining and illustrating principles of oneness through various religious doctrines, metaphors, and personal experiences. It also demonstrated how all man-made institutions and organizations had not only failed to bring about this oneness (integrity), but because of man's unrighteous dominion, had become diabolical and diametrically opposed to oneness. (The Greek prefix "dia" means "through or between," and "di" means "two.")

In my book I outlined the sequence of events in an average person's life. An average person is born in a hospital institution, which is often a hostile and alien environment for both baby and mother. Almost immediately after birth, the baby is taken away from its primary source (mother) to be bathed, weighed and measured by a hired attendant. The infant immediately suffers feelings of pain and separation. Unless the mother requests in-room nursing, the baby is cared for by a hired attendant for those first few hours or perhaps days of the infant's life. If the baby is a boy, he can expect the added trauma of circumcision performed a few days or so after birth. In the course of the next few years, that same infant is weighed, measured, and pierced by needles again by a hired attendant, causing more pain and feelings of separation.

Then at the golden age five, the child is again taken away from its primary source (mom and dad) and institutionalized in an alien environment to be programmed in whatever agenda the institution has currently chosen—again by hired attendants. This process goes on during the child's formative years—ages five to seventeen—until any connections with the child's primary source (family) has been seriously challenged. After the disengaged young adult has been programmed with enough media propaganda via TV, movies, magazines and novels especially promoting the sacrilegious subject of sex, and is desensitized towards violence; then the young adult is encouraged to engage in intimate, non-committed relationships either inside or outside the institute of marriage.

Since most young adults have personally witnessed few examples of deep, long-lasting, committed relationships in their own lives or in modern society, their own relationships rarely last longer than a few years. The young person is doomed to believe that life is an unloving and fearful place, and feels isolated in the illusions of separation. Because of these feelings of isolation and fear, it is easy for the young person to commit acts of violence because there is no real feeling of conscious connection to the individuals around him. Then the institutions of our society reclaim these diabolical products they have created within their prisons, mental institutions or welfare systems because they have cracked under all the stress.

And the great corruption conspiracy begins all over again in the next generation. And conspiracy it is. *Any institution which inhibits a human soul from following the path of Spirit is evil and corrupt.* Evil spelled backwards is live—it is the opposite of life. We can no longer live in an evil environment or our very integrity begins to disintegrate. And thus the very fiber of society begins to unravel and disintegrate.

The conspiracy problem of division and separation is complex requiring a total revision of our present-day belief systems. Though discouragingly difficult, it is not impossible. I have obtained positive results with my own children who are home-birthed, home-health-cared, home-educated, and raised in a natural environment without TV or other intrusions. But these results require dedicated investment from parents who truly care about the welfare of their children. If our society is to survive and evolve into the twenty-first century when everyone's personal integrity will be challenged—then these principles must be taught. And so I became a "voice crying in the wilderness" for people to have ears to hear and eyes to see. I yearned for a simple metaphor to explain this concept of oneness to others, something easier than reading my still unpublished 500-page manuscript.

Then one day as I was listening to a tape (recorded at the last and final Windstar Symposium), reminiscing on how powerfully this one song of John

Denver's had impacted me when I was there in person. The words to this incredible love song again hit me like no other. No title had been announced, so I simply named it "John's Song."

In this magic hour of softening light
The moments in between the day and the night
The instant when all shadows disappear
The distance in between the love and the fear
There's a longing deep within the wandering soul
It's like the half that understands it once was whole
Like the two who only dream of being one
Like the moon whose only light is in the sun
There's a danger in forever looking outside
You start to believe that all your prayers have been denied
And you forget the sound of your own name
Thus begins the suffering and pain

I wanted an answer
I wanted a way
I wanted to know just what to do
And what to say
I wanted a reason
I want to know why,
Can there never be heaven right here on earth
And peace inside?
Inside my heart
Deep in my soul
Within each part
And in the whole

There's a promise in the journeys of the mind
You begin to believe that there are miracles you will find
And that someday you'll remember who you are…
The seed within a bright and shining star
It's like the flame that lives within each hungering heart
That only awaits the gift of love for it to start
Into a fire that burns forever endlessly
Like the river that can't help but meet the sea
In the moments in between the dark and the dawn
In the space between the silence and the song
Suddenly the mystery is clear…

Love is only letting go of fear

Love is the answer
Love is the way
Love is in knowing just what to do
And what to say
Love is the reason
Love is the why
Love is in heaven right here on earth
And peace inside
Inside your heart
Deep in your soul
Within each part
And in the whole...

After the usual shedding of tears over the intimate journey John always takes me on into a communion of hearts, a profound feeling of ecstatic revelation started to flood my consciousness, bringing me into a mystical feeling of oneness with John and with my Creator.

Divine revelation started to flow into my mind...Heavenly Father—the Creator, Jesus Christ—the Redeemer, and the Holy Spirit—the Testifier, though represented as three, were one entity manifest in different personages or roles. That one entity called "God" was attempting to court us all back into oneness with him/her. We were all there in the beginning with God as part of the Holy Spirit essence—like seeds within a bright and shining star. Our very being, our very make-up, our very DNA was and is God-substance, God-created, God-spawned; and like seeds from their primary source, we had been planted down on earth to see if we would sprout, flower, and produce fruit. The only problem was—we hadn't a clue as to what this mystical experience was all about until...yes, until we became firmly established in good soil and began to grow...and blossom...and then start to produce fruit. We hadn't a clue that we were God-seed until we produced it for ourselves and became as God!

Then the thoughts continued to become even more clear. No, we *had* been given a clue—in fact there were a myriad of clues and metaphors all around us about who we are and what are final destiny is. And the biggest clue was the life of Jesus Christ, the supreme example of what divine, unconditional love was all about. That love wasn't just a feeling of the heart, but was a committed act of total unselfish compassion. The caring essence of love.

Yes, love is the answer, love is the way. Jesus Christ—God incarnate—showed us the way by hanging upon the cross in a supreme act of compassion to demonstrate the at-one-ment. He offered a way for us to repent (turn around) from all of our sins (separations within) and become whole again. The image of the cross came into my mind and what a simple yet profound metaphor it is. The two arms or poles come together at one intersection, one point of contact. And the profound thought came to me that at that point of intersection was where the very heart of Jesus was as he hung upon it. At this point of Christ-consciousness, of unconditional love, of balance, of beauty—everything comes together in oneness.

I thought of how all paradoxes in life, or seemingly opposite points of view, all have their point of intersection contained in the cross. John had described so beautifully some of these paradoxes in his song. How light and darkness had their point of intersection in the moments of dusk and dawn—that mystical, magical hour of twilight when the birds and creatures of the earth sing their prayers to their creator. The inspiration that comes to a singer in that space between the silence and the song. Two lovers become one in the most delightful experience available to us—the marriage act or consummation of two physical bodies.

The divine revelation continued…that this was what relationship was all about—these divine "marriage-acts" of God. All dichotomies, all contradictions, all opposites, all paradoxes, all differences of opinions—all come together in divine consummation. The word "consummation" came to mind, so I looked it up in the dictionary:

1. To bring to completion; to complete; achieve.
2. To perfect.
3. To complete by intercourse; said of marriage.

The cross. The mystical point of intersection where all things come together in intimate consummation is where all miracles happen. It is where completion and perfection happens.

The consummation between the sun and rain produced the miracle of rainbows.

The consummation between seed and soil produced the miracle of life.

The consummation between hot and cold produced the comfort of warmth.

The consummation between ocean and land produced delightful beaches and coastlines.

My favorite seasons—spring and fall—were the consummation between summer and winter.

The consummation between food and taste-buds produced the deliciousness of taste.

The consummation between your fingers and skin produced the sensation of touch.

The consummation between music and lyrics produced the wonderment of song.

My mind was racing, thinking about all the miracles produced from the marriage between paradoxes or seemingly opposites. And then the thought came to me—that this was the truth in all relationship conflict—that it was simply our belief in polarities that kept us apart in a state of separation or "sin." But the real "sin" was our belief system that fixed the illusion in our minds that we are "polarized" from each other—like the north and south ends of a pole—when we are in disagreement. In reality, we had just chosen a fixed position on one or the other arm of the cross. But if we could just realize (real eyes) our false belief system and see instead that divine point of intersection on the cross where all paradoxes, all points of view, all differences of opinion can be resolved. Then we would find the perfect truth, balance, beauty...and love...and a hope for healing, wholeness, and holiness for this fragmented world.

For example, if one person in a relationship has taken an ultra-conservative viewpoint about cutting down timber, believing it wrong to cut down *any* trees to sustain a joyful existence; and he was put in relationship with another person who took an ultra-liberal stance that man has every right to take whatever resources he desires, then any rational person could see that there is a balance between these two arguments. And if the two parties agree that perhaps they need to surrender their fixed position on either the conservative or liberal arm of the cross, then they can come to that place of peace, resolution, consummation...at-one-ment.

And coming to that place of consummation and at-one-ment is just a matter of communicating effectively our own particular viewpoints and issues surrounding those views so that they can be expressed, acknowledged, honored, respected—and then surrendered if necessary, to come to that perfect place of peace...of Christ-consciousness. Yes, that is where we all want and need to be—at that Christ-consciousness perspective contained in that point of intersection on the cross. That perfect point of at-one-ment.

All conflict could be erased, *all* fighting resolved, and *all* wars prevented, if we would *all* chose in *all* relationships, in every moment of our lives to surrender to the Christ-consciousness viewpoint of the cross. And if our position or view-point is already there, then there is no need for us to move or change.

I thought about some of the volatile issues that were dividing us individually and as a nation. Abortion, for eample; one segment of society has chosen a conservative "pro-life" viewpoint, while another segment of society has chosen a liberal "pro-choice" viewpoint. But I believe there is balance between these two arguments by acknowledging and respecting each, and then by finding the place of agreement and consummation. For me, Christ-consciousness is acknowledged in the popular slogan: "Pro-choice before conception—Pro-life after conception" as it acknowledges and honors both points of view. And the rights of the unborn child. I thought about some of the popular slogans I'd heard capturing this image of the cross:

> Unity in diversity
> Walk your talk
> Think globally, act locally
> Don't think you or me. Think we.

And some of my favorite scriptures came to mind:

> I am the Alpha and Omega, the beginning and the ending.
> (Rev. 1:8)
> Faith without works is dead. (James 2:17)
> The letter killeth, but the spirit giveth life. (2 Cor. 3:6)
> Weak things of the world shall break down the strong.
> (D&C 1:19)
> Spirit and element inseparably connected receive a fullness
> of joy. (D&C 93:33)

I thought about the concept of male and female energies coming together in the mystical consummation of marriage and how this concept was taught in practically every religion. The yin/yang of Taoism; the Shakti/Shiva of Hinduism; the Serifot in the Jewish Kabbala; the expansive/contractive energies in Cosmology—all were examples of the same metaphor, the concept of the cross.

The male, yang, Shiva, contractive energy represents the vertical arm of the cross; in Kabbalic terms, understanding, judgment, victory; the rational mind that is grounded from heaven into the earth like a huge lightning rod, the erect phallus, and the cosmic elements of fire and earth.

The female, yin, Shakti, expansive energy represents the horizontal arm of the cross; in Kabbalic terms, wisdom, mercy, glory; the intuitive and receptive mind, the elements air and water, and the open female vagina.

Yes, God uses all of his/her exquisite, glorious metaphors to court us back into that mystical marriage of communion with him/her. All we have to do is give up our resistance and surrender all of our illusions of separation, consenting to the marriage act of allowing our finite souls to be joined with his/her infinite oneness...or at-one-ment.

"Like the river that can't help but meet the sea."

Again, I was transformed back to John's mystical, untitled song..."Suddenly the mystery is clear. Love is only letting go of fear."

Yes, fear is what keeps us trapped in our illusion of our separation—our fears of letting go of past, present and future pain, fears of change, fears of the unknown, fears of being wrong, fears of making a mistake, fears of not being loved—but most of all, fears of separation, which ironically keeps us in this awful state of separation. And so what is the answer to getting out of the misery of separation? Surrendering to love. Surrendering to the consummation of perfection.

> Love is the answer
> Love is the way
> Love is in knowing just what to do
> And what to say
> Love is the reason
> Love is the why
> Love is in heaven right here on earth
> And peace inside...

And then I contemplated my own perfect place of beauty, my own heaven on earth and how it had been so prophetically, poetically named—Higher Ground.

Chapter Fifteen

Magumba

"Hey, kids. What d'ya say we all take a break from Grandma's story-telling and play some softball!" It was Joshua, the children's favorite uncle wanting to give his mom a break. The grandchildren scramble to their feet in response to Josh's invitation. Their mothers join in to organize teams and get the bases set up. Grandma Jesse and her daughter, Serenity, remain behind.

"Mom, I loved your sharing the beautiful story of how you discovered oneness or the at-one-ment. What I don't understand is how you knowingly went against that oneness when you left Dad and got a divorce. It seems like such a contradiction and the pain you caused me and the rest of us was nearly unbearable..." Serenity's voice tapered off in unchecked emotion. Jesse's arm came around her as the tears that she'd held back for so many years, overflowed.

"Well, my sweet Serenity. That was your mom's time of Magumba."

"Magumba. What does "Magumba" have to do with it? You left us..."

"Let me tell you the story of Magumba and maybe you'll understand. And then I'll tell you the rest of the story of why I *had* to leave. Magumba was a story John Denver told us at his last Windstar Symposium...and if my memory serves me correctly, that was the last time I ever saw him."

Jesse closes her eyes as she holds Serenity tenderly in her arms. She fades into blissful reverie, recalling the story told by her favorite celebrity.

Magumba

Once there were three explorers who got captured by a tribe of African headhunters in the deepest parts of the African jungle.

Now you can just imagine how frightened these three young men were as they were tied to a stake contemplating that they would be the next meal for these cannibals. As they listened to the drums beat and the fires roar, each of them wondered who would become the first victim of these savage headhunters. Finally as the "feastive" spirit of the African headhunters reached its frenzied peak, the chief of the village appeared, along with his indescribably ugly daughter.

Now, you can't even imagine how ugly this chief's daughter was. I mean, *she was ugly!* She must have weighed at least 300 pounds, had raised tattoos all over her body, huge lips to hide a broad smile with a couple of front teeth missing. And not only did she have a couple of teeth missing, but where there should have been hair was a little black topknot on top of her head. I mean this "beauty" could have frightened the daylights out of *any* man who was brave enough to venture close enough to get a good look at her. I mean, *she was ugly!*

Anyway, it was apparent that the chief was looking for a candidate to marry his "fine daughter," and since he couldn't get any of the other tribesmen to volunteer, he was now looking at these three young men for potential "son-in-laws."

He had the first man untied from the stake and brought over to where the young man could get a good look at "Mahonaleelee." (That was her name in African.) After a few moments of sizing up the young man, the African chief points his staff at him and then points it at his daughter and shouts, "Mahonaleelee or Magumba!"

Then came the silence of indecision as the young man takes a closer look at Mahonaleelee. This close inspection sends shivers of sheer terror down his spine at the prospects of spending even one moment alone with this creature. He thought to himself, "Anything's got to be better than marriage to this... creature. Perhaps 'Magumba' is another female of the village that hasn't been revealed yet." (Kinda like "bachelorette number two" in the "Dating Game.")

Following this line of thinking, the first young explorer cries out "Magumba!" With this response, a group of tribesmen is called by the chief to carry him off to a nearby grass hut. A few moments later, the sounds of screaming and wailing of intense pain and torture are overheard by all.

Then the second young explorer is untied from the stake and brought over to meet with the chief and his "lovely daughter." By this time "bachelor number two" is fully aware of what is behind the "two doors" of the "Dating Game"—Mahonaleelee or Magumba—life or death. As bachelor two gazes into the deep-set eyes of Mahonaleelee and she breaks out into a toothless grin, he can find no warmth inside his heart for her, but only cold chills of terror fill his soul.

When the chief then shouts out—"Mahonaleelee or Magumba"—there is only one decision he can make—"Magumba"—because the thoughts of marriage to Mahonaleelee is a fate far worse than death.

And so the fate of the second young explorer follows that of the first as the sounds of anguish and torture issue forth from the grass hut he is hauled away to.

Now it's "bachelor number three's" turn to make a decision between life and death—Mahonaleelee or Magumba. By now bachelor three is shaking in his jungle boots as these two prospects are placed before him to decide between. He looks at Mahonaleelee...then to the grass hut that held his two comrades... and then back to Mahonaleelee...then back to the grass hut, back to Mahonaleelee, back and forth, back and forth, trying to decide.

Then the fear of torture and death overwhelm him, and he starts to cry out in panic, "Anything but Magumba, please, anything but Magumba."

Then the chief of the tribe lifts up the chin of the frightened youth and looks deep into his eyes and speaks, "You say, you choose Mahonaleelee?" Both the chief and the young man nod their heads in agreement while the youth continues to mumble, "Anything but Magumba, anything."

Then the chief again takes the young explorer's chin in his hands and lifts it so he can look straight into his eyes. This time he looks deeply—into his very soul. He could tell by the looks of this frightened young man that there is no love or warmth in his heart for his beloved daughter, Mahonaleelee.

He then raises his staff and speaks. "Wise decision, you choose Mahonaleelee. But first—Magumba!"

Everyone has their own personal "Magumbas" in life. These "Magumbas" are the painful issues we must move through and resolve in our relationships so that we can eventually learn to love and embrace the "Mahonaleelees" who come our way. I suppose my own personal Magumba and Mahonaleelee came in the form of Marcie—Karl's third wife.

I met Marcie for the first time in Manti in November of 1994. Karl and I had made several visits to some old friends, who were also polygamists, who had moved to Manti to live with the Jim Harmston group. Marcie, a friend of theirs, came over to their home one evening when Karl and I were visiting them. She and Karl immediately felt a strong connection with each another, revealing to us all that they probably had a spiritual contract with each other that they needed to fulfill in this physical dimension.

Marcie was an attractive blonde with brilliant blue eyes, a few years younger than me. She had so many characteristics which appealed to Karl yet lacked in me, that I soon became convinced that Marcie was Karl's "soul-mate"—the perfect complement whom he'd been looking for all of his life. The physical and spiritual magnetism was so strong that Karl and Marcie became physically affectionate with each other after only a few meetings—desiring more than anything to come together in marriage. I was pregnant with our tenth child and vowed I would never again accept a sister-wife while I was pregnant. It was just too stressful on me and my unborn child. Furthermore, our experience with Kirstie had made it clear—at least to me—that certain issues needed to be resolved *before* making any more marriage-contract agreements. The biggest issue for me was the issue of inequality and I was secretly hoping that God would bring a *man* into the relationship, rather than another *woman,* to balance things out. Nevertheless, I figured a long courtship was in order so these issues could surface and be resolved.

For one thing, Marcie was recently divorced with three children from her previous marriage. The issues regarding custody and visiting privileges hadn't been completely resolved with her ex-husband, Tom. I also felt Marcie hadn't healed completely from the "fall-out" caused by this divorce and was somewhat of a "free-radical" attempting to attach herself to the first available relationship so she could feel a sense of completion. I knew she would be successful in a relationship only by going through the sometimes long and painful process of healing herself and making her own self whole and complete. If this healing didn't occur, her relationship with Karl, Kirstie and me would be imbalanced and co-dependent, potentially destructive to all of us. But the more I tried to convince everyone of my concerns, the more everyone tried to convince me that I was simply feeling vulnerable because of my pregnancy and acting out in fear and jealousy.

Despite my objections, Karl insisted on moving Marcie and her three children up to Higher Ground—just four months after their first meeting. Kirstie and Marcie immediately bonded and none of them could figure out why I was resisting what all of them felt was inevitable—marriage. They pointed out that all three of them—Karl, Marcie and Kirstie—were enjoying the radiant love-energy produced from the courtship, while I was up in my room alone, crying my eyes out because of the consequences I could foresee.

Two days passed as I wept alone in my room, praying constantly for answers. As if in the language of God, I was impressed through the emotions of my heart that I had two choices, and I was given glimpses of each. First, I was impressed in my heart that Karl and Marcie were already too physically and emotionally involved with each other at this point to reverse the direction they were going. Their physical affections were driving them, and I saw if I resisted their pleadings for my consent in marriage, that they would go ahead and have sex without consent, causing adultery and consequent separation between Karl and me. I would probably end our marriage of nearly twenty years, and our chief victims would be our eight children.

The second choice was to give my consent, despite my concerns, in order to preserve our marriage. Karl, Marcie and Kirstie had already chosen this path and it was more than I could do to resist this strong direction, especially in the emotionally-charged pregnant condition I was in. I was also shown what these consequences were.

Marcie, in her unresolved condition, wouldn't be able to handle the emotional challenges of plural marriage since she hadn't been completely healed from a male/female monogamous relationship that had damaged her. Marriage to Karl would distract her from the inner work she needed to do. This marriage would also breach her contracts with her ex-husband to raise their children together—with integrity lost and fall-out occurring. I was shown that Marcie would eventually leave the relationship after a short time, causing another breach of contract and divorce. It would be difficult for all of us, but the Spirit told me that this choice would cause less fall-out and damage fewer people.

My last effort was to write Karl a letter pleading with him to wait just two weeks until the baby was born to complete the act of consummation. But his physical and emotional affections were driving him and with the emphasis of Kirstie and Marcie, I had to back down and surrender. Being eight and a half months pregnant, I didn't have any fight left in me. But I did ask for one agreement from all three of them. That they would not participate in oral sex before the baby came. Karl had contracted genital herpes early in our relationship, which is known to be incurable. I had avoided oral sex with Karl during pregnancy knowing full well the possible outcome to me and the baby if I contracted it. Genital herpes can cause death to an unborn baby in utero and cause sterility to females. And so we all made this agreement before all four us consummated the marriage together.

The children were all watching a movie on the TV with the generator running when the four of us came down to tell them the news—tonight their dad was going to marry Marcie. None of the children liked Marcie and my older children were shocked and appalled that we had brought Marcie into the family without *their* consent. Ashley, Delaney, and Jacob eventually moved out and down to their grandmother's house in Logan or their grandmother's house in Salt Lake, feeling that their home had been invaded and there wasn't any room left for them. With Marcie and her three young children moving into our small, five-bedroom cabin, I could understand their sentiments. It was *extremely* overcrowded and felt like a three-ring circus day and night. Marcie's two young children would cry incessantly at night, driving us all nuts. The housing situation was another issue I had with Karl that was never to be resolved.

Of course, there were many positive things Marcie brought into the relationship. She had a great sense of humor and her training in midwifery was a big help in my delivery of Jasmine. We both called it my "greased-lightning" delivery as she came so fast that I ended up delivering her on the bathroom floor as I couldn't make it upstairs to the bedroom in time.

Then a few weeks after the delivery, I started having a recurring dream that Karl, Kirstie and Marcie were having oral sex behind my back. It angered me in my dream to the point that I emotionally divorced them all for their betrayal. The third night it happened, I was in bed with Kirstie with sweet Jasmine sleeping between us. When I awoke I shared with Kirstie my dream and confronted her about its authenticity. She nonchalantly remarked that it was "only a dream." I then went into Marcie, after Karl had left for town, and confronted her with my dream. She then retorted smugly, "Well, was it good?"

"What do you mean by that?" I asked her blankly.

"You figure it out," she said as she got up to leave.

I was confused and frustrated and so I asked Kirstie to tend the children while I drove into town to talk with Karl at his job-site. He had been sawing lumber with his new portable sawmill and so I packed us both a lunch. When I got there, he greeted me with mixed emotions, the sternness in my face revealing that something was up. As we both sat in the car eating our lunch, I asked him point-blank, "So, have you been having oral sex with Marcie?"

Karl's face flushed and I knew the answer. My heart sank. "So why haven't you told me or even asked me if it would be all right with me?!" My voice was piercing but nothing compared to my heart. I started to cry. "If our relationship isn't based on truth and honesty than there really isn't any relationship at all." Karl still remained silent. "So, did you have oral sex with just Marcie, or was Kirstie involved, too?" I didn't really want to know the answer—but I needed to know.

"Yes, we've all been having oral sex together for some time now. I'm sorry. What more can I say?"

I'm sorry...what more can I say? WHAT MORE CAN YOU SAY!!! My guts were being wretched out of my stomach and *what more can you say?*

"That's interesting. When I confronted both of them this morning after having a dream *three nights in a row* that you were all doing it behind my back, they both pretty much lied to me. Is this what I'm married to—a bunch of liars?"

I felt so betrayed that I didn't know what to do next. I wanted to hit Karl, to drive the madness out of him and me. I cried as my heart again shattered into pieces. I refused to let Karl comfort me because I knew he offered no comfort this time. I needed to get away from him and so I bolted from the car and started running recklessly through the woods. I didn't know or even care where I was going; I just needed to get away from him...from me. I tripped over a log and fell to the earth. The warmth of Mother Earth felt good against my cold body. Karl soon arrived and again tried to comfort me. I thrashed out at him as he tried to hold me. "No, don't...don't even try."

After an hour or so spent crying in a heap upon the ground, Karl convinced me to get in the car and go for a ride with him so we could talk. I consented. Talking was always a good way to sort things out. When we got to the Mall parking lot, I asked him again, point-blank, if there were any other secrets he was hiding that I should know about. Now was a good time to come clean with any more dishonesty.

He then shared with me that there were two other incidents that he'd kept secret from me for many years. That he had had two different affairs with other women when he was out on the road. He hadn't had intercourse with them, but he'd done everything else. It was during the time just before Jadon's death—which had brought him to his senses. He couldn't tell me then as I was already in enough pain and dispair from the death and the whooping cough. He thought it was best to keep it a secret.

I went blank. I just wanted to die. At that very moment I just wanted to die. Death could never be as painful as what I was experiencing in *that* moment. I couldn't even cry anymore...the tears had all been spent. I got out of the car and collapsed on the Mall parking lot. I couldn't run, I couldn't move. *I just wanted to die.*

Karl picked me up and hauled me back into the car. He drove me home in silence. He carried me up the stairs and put me in bed with Jasmine who was eager to nurse. The warmth of her tiny body revived me and my love flowed out of me to her. And so I chose to live another day...for her.

Marcie had packed up her bags and left with her three children. I was glad. I didn't want to have to deal with her. Kirstie, on the other hand, I needed to deal with. Her betrayal was almost as severe as Karl's. I'd come to love and trust Kirstie, and now our trust was broken. Karl agreed that the three of us needed to talk, but not now. He begged me to wait until morning but I knew the anger would fester if I waited until morning to confront Kirstie. But I gave him his way.

The next morning, the three of us climbed into Karl's truck and drove down the mountain to a small clearing. Kirstie sat in the middle between Karl and I, armed and ready. But she didn't realize what she was in for.

"So, Kirstie, why did you lie to me yesterday when I confronted you about my dream?" I questioned angrily, ready to explode.

"Because I didn't think it was any of your God-damned business what Karl and I do in bed together. You're just a controlling bitch and I can do anything I *damn well please* with *my* husband."

It was too close for comfort, and my fist swung out uncontrollably and connected with her face. Both Karl and Kirstie were stunned. Karl grabbed Kirstie's hands as she tried to get back at me. I fled from the truck and headed down the mountain. This time I was ready to leave for good. Karl came after me again and grabbed ahold of me.

"Enough is enough, Jesse!" he shouted. "You are letting your emotions get way out of hand! I can't believe you just hit Kirstie! Come on, get control of yourself! I've never seen you act this way!"

"I've had it, Karl...I've just had it! You either get rid of her...and all your bitches...or I'm taking all the kids and leaving...today! If I'd known all of this before, I'd have made other choices. *Now, I'm making other choices.*"

"Okay, okay, Jesse. I get that you're really upset about everything. If that's what you want, then that's what you'll get. I'll send Kirstie and her kids on a bus back to Lovell tomorrow. I love and care about you *that much.*"

"No, Karl. They leave *today.* They leave or I leave."

Kirstie was ever so willing to leave that day. We both knew it would end in an enormous cat-fight if she didn't. The only other secrets I didn't know about until later was that she and Marcie were *both* pregnant at the time they *both* left.

But Karl and I needed some time alone, with the remainder of our children, to work through all of our unresolved issues. And there were mountains of them...more than I could have ever imagined. The lies and betrayals of trusts were monstrous and I didn't think we could ever get past them. Karl agreed not to have any communication with Marcie, but Kirstie insisted on calling him ever so often to keep him posted on how *his* children were and how she was getting along with her pregnancy. I resented him each time he talked with her and I insisted on being there during the entire conversation as I didn't trust either of them in the slightest. Kirstie begged Karl to come to the delivery of their child—she needed and missed him so. I reluctantly consented, but never felt good about the week he was gone. After that, both of them begged me to let Kirstie and her children come back.

I was pregnant again with my eleventh child. By that time the idea of having Kirstie around to help out with household chores appealed to my exhausted body. I finally surrendered my need to control the relationship, but insisted that Karl not sleep with her until after the baby was born, as I didn't trust either of them with the issue of oral sex.

Anthony was born in the hospital this time, because he was so big—over ten pounds—and my contractions pooped out in the end. An hour's worth of Pitocin and Anthony was ready to deliver. The doctor surprisingly allowed Karl to deliver him after hearing about all of his previous experience delivering his own children. He was a handsome baby and I was proud when I took him home the next day to show him off to the children. They were delighted with their new brother and it was good to have Kirstie around the house to help out. But our relationship was never the same again after our blow-out. Both of us kept guarded and I often found excuses to leave and go down to Salt Lake. Karl never made any efforts to resolve the issues of inequality and inadequate housing.

One time while I was in Salt Lake, I told him I wasn't coming home because I'd found someone new—a Native American shaman—I'd felt spiritually connected with. Vince was also out of prison and I felt free to develop a romantic relationship with him. Karl insisted that I come home, but I insisted that I wouldn't come back until the relationship was balanced. And so he sent Kirstie away again to Lovell so we could work out these issues.

And so I came home reluctantly, if not for Karl, but for the children. Kirstie felt it was unfair that she'd been sent away again when it was all about *my* issues. She was completely satisfied with the status quo. I told them both that I wouldn't live in an imbalanced plural relationship anymore. But Karl never did well under pressure and strong-armed me with his patriarchal authority: "that it was his Biblical right and duty as a man to live and take care of *all of his wives and children.*" And so I gave him the ultimatum. If Kirstie came back—I would leave for good. He then gave me the ultimatum. That Kirstie was coming back regardless of my choice—but if I left, I would have to leave without *any* of our children. I insisted that it was my God-given right as a mother to care for *all of my children* since I'd birthed them.

Then things turned violent. Karl told me if I took *his* children away, that he would "track me down and gut me open." I slapped him in the face with a dishrag and he then smacked me in the face with his fist—knocking me to the floor right in front of the children. It was all over after that. I left with Amber—my only teenager still around—and fled to Salt Lake the day before Kirstie was to arrive.

"And you know the rest of the story, my dear, as you were left as the oldest child to help sort out the mess. Thank goodness, Ashley and Delaney returned home to help out Kirstie with the children. And that, my dear Serenity, was my *Magumba.*"

Chapter Sixteen

Sisters

It's mid-afternoon, and a billow of clouds hangs low in the sky over a mountain peak across the green valley from Marriage Mountain. It looks like a dollop of whipped cream on a mountain of Starlight Mint ice cream—deliciously covered with rivers of hot fudge. It reminds Jesse of the times her dad would take the family out for hot fudge sundaes at Fernwoods on Sundays. Mom would complain as she didn't like "breaking the Sabbath Day." But after she was served up her hot fudge sundae, her objections would melt.

As if on cue, an elegant, gray-haired woman approaches, carrying a beautifully wrapped gift. Jesse springs from her chair (as quickly as a seventy-year-old woman can) and lovingly embraces Rosalie, her sister.

"Don't you want to take a break from your story-telling, old woman, and finish unwrapping your gifts? I'm sorry I'm late, Jesse. I hope I didn't miss *too many* of your stories."

Both women cackle as Jesse collapses onto her padded stool to open another gift. She carefully unwraps it in her traditional fashion—trying not to tear any of the beautiful wrapping paper. A heart-shaped wooden plaque is revealed with a hand-carved inscription in intricate calligraphy. Jesse reads the inscription aloud:

> Fate Made Us Sisters
> Hearts Made Us Friends

"Oh, how precious! This is absolutely exquisite! But how could you have possibly known, my dear sister?"

"One of your children told me when I asked them what to give you as a birthday gift. They said that the plaque I'd given you years ago had fallen off the wall and broke, and before you could repair it, one of your little ones had scribbled on it with permanent marker. They said you'd kept it hidden in one of your desk drawers hoping someday to find time to make another one. They said it had been one of your favorite keepsakes. Well, now *I've* made you another one which I hope won't be broken or scribbled on by your... grandchildren." Rosalie explains as she scans her captive audience.

"Oh, thank you, Rosalie. How very thoughtful you are!" exclaims Grandma Jesse, turning the plaque over and over to admire the beautiful handiwork.

"You certainly still have a knack with your hands, Sis...but you don't know my grandchildren. This time I will hang it up in a place where it won't be bothered and where I can look at it every day and think about you and how you helped to make the vision of Heartsong Living Centers come true."

"Oh, Mother," Serenity implores. "Tell the story of how you and Aunt Rosalie made Heartsong come true."

Well, I guess it all started right after we got back from our trip out to Aspen to deliver my "Dear John" letter. Up until that time Rosalie thought I was a bit crazy with all my visions and dreams about starting a community up in Montana. I always wanted her to move up there with us so that our combined energies could really "move mountains" so to speak (as we'd experienced on our trip to Aspen moving through obstacles). But she always felt that her work was in Salt Lake, as many people there were right on the verge of waking up to this new concept of intentional community. She drew me down to Salt Lake occasionally when the Spirit would direct to help her with community-building, and then the two of us would really stir things up.

I remember once when the Spirit strongly directed me to come down to Salt Lake before my parents left for Yuma that fall. Karl was supposed to meet me in town that day, so I could leave in our other car that we had up for sale in a parking lot. When he didn't show up on time for me to leave, I took the one car to Ashley and Delaney's ballet class and left it there with a note saying, "Girls—drive yourselves home safely as I need to go to Salt Lake today." I then had to walk several blocks to pick up the other car to drive down there with.

Ashley was only fifteen, and although she knew how to drive, she didn't have her driver's license. But I just trusted the Spirit that things would turn out all right. I was relieved to find out later that Karl showed up just in time to drive them home safely.

I didn't know it at the time, but I barely got there just before Dad and Mom left for Yuma. So my dad and I made an occasion of it by going out to lunch together. We enjoyed a good conversation about his estate and what he desired of me to do concerning it. He'd asked me earlier to get my children's Social Security numbers so he could put his estate in order, but Karl refused to get Birth Certificates for any of the children who'd been born at home. He was convinced that these were concessions toward the "mark of the beast." Sometimes I was embarrassed by Karl's fanatical beliefs, but what could I do? I was stuck in a marriage with someone who was non-negotiable. And so I told my dad that I'd try to get what he'd asked for—knowing in the back of my mind that would be impossible.

I then steered the conversation to what I considered more important matters than finances—family memories, fun things he and Mom would do in Yuma, and how I wished I could come down for Christmas. But I knew going down to Yuma with my large family would drive both him and Mom out of house and home. And Karl would never approve of me going down there by myself—although the thoughts of a warm vacation in the middle of winter sounded fabulous.

My parents left the following day and with a few days on my hands, I felt an urgency to get my brothers and sisters together for a family portrait as a special Christmas gift for our parents. I convinced my oldest sister, Carol, to fly in from San Diego. She was another sister who was very intuitive and had similar feelings as I did—that this might be Dad's last Christmas. And so all six of us went down to a local portrait studio and had a family portrait taken.

We were so glad that we'd made the effort to give Dad his most beloved Christmas gift—a portrait of his six children—as he passed away a month later. At the end of January he underwent quadruple by-pass surgery and never regained consciousness after the surgery. Our entire family gathered together to make the difficult decision whether to take him off the life-support system (which was what he wanted) and release his spirit into the next dimension.

We all sat in the hospital waiting room to make the most difficult decision many of us would ever make. After we all agreed, we held each other in a family circle, bawling like little lambs. After a few moments of grace, the attending nurse gave us our instructions; we would each be given the opportunity to say our final farewells before he was unplugged, or we could wait until after he was unplugged from the machines in hopes that he'd hold on a few minutes on his own. I decided to take the opportunity before he was unplugged to pour my heart-felt love out to my dad.

I went into the ICU and tried to ignore all the machines pumping life into my dad's frail body through plastic hoses and tubes. It overwhelmed me as I stumbled to find a chair. I sat down next to my father and took his tender hand in mine

"Dad," I began, trying to choke back the encroaching tears. "I just want you to know how much I truly love and appreciate *your* being *my dad.*" A tide of emotion swept over me and spilled over into our clasped hands. It took a few moments for it to recede. "And, Dad, I want you to know that I forgive you for any pain you may have caused me." I looked at his tired, worn-out face and thought, *what pain could this gentle man possibly have caused me?* "I always loved you, Dad, no matter what…and I understand that whatever you did to the others…you were simply reaching out for love." The thoughts of Kent and Bryce in the other room waiting for their turn with Dad flashed through my mind. "We all make mistakes, Dad, and I know you've made your peace with God. I just want to thank you from the bottom of my heart for being the *very best Dad* you possibly could be. *I'll love you forever, Dad.*"

This time I didn't attempt to hold back the tears that flooded through me. I figured in his unconscious state hooked up to all the machines, Dad probably couldn't hear a word I'd said. I blotted my eyes with a Kleenex so I could look down at his face…one more time. Were my eyes deceiving me? Was that a tear gathering in the corner of his eye? Dad's lips started to quiver as if he wanted to speak. He struggled for a moment, and then the tear escaped his eye and flowed down his cheek. I sobbed again knowing he'd heard my words.

I went back to the waiting room to tell the other members of my family what had happened. I encouraged them to say their good-byes before the nurse unplugged the machines. The nurse reassured them that they would have a few moments after the machines were off to say their final farewells, and so they all opted to wait. Unfortunately, Dad died only seconds after the machines were unplugged. I will always cherish those last few moments I spent with my dad, and also the memories of our last lunch together before he went to Yuma.

Mom never shed a tear during this whole process of Dad's dying and his funeral. I wondered if it was her inner strength or she was simply in a state of disassociated denial. It was my mother's family pattern to never show any emotion. My grandmother was that way and it had carried over to my aunts and uncles. Of course, I broke the family mold—I had enough emotion to make up for everyone.

Rosalie got deathly ill right before the funeral and was barely able to make it, let alone sing with me in our prearranged duet. My ex-brother-in-law, Ben, filled in for her and everyone commented that we sang beautifully together.

The next time I phoned Mom to find out how everything was after coming back to Montana, I discovered that Rosalie had been taken to the hospital. She had been doing a series of colonics prior to the funeral and had ruptured her intestines causing peritonitis to set in. The doctors had performed emergency surgery to barely save her life. I was shocked by the news but I knew I couldn't afford another trip down to Salt Lake to see her and talking to her on the neighbor's phone was a bit inconvenient at times.

The next time I was able to talk with Rosalie, heart to heart, was in July after Kirstie had delivered Alma and things around our place had settled down a bit. I brought my children down with me to give Karl and Kirstie some time alone and also so the children could visit their cousins in Salt Lake. Rosalie with her four children and I with my six all went swimming together. As Rosalie and I basked in the sun on the lawn by the swimming pool, she shared with me the details of her "near-death experience."

"I suppose Mom never told you this, but I actually died on the operating table while they were cutting me open. I even asked the doctor who'd operated on me if it really did happen...if I *really did die*. He was reluctant to tell me the truth but, yes, he had lost me for a few moments on the operating table."

"Wow," I gasped, trying to grasp the implications of how I'd nearly lost my dearest sister. After a moment of contemplation, I became curious. "So what happened to you while you were...dead?"

Rosalie explained that she had traveled through a tube of translucent light and was brought into the presence of a radiant being whom she recognized as Christ. Her entire spirit completely merged with his, causing her to experience the most incredible, divinely penetrating love she had ever felt before. She could hardly describe her feelings as tears filled her eyes.

"You know, Jesse," she continued as she regained her composure. "The worst part of the whole experience was when Christ told me I had to go back into my body as my work on Earth wasn't completed yet. I just didn't want to go back. I didn't know how I could ever face such a darkened world after being in a world filled with such love and light. But the Lord insisted that I go back so that I could help build the light centers or places of healing that Christ showed me needed to be built so that His Kingdom could come down and dwell on Earth.

"You know, Jesse, I used to doubt your visions about the path you felt so inspired to follow. But I don't any more. God himself showed me what heaven is like, and it is based on the concept of perfect love and perfect freedom. Everything just *is*, Jesse...just as you said it would be. No more feelings of separation—only pure, unadulterated love and oneness. And it is *so real!*"

I held Rosalie in my arms as we both wept. Our love flowed in ways it had never done before. We both shared our heart-felt love for each other and our concerns for each other's happiness. Rosalie was currently stuck in a relationship which was stifling her, and she asked me to pray for her that she would be able to find her "covenant mate" or "soul-mate" so she could complete that contract with him before she was called "home" again. I said I would pray for her as the Spirit led me. I also asked her to pray for me to resolve some of the "irresolvable" issues which plural marriage brings. She promised she would.

The next time the Spirit called me to Salt Lake was a few months later. Rosalie handed me a white book only moments after I'd arrived. "Read the passages I've highlighted in yellow," she insisted. I looked at the title at the top, "Shulemna" and observed that it was divided into books and verses like scripture. I started with Chapter 3:

1. And now as I was saying concerning the many records, for we did perceive that there were many records kept that we knew not of and we did see that they were in God's hands and, therefore, were preserved to come forth by the will of the Father. And as we did perceive the records we did also perceive in our consciousness the content of the records and we did know and bear record that they did tell of the many marvelous works of God in every time and every place.

2. And we did see that Jesus did visit all people everywhere who were of the house of Israel, for they were scattered on all the face of the earth and on the isles of the sea. But Jesus did truly visit them according to His promise and there were none who had kept the covenants of their fathers that He did visit.

3. And behold we did perceive that some were like unto our people at the time of the coming of Jesus in His resurrection, dwindling in unbelief. But they did receive Him like unto our people and He did bring in a new order of things in whatsoever place He did visit.

4. And they did keep their sacred records, and those who did become the Shulemna did take charge of those records and they have them unto this day; and thus God's people are gathered into the Fathers, for behold you see that all God's works, both His people and His words and His holy treasure, are gathered into one; for thus was it stated by the prophet Ether and many others in his time and from his people were

taken up and did not taste of death, for I have seen them and they have ministered unto me.

5. Yea, I do know of all their marvelous words which are the works of the Fathers and it is not preserved in your records because you know not any of the Fathers' works.

6. And the brother of Jared also, and his family, for behold they did fulfill all the promises of God therefore they did obtain heaven; yea they did obtain heaven and their history I have written and sealed it up. For behold the brother of Jared did look into heaven and behold the family of God and did know and did understand that priesthood which is the family of God. And he did see that it did encompass all the peoples of the earth who did come unto God, yea, from the beginning even unto the end of time.

7. And he did see that as our Father Adam did go forth on the earth and they did multiply, for behold they were many to begin with, and our Father Adam was the first of many; therefore they were all organized from the beginning in a heavenly manner and they did know from whence they came and did continue that type here upon the earth, for that order did exist among them which had always been from everlasting to everlasting.

8. For they were of one heart and one mind, and one flesh, being in harmony with one another; and, thus, there was peace and love amongst them, for there was no separation because of the harmony. And they did not set one before the other, for all were equal and as one. And because of this oneness, the earth did flourish under their hands for the earth did recognize and respond to their dominion and did bring forth abundantly for the joy of the Lord. And when children were born unto them they did continue the heavenly order for the love of God, which is the priesthood of God, was in them to its perfection.

9. But behold, as the children began to grow up and exercise their own will contrary to the love of God, the disharmony began to destroy the Holy Order of God, for the oneness began to dissipate. And they began to divide off from the order which had been established by their fathers and go forth two by two; therefore, there began to be a great division in the Holy Order and the oneness which once existed in that

priesthood remained only with a select few who did follow the Holy Order.

10. And behold when Cain did slay his brother Abel, it did cause great havoc in the Holy Order, for it did introduce the works of Satan for the first time into the Holy Order itself, for previous to this time Satan did have no hold on the hearts of the children of God, the only evil they did before this time was the consequence of their own choices being out of harmony with the Holy Order, which order existed because of God working in man.

11. But behold when Cain did rise up and slay his brother, he did it by covenant with his father, and thus power was given Satan to begin his reign in the children of God in the flesh. And thus did the work of destruction run rampant in the Holy Order, for Satan began from that time forth to rage in their hearts.

12. And behold the children of God did from that time forth begin to choose Satan as their father, for they chose not anymore to follow after the Order of the Ancient of Days. Therefore did Enoch see that heaven did weep over her children for they did choose Satan as their father and chose some other law or order than His priesthood. Therefore they chose Satan and his priesthood; and thus did Satan's kingdom grow up and he rules his kingdom unto this day.

13. And the children of this world know not that Satan is their father and that he reigns in their hearts, even all. And even those who have chosen Jesus Christ the Son of God have not chosen Him as their Father for verily, verily, if they have chosen Him as their Father then will He lead them unto the Father; for did He not promise that He would even introduce the Father to them and both the Father and the Son would abide in them? (Shulemna 3:1-13, *Sacred Scriptures;* Orem, Utah: MAP Publications, 1993.)

"Wow!" I exclaimed in amazement. I closed the book, my finger holding the place, in order to discover the title—*Sacred Scriptures.* "Where in the world did you get this book, Rosalie, and how can I get a copy?"

"As for your second question, you already have one as this is my gift to you. As for the first—well, that's a *good* story."

"Go ahead...I'm wide open for a *good* story."

I settled back as Rosalie explained how she'd encountered a group of Latter-Day Saints who were seriously studying the mysteries of the gospel in a study group. The more they studied deeper and further into the gospel, the more frequently they received direct revelations from God—or what they referred to as, "the Fathers." Some of them had written down these revelations, then combined them and published them as *Sacred Scriptures*.

"Wow!" I was amazed at the grace of God's hand in all things. "So how has the Church responded towards these *Sacred Scriptures?*"

"Oh, the Church is *totally* against them. In fact they've threatened to excommunicate anyone who even owns a copy and believes that it's revelation. Most of those involved in the study group have already been excommunicated—especially after they published this news release to the Salt Lake Tribune."

Rosalie handed me a page of the newspaper dated Sunday, May 21, 1995. Thoroughly fascinated, I read this proclamation:

A WITNESS, A WARNING, AND A BLESSING

Be it known unto all nations, kindred, tongues, and people: That we the undersigned, through the grace of God the Father and the Lord Jesus Christ do declare that the work of the Father has now commenced upon the earth. And this work is a work of love and of gathering into one body all nationalities of the world, regardless of race, color, or religious affiliation. We declare with words of soberness that angels have administered unto many of us and have brought into the light of the day many sacred scriptural writings which have been withheld from man that they might come forth to a more pure and believing generation, even portions of the sealed part of the Book of Mormon, which portion is a testimony of the Father and the Son and their love for all the generations of mankind.

And He has shown unto us that the great cleansing of the earth is about to begin and that it will start with those who have been given the most light and yet deny his power among them. We have seen that it will start with his own house being set in order and then shall commence forth until is shall fill the whole earth. We plead unto all men and women everywhere to seek the spirit of God in their lives and to come out from under the bondage of relying on the arm of flesh. Listen and do His promptings and seek

His face continually without putting your trust in man. We who have bound ourselves together with God do not put one man above another and there is no appointed leader among us. We hold all things in common and are given by God to know the needs of each individual as they arise.

All of the gifts of the spirit (healings, visions, prophesying, speaking in tongues and interpretations of tongues) are manifest among us, for God cannot withhold them when we unitedly seek His will and do it in all things.

And now we declare unto the world that His works and way of life shall be that order which shall proceed for a thousand years when Christ shall reign as King of kings and Lord of lords. And glory and honor and power be to the Father, Son, and Holy Ghost, which is one God.

The declaration was signed by seventy-five men and women.

"So...when do I get to meet this group of friends of yours?" I inquired eagerly.

"Tonight, if you'd like. In fact, if you'd like to come with me, you might get to meet Hanah, the one who wrote Shulemna. Someone from the study group told me she was in town and was going to be at the meeting tonight."

"For sure! I'd love to go to your meeting and meet this lady, Hanah."

The meeting was held in an old abandoned restaurant near Bountiful. A group of about thirty or so had gathered to listen to a talk given by a gentleman from Missouri. Though the talk was quite interesting and inspiring, my attention was distracted, trying to figure out which person could possibly be this mysterious woman, Hanah. Then an elderly woman walked through the door with blue-gray hair, and a radiant face. Immediately I knew by the Spirit that she was Hanah.

It had grown late by the time the meeting was over, and our conversation with Hanah afterwards was brief. We arranged a meeting for tomorrow near her son's home where we could have a lengthier conversation.

The following day all three of us—Rosalie, Hanah and I—settled down at a picnic table in a school park near her son's home. I'd brought a copy of my own thick manuscript, *Becoming One*, in case I felt prompted to share it with her. Hanah had brought a stack of her own books—the Mormon standard works, the *Sacred Scriptures*, and another book entitled, *The Keys of Enoch* by J. J. Hurtak.

We began by exchanging some personal history. Hanah had also been a plural wife and was familiar with the Allred group in Montana. They had become so-called "independents" and had lived with her husband and her sister-wife in a small town just outside of Whitefish, less than a hundred miles from Pinesdale.

She then told us the tragic story of how she'd left her first husband and ten children in order to live the fullness of the gospel as the Spirit had strongly directed her to do. Tears welled up in my own eyes thinking of how I'd had to leave Karl, Kirstie and my own nine children in order to come down on my visit to Salt Lake. It had been especially hard this time because Karl was totally objecting to my frequent visits. The more I insisted that the Spirit was calling me down, the more he resisted. Ever since my four-week Vision Quest to Aspen, Karl had always resented being left with the kids. But I figured things were different now. He had Kirstie to help take care of him and the children while I could meet the needs that the Spirit was calling me to do.

I didn't share my inner turmoil with Hanah, allowing her to get on with more enlightened subjects. I could tell by her armful of books that she had come prepared for a lengthy gospel discussion.

She explained how Moroni (a Book of Mormon character) was directing her through the Spirit to begin to form a Holy Order again—as explained in her book, *Shulemna*—in order to reconnect the Earth back to the Fathers. She explained that during the time of Adam and Eve in the Garden of Eden, that Heaven and Earth had been connected by a kind of spiritual umbilical cord, a conduit, so to speak, allowing a free-flow of exchange between heavenly and mortal beings. She called it the River Keshon. But at the Fall—the partaking of the forbidden fruit representing human judgment between good and evil—the Earth had shifted on its axis, reeling to and fro. This shock severed the umbilical cord and separated God and humans...Heaven and Earth so to speak.

It was prophesied that, in the fullness of times, another shift would occur to reconnect Heaven and Earth again by way of this River Keshon. Heavenly and earthly beings would again be reunited by the divine process of translation and resurrection.

"And so you're trying to tell me that to reconnect Heaven and Earth together again, that a Holy Order must be formed to generate enough unified magnetic field to cause a polar shift?" I repeated her ideas as clearly as I could.

"Precisely!" she exclaimed, delighted that I had grasped her concept. She then explained the specific details and dynamics of the procedure through scriptural references and referring to her *Keys of Enoch* volume, which she described as containing the principles by which the City of Enoch was translated. Its author, J. J. Hurtak, was a Jewish scholar who was adept in the Hebrew language and Jewish mysticism.

The procedure involved *chakra* opening and energy vortices, which I was somewhat familiar with through my yoga training and my personal experiences with *kundalini* energies. Although some of the deeper cosmic technology I had a hard time grasping, I became quite convinced that Hanah was on to something—especially since the Spirit had witnessed to me years earlier of similar revelation. My only problem was the timing.

"So when this energy vortex is created, causing the polar shift, everyone who isn't on "higher ground," so to speak, will be destroyed because of the earthquakes, tidal waves, and God only knows what?" I queried.

"Well, yes," Hanah said calmly, "It will cause tremendous damage upon the earth, but I'm sure God will lead his children out of harm's way. Besides that, once the vortex is opened, translated beings will help us build the Zion communities we need in order to bring in the millennium."

"But why not build these Zion communities *before* the polar shift takes place so that more lives can be spared?" I insisted.

"That would be wonderful, if it were possible!" she exclaimed. "But I just don't see how we have the time or resources to do it. You, yourself, know how hard it is to awaken people to the truth. Most people won't make the move to unite in community until they are humbled or compelled to do so. You know the history of mankind as well as I do."

"You know, Jesse. Hanah's right," confirmed Rosalie, who'd been noticeably quiet during our entire conversation. "People are never going to be convinced that the world is coming to an end. Everyone's just *sick and tired* of hearing about it. If they haven't believed the prophets by now, what makes you think they're going to believe *you*—or anyone else for that matter?"

I knew in my heart that Hanah and Rosalie had spoken the truth. No one wanted to hear another whacked-out prophet telling them that the world—as they knew it—was ending. I, myself, was sick of hearing it from Karl. But still I had to do something. I just had to try and establish at least a few places of refuge—perhaps in Utah and at Higher Ground—as my vision at Windstar had directed me to do. Oh, what little progress I'd made since then. It was like trying to roll a heavy rock uphill against tremendous downward resistance. It was so difficult trying to maintain a sense of community in my own family—let alone among strangers. But I knew Hanah's vision for assembling a Holy Order to open the vortex may take years. At least this would give me some time. Maybe something I could do would awaken people to the need to gather to higher ground.

As Hanah rose to leave, I handed her my bulky manuscript. "The Spirit has directed me to give this to you," I told her.

"Oh, thank you," she acknowledged sincerely. She closed her eyes for a moment in deep contemplation. "Oh, yes, very good! A book on the principles of translation."

Well, I didn't know anything about that—I had never "translated" any books before. And then I got her meaning.

Chapter Seventeen

Hidden Valley

The idea for Hidden Valley Health Resort was born after much contemplation, labor, and prayer. Together, Rosalie and I hoped to create a vehicle to facilitate healing in individuals so they could begin to manifest the reality of their wholeness and oneness in community. In this way we felt we could halt the disintegration and destruction of the planet and turn the prognosis around to achieve the planet's divine integration and salvation. Of course, we were idealistic in our vision, but we had to start somewhere. And, as we believed and witnessed on many occasions, if God was behind us—all things were possible.

Rosalie, and her new-found husband and soul-mate, Randy, felt the pull to build a "light center" down in Salt Lake, under the guise of Hidden Valley Health Resort. Karl and I strongly felt the draw to finish our project up at Higher Ground—putting in a hydropower plant, greenhouses, and a community center/complex there. Since none of us had any liquid resources to speak of, Karl and I decided to help Rosalie and Randy with their project, since Rosalie seemed to be drawing a lot of energy to it.

Rosalie and I both held equity in a piece of land held in a family trust next to the Hidden Valley Golf Course. Our combined interest was approximately two acres at the current market value of around $100,000 an acre. We thought that with this kind of leverage we could find financing that would let us start building the health facility on our own two acres. We also had a lot of genuine support from some influential people living in Salt Lake, many from Rosalie's study group who were also looking for a facility to start manifesting their vision of community.

Our difficulty was the need for start-up capital so that we could convince both the golf course, which wanted to purchase the majority of the property from Mom's family trust to put in nine more holes; and Mom's siblings, who shared control over the trust—that we were legitimate. That and the land was not subdivided, and so we couldn't realistically utilize our two acres to start building on.

The land was located in Draper, a prime location next to the eastern foothills of the Wasatch Mountains in the southern part of Salt Lake Valley. The family trust held the deed to the land and all of the water rights. The property was still listed in the "green belt" as it had once been rich agricultural land.

As I stood atop a small summit surveying the land to determine where the best location was for Hidden Valley Health Resort, a feeling of connection to my grandfather, who was a visionary man, came over me. I felt he wanted this land to fulfill a special destiny—to bring his family together in a place of healing and perhaps sustain them in the face of global transition.

During the week I was down in Salt Lake, Rosalie organized a meeting with the Hidden Valley Health Resort Committee, consisting of many outstanding members of the community; including investment and mortgage bankers, owners of construction companies, store owners and managers, professional health practitioners, publishers, sales directors, etc. Each was impressively qualified, I thought, to get her project off the ground.

"So what's holding up the show?" I inquired, looking over Rosalie's roster of guests. "You have enough qualified people here to make just about anything happen. What's the hold-up?"

Rosalie was busy getting her executive suite apartment ready to entertain her guests. "Nobody wants to put up the investment capital in order to get a bank to loan us the five million dollars for a health resort," she said matter-of-factly.

"Five million dollars!" I exclaimed, nearly choking on the amount. "Why so expensive! I thought the health resort bit was just a front for a self-sustainable healing center?"

"Well, you and I know what it's all about. But tell anyone else and they'd think you were fanatics, and everyone would pull out their support—or at least the ones with any money. With everyone anticipating the 2002 Winter Olympics being held in Salt Lake, an exclusive health resort right next to a well-established golf course is just the concept that will interest the big investors in Salt Lake. You just don't know the climate of Salt Lake anymore."

And frankly, I was glad I didn't. I suppose living so long in the mountains had made me a bit naive of big city life, even though I was born and raised in Salt Lake. I didn't envy Rosalie and her task of trying to rally people behind her project in this fast-paced, fractured environment.

"Oh, by the way," suggested Rosalie, "Why don't you see if you can get a hold of Norman again. He seemed real interested in the project the last time I talked with him—especially when he found out *you* were going to be involved."

"Oh, all right. If you insist," I conceded. I dialed the number on the slip of paper Rosalie handed to me, repulsed at the idea of being a carrot on a string. Norman's number gave me his answering service so I left a message about the meeting.

Granted, Norman was wealthy having made his fortune as a computer-programmer. He was vice-president of a computer-programming company he helped create in Salt Lake, and because of his genius with computers, was hired as a consultant by businesses world-wide. And I had to admit Norman had helped me out a few times. He'd given me a hundred dollars to get to Windstar in 1983 when I divorced Karl. He'd also loaned me his yellow Audi, which died in Snowmass shortly after I arrived. Despite all his favors, it didn't squelch the uneasiness in the pit of my stomach at the thoughts of seeing him again. I felt Rosalie had gone a bit too far in using whatever connections she could as a "means to an end." Sometimes "old flames" weren't the most reliable resources.

I nursed four-month-old, Adam, to sleep and slipped him into Rosalie's bed upstairs before the guests arrived. Rosalie greeted the guests and made the introductions. As the meeting started, I chose a seat on the back row next to the stairs so I could listen for baby Adam upstairs.

Rosalie looked elegant in her black and gold Oriental pantsuit complete with matching black and gold filigree earrings. I felt out of place in an olive rayon blouse Kirstie had loaned me, flowered second-hand stretch pants, and imitation Birkenstocks I'd scored at a garage sale. Rosalie assured me I looked gorgeous in anything I wore, but I was glad *she* was the one up front.

As I continued to admire my younger sister's eloquent executive style, the doorbell rang, indicating a latecomer. Rosalie interrupted her speech to open the door. To my surprise and dismay, in walked Norman dressed in a fire-engine red corduroy shirt, tight Levis, and cowboy boots. Still the same old Norman trying to make a dramatic entry, I surmised, as he glanced in my direction. He combed his sun-bleached bangs from his tan face with his fingers—a dramatic technique left over from high school.

"Well, get off your ass and come over here and give me a squeeze!" bellowed Norman, beckoning me with his hand.

Everyone's eyes turned in my direction as I shrank in my chair trying to make myself invisible. I blushed in obvious embarrassment.

"So, what are you waiting for, beautiful? Hell knows I ain't gonna move from this spot 'til you come give me a hug!"

I winced at the very thoughts of touching the man—let alone showing him any affection in front of anxious onlookers. But Rosalie and a few others were glaring at me. For her sake and the sake of the meeting, I stood up and walked over to give him his requested hug. I could smell beer on his breath as his fingers caressed my back. My spine tingled uncomfortably as I realized he'd brought a few uninvited "spirits" along with him.

Rosalie seized control, introducing Norman and commenting that we had a "thing going on in high school." Norman found a chair directly in front of me and kept turning around to make indecent remarks, grope my leg, and shout boisterous interruptions as Rosalie continued to outline her proposal for the development of the health resort. Rosalie got flustered as both of our patience was more than tried. She cut the meeting short as it was obvious that the entire continuity of the meeting was lost.

As everyone got up to leave, Norman grabbed my hand and pulled me through the crowd to the door. "Come on. Let's get a little fresh air," he suggested, yanking me outside.

I thought I'd had enough "fresh air" for one night as I looked for a way to escape.

"Are you thirsty?" he inquired, pulling me over to his blue Jaguar. "I've got a cold six-pack in the car."

"You *know* I don't drink, Norman," I replied.

"Oh, still doin' the 'straight-act' are you, Jesse? Well, honey, you don't mind if I do?" he suggested, exploding a can of warm beer all over himself and his Jaguar.

Still the same klutzy, arrogant self, I mused silently. I tried to ignore the pity glances of the other guests, who were leaving without speaking.

"Come on," he blurted. "I'll buy us both a cold one over at that corner-mart."

He grabbed my arm just above the elbow and escorted me to Towne Pump. I selected a cold Snapple while he picked out a six-pack of Coors Lite.

Back at his Jaguar, Norman opened his trunk to drop in the six-pack minus one. He grabbed an envelope lying on top of what looked like his mail. He ripped opened the envelope and handed me the bank statement inside. It was for his current savings account and the amount was well over $300,000. I handed it back without a word, my features expressionless.

"And that's only in one small savings account," he remarked, gulping the beer and keeping his eyes riveted on my face. "I've got other savings accounts all over the world with a lot more assets than that."

"So why don't you invest a few hundred thousand into Rosalie's health resort?" I inquired. "I'm sure you'll get back your investment...and then some."

Norman's eyes glared. "Is that why you invited me here—to invest in your sister's wild imagination?"

I was becoming impatient again. "It's not just her *wild imagination* you'd be investing in. You'd be able to help a lot of people get healthy... maybe starting with yourself!" I poked at his beer gut hanging over his belt buckle.

Norman's eyes brightened as if I'd made a pass at him. "Well, I suppose if I were guaranteed the right kind of benefits," he sneered, "I could see myself investing a few thousand—just to throw away at it."

"You know, you really make me sick," I retorted, starting to walk towards Rosalie's apartment.

"Wait a minute, wait a minute. That's no way to swing a deal, is it now... Princess?"

His pet name had endeared me to him in high school. How dare he call me that after I'd been married for over twenty years to someone else?! But I held out a few minutes more for Rosalie's sake.

"To tell you the truth, Princess—you're not even going to have enough time to build your God-damn health resort before the system collapses."

"So what do you know about all that?" I responded curiously.

"Believe me. I know what I'm talking about." He sounded sober this time. Almost serious. "It's all coming down in about two and a half years and there's nothing anyone can do to stop it."

"Oh, so what are you telling me, Norman—you've got *inside* information about a conspiracy plan to collapse the economic system?"

"You know, Jesse, I used to think you were crazy talking about this one-world conspiracy crap your mom used to brain-wash you into believing. But just last year I visited Stockholm. I was hired to help program one of the largest computers I'd ever seen. It took up an entire room and they called it 'the Beast.' Its access number was 666."

"Whoa!" I exclaimed. "Then it *is* for real."

"Yeah, and all the computer programmers know that there's been a virus planted in all the computer systems ever since the computers got popular. They call it the Y2K problem. When the year 2000 rolls around, all the major computer systems will shut down. And that will automatically shut down all electricity, all telephone services, all communications systems, all transportation systems—you name it—it's history!"

Norman started chuckling, which turned into an awful hacking cough.

"Just think about it, Princess. The hangover everyone's going to have New Year's Day, 2000, when they go to their refrigerator to grab a cold one and the only cold one they're going to grab is their own...well, you got the picture. No electricity, no heat, no refrigerator, no lights, no phone—no life for most of the losers who haven't got a clue about what's coming down. Then the ones in charge just plan to wait it out a year or so to see who survives."

I was beginning to get sick to my stomach. I wanted to throw up or scream in a frenzied rage! Instead I held my peace as Norman continued.

"The drones will be the first to go. You know...the ones who are just burdens on our society anyway. The old geezers who can't get their medications from the grocery store in time. The terminally-ill whose plug will be pulled the minute the power goes out." He paused to let the words sink in and then emphasized, "Just like they did to your dad, I hear."

His words struck deep, but still I let him continue.

"And then there's the ones like your mom and brothers and sisters living in the city who're dependent on the system for food, heat, gasoline...even water, 'cause the water system uses electricity to pump it. Well, you can kiss all your family good-bye as in a matter of a few days everything will be gone—all the food out of the grocery stores—if they can figure out a way to cook without electricity...or keep warm for that matter. And then if they get the brilliant idea to finally try and get to your place in Montana, it will be too late. The gas pumps won't pump gas without electricity and the gas prices will have gone sky-high by then 'cause those in the know will have planned it that way to prevent people from hoarding."

"And then there will be the ones like you, Jesse—people thinking they've gotten it together enough to survive the catastrophe. Well, given a few months or so of not being able to buy anything at the store, you'll cave into the New World Order just to buy the things you need. And if not, you stubborn 'die-hards' will be hunted down like Jackrabbits and exterminated."

"So why are you telling me all this, Norman?" I demanded, wanting to strike out at him with a two-fisted rage that had been boiling inside of me. But I held my composure. I wanted to find out what all this insanity was leading up to.

"Because *I really do care about you, Princess,* and I don't want to see you and your family go through this horrible devastation. You know, Princess, I've *never* stopped loving you. No, not even when I was married to my gorgeous wife, Linda, could I ever stop loving you. *You* were in my heart...*always.*"

Norman paused, his voice thick with emotion. "You see, I have this piece of property I bought years ago tucked away in a beautiful spot in the Swiss Alps. We'll be safe there. I even made a deal with 'them.' That if I helped program their computer, me and my family would be taken care of... royally."

"You and your family? What about *you and your family?*" I asked emphatically. "When I was trying to get your phone number, your brother said you'd just gotten divorced from your wife and left her with two kids. Is that what you want me to do with Karl and my children up in Montana? Throw them away so that I can go live in the lap of luxury with you?!"

"Oh, Jesse, you know I wouldn't want you to give up your kids," he stammered. "How could I expect that from *any* mother? But you know your husband's always been a loser. He's never provided for *any* of your needs throughout your *entire* married life! You left him once before when he wanted to become a polygamist. You could do it again, especially considering all the lives you'd be saving—you, your children, your mom, Rosalie, all your brothers and sisters. I'd be willing to provide for all of them if only..."

"Jesse!" It was Rosalie at the door of her apartment holding a fussing Adam. "I think he's hungry. Are you about ready to come in?" she called.

"Yeah, we were just about *finished* with our conversation," I called back, hurrying across the parking lot. To my dismay, Norman followed at my heels.

"Oh, what a darling baby! Let me hold him," insisted Norman, pulling him from my arms before I could object.

As Norman cuddled Adam in his arms, I felt panicked. I wanted to cry out some magic word to make Norman disappear. "Rumplestillskin," I cried to myself, hoping the word still held some leftover magic. Fortunately Adam started to scream loudly, indicating he wanted to be nursed...and now! Norman relinquished the baby as I plucked him from his arms; relieved to have him back in my arms again. I sank into the comfort of Rosalie's armchair and lifted my blouse to begin nursing. Norman found a spot on the sofa next to Rosalie—directly across from me.

"Think about what I shared with you," was his final remark as he strained his neck to get a cheap thrill. I did think about it as I sat silently nursing Adam while Rosalie and Norman talked business.

Sure, life had been difficult being married to Karl. He had a bit of royal arrogance and his good looks had given him more than his share of male ego. But leave him? Lately, the marriage relationship was more than a bit rocky. After Marcie left and I allowed Kirstie to return to the family, all of our unresolved issues kept resurfacing. No matter how hard we struggled, we could never resolve the main issues of our conflicts—equity, justice and freedom. I still believed in the principle of polygamy, but I believed polygamy went both ways for it to be fair. And Karl just wasn't willing to give me the freedom I desired to develop my own intimate relationships with other men. He was too afraid of losing me to "someone else" even though while I was away, he was going to bed every night with "someone else" while I slept alone.

Did I really want to go back to Montana and struggle with the nagging issues of never enough money, never enough intimacy, and never enough peace in relationship? No, not really. But would I trade my difficult lifestyle of living in God's country with no electricity, no phone, no neighbors for what Norman had generously offered? No, never!

I had freely chosen this lifestyle out of love—love for Karl, love for my children, love for Kirstie, but most of all, love for God. I knew God had led me on my life's path to marry Karl, bear eleven wonderful children, and shoulder the burdens that plural marriage would bring. And somehow I knew that God would see us through...come what may. And that through His love and our love for each other, we'd find a way to survive. Not only survive, but thrive.

Could I ever find this kind of love in the arms of the red-necked, beer-bellied man sitting across from me? Again the answer was clear. No, never!

"You actually were alone with that creep and even allowed him to hold our baby!" Karl shouted, after I confessed my story to him on my return home to Montana.

"I only asked you to promise me two things—*two things*—and you couldn't even do either of them! I asked you *not* to be alone with *any* men, and I asked you *not* to allow *anyone* to hold our baby. How can I *ever* trust you to go down to Salt Lake by yourself if you don't even have strength enough—*the guts enough*—to keep two little promises?"

"It wasn't like I wanted to break those promises..." I began, trying to defend myself against Karl's verbal attacks. "It just...happened. I felt by the Spirit not to contend with him, like the scriptures say...'agree with your adversary while in the way with him'—and then move out of the way."

"Oh, you and your *spiritual justification*," mocked Karl, cynically. "Well, I just hope nothing bad comes of it."

But something wicked was in the making. Tempers flared, tongues fired, and temperatures rose as "dis-ease" spread rampant through our family like wildfire. We all came down with some unknown virus which brought on fevers, chills and the same hacking cough that Norman had exhibited the night of our conversation.

Adam developed an extremely high temperature, which I tried to treat with elderflower and peppermint tea, a favorite herbal remedy for fevers. His fever had dropped a bit when I tucked him in bed with me. I set a tincture bottle full of tea next to him to give him during the night. I wanted to give him some baby aspirin to assure that his temperature wouldn't rise any more during the night, but Karl, who was against any type of medication, insisted that Adam would be all right with just tea. I felt Karl was a bit of a fanatic when it came to modern medicine. I believed there's a time and place for everything and I believed Adam's fever was severe enough to warrant medication.

At about two a.m. I awoke restlessly and felt Adam's head. It felt like a furnace. Quickly, I turned on the flashlight and tried to coax some tea into him. He was completely lethargic, staring at a point just above my head. The hideous memory of how Jadon had done this just prior to his death flashed through my mind. I kept trying to get tea down him, but noticed that he wasn't swallowing. Oh, my God! He wasn't breathing either, and he was starting to turn blue!

"Kirstie!" I screamed, scooping Adam up in my arms. "Adam's stopped breathing!"

I ran out into the hall. Karl, who'd been sleeping on the couch downstairs, met me on the stairs as he grabbed Adam from my arms.

"Go run a cold bath!" commanded Karl. Kirstie, who'd followed me down the stairs, ran into the bathroom and cranked on the cold water. I collapsed on the couch, trembling, my hands pressed against my eyes...and prayed. I prayed with all the energy of my soul that God would forgive me... for the broken promises, for my stupid neglect, for anything I'd done to have caused this to happen to me again.

"Oh, no, God no," I moaned. "Please don't make me suffer through losing another child because of my blasted stupidity!" Tears ran down my face as I petitioned the Lord again. "Please, Lord Jesus, help me. Help us save the life our baby, for God's sake!"

I got up and walked unsteadily into the bathroom to see if...yes, God yes! Adam was moving slightly, starting to breathe again as Karl held him in the cool water, solemnly pronouncing a priesthood blessing over him.

"Oh, God, thank-you, thank-you!" I praised out loud. Karl lifted the baby from the water, and Adam started to cry. I grabbed a clean towel from the shelf and wrapped it around my precious, crying, squirming baby. I held him close to my heart and whispered a final prayer.

"Thank God, Jesus—your power is greater!"

Karl was a changed man after that, as he realized the miracle that had taken place in our life through Jesus Christ's atoning grace. He felt as if he'd passed through the veil of death, himself, to bring back our baby from the dark abyss. He'd offered his own life in exchange for Adam's. And God had acknowledged his sincere, heartfelt sacrifice—bringing Adam back to life again.

I could relate so well to what Karl had experienced. Eleven times I'd gone to the veil of death's transition where I felt like I was going to die—actually wanted to die—in order to bring my precious new-borns their first breath of life. Karl now had a deeper knowing…a deeper appreciation for the sacrifices I'd made in order to bring forth his children. And we both had a deeper appreciation for what our older brother, Jesus, felt as he hung on the cross for all mankind to bring us the greatest gift of all—Eternal Life.

Chapter Eighteen

Heartsong

"So Mom, what ever happened to your vision of the Hidden Valley Health Resort? It seemed like such a great idea. Did Rosalie ever get the financing to build it?"

Obviously Serenity, having been left up in Montana at the time, was unaware of some of the family history. But now was a good time to fill her in on "the rest of the story."

A month or so passed since the meeting that Norman attended. At the end of September, Karl and I went down (together this time) to see if we could help push a land deal through with Mom's family estate. We were hoping the family would sign a contract for us to get control of the land next to the golf course and secure the financing to begin construction. But it was pretty clear as we explored the options that other parties had control over the land and they weren't willing to budge for what we were offering.

While we were still in Salt Lake, we connected with an herb company that was interested in investing some substantial capital into the health resort as they could see the market potential for their own products. They were also interested in marketing my herbal Green Drink formula. Karl and I created a product information sheet for them to present to the Olympic Committee, as they were already testing a few of their other products on some of the Olympic athletes.

After two exhaustive weeks of "busy-ness," Karl and I were ready to be back home with our family in the rejuvenating Montana mountains. We decided we could finish putting together the rest of the Green Drink formula there. Even so, I felt some reluctance and heaviness in my heart about returning to Montana. When I got back I would face two weeks of sleeping alone. It was only fair to Kirstie who'd tended the house and family for two weeks deprived of the comfort and intimacy of a husband.

As we approached our home, we noticed a strange vehicle dropping off two Amish couples dressed in their traditional black clothing. I'd totally forgotten that we'd arranged for them to visit that weekend after several years of correspondence. We'd been sharing back and forth our success stories of living off the land and building community. They'd wanted to visit us to see what we'd been able to accomplish. I did my best to be cheerful and welcoming and probably would have really enjoyed their visit and my reunion with the children, if I hadn't been so full of anxiety at the thought of sleeping alone.

That night Karl and Kirstie slept in the bedroom next door to mine. The tongue and groove walls, which divided the two rooms, didn't go all the way to the ceiling as Karl had run out of wood. Through a gap of a foot or so, sounds and even smells passed freely from room to room. It was the worst torture I could think of—listening to my husband making love to another woman just a few feet away. And with the house full of guests, I couldn't even seek refuge on the couch downstairs. I longed desperately for another man to comfort me, as my loneliness was excruciatingly painful some nights. I would often fantasize about John Denver holding me and singing me to sleep with his love song, "Lady."

I worked hard all weekend to keep up the façade that our polygamous relationship was actually working. We showed our Amish guests around our humble estate—a small raised-bed garden, a llama corral, a chicken coop and goat pens. I was certain it suffered in comparison with their well-developed, self-sustaining farm in Pennsylvania. Nevertheless, they enjoyed our herb-gathering walk during which I identified and picked the ingredients for my Green Drink formula. Even though it was the end of the season and the plants were a bit bitter, they enjoyed sampling the concoction and raved about its taste.

On Sunday morning, we exchanged scriptures in a gospel discussion that Karl led, and we shared with them a message about the restored gospel and the Book of Mormon. Then, as a special treat, we sang for each other our favorite "heartsongs." Our family sang an unrehearsed rendition of "I Am a Child of God," and their quartet sang a German hymn which one of them translated:

> O God Father We Praise Thee
> And Thy Goodness we Praise

That you O Lord have so Gracefully
And has newly shown unto us
And has Lead us, Lord together
To exhort Ourselves With Thy Word
Give us Grace unto this

Open the mouth Lord of thy Servant
Give him the Wisdom
That he may speak Thy Word right
What Leadeth to a Godly life
And is worthy to Thy praise
Give us hunger for such food
That is our desire

Give our heart understanding
To enlighten us on Earth
That we may become Godly
And live in righteousness
Thinking on Thy word Always
So man is not Deceived

Yours O Lord is the Kingdom alone
And also the Power together
We Love you in the Congregation
And Thank Thy Name
And pray unto Thee from our Heart
That Thou will be with us this hour
Through Jesus Christ. Amen

At the end of the meeting, we exchanged hugs and fond farewells. Karl drove them in our pick-up truck to the bus station; the two gentlemen riding solemnly in the back wearing their best-starched Sunday suits complete with black top hats. Normally, the sight would have tickled me with delight, but I was holding onto dark resentments. I knew I needed to get these bitter feelings out of my heart and that the only way was to take them to the Lord. I set things in order at home and asked Kirstie to take over while I went for a walk.

It was a beautiful, autumn afternoon as I hiked to one of my favorite sacred spots—a grove of Cedars along the babbling stream. There I felt safe to cry out my bitterness to the Lord and to the mountain; lamenting how unfair and unjust it was to be living in such an inequitable marriage. I told the Lord I just couldn't handle it anymore. I begged him to release me from this heavy burden even though I had freely chosen it.

I wept deeply for over an hour, clearing my heart and soul of all the resentment I felt towards Karl, Kirstie, and the other so-called "saints" who'd created this hellish system of inequality. It was necessary for me to be able to go on living it.

After Karl got back from town, Kirstie suggested that I sleep with him that night. She sensed my need for his comfort. I argued against it, knowing how difficult it had been for her to be alone on the mountain with nine children for two full weeks. But I yielded when Karl joined Kirstie's side of the debate. Besides, I felt flu symptoms coming on and needed the comfort of a warm body next to mine.

Monday morning arrived, and with it came one of Karl's extraordinary massages, which he always gives me when I'm feeling especially deprived. As his hands played a symphony on my body, opening up all my chakras and sending me into a pleasant alpha state, a song kept playing in my heart as if someone were actually singing from the Spirit World. I kept hearing John Denver's voice singing to me, and I even felt guilty that I was thinking of him with Karl there loving me.

Karl could sense that my thoughts were far away and asked repeatedly what I was thinking about. I just smiled to myself and replied, "Nothing much." But the song kept filling my heart as if it were being sung to me directly by John even though it wasn't one of his songs I was familiar with.

Kirstie prepared a fabulous breakfast and then Karl took thirteen-year-old Amber and went to town to mail our Green Drink formula. I was still having attacks of intestinal flu and decided to rest in bed that morning. Amber wouldn't be there for home-school and Serenity really wasn't in the mood for school with the nice weather outside.

I propped myself up on pillows and wrote the words of the song that had been playing on my heart that morning. I was very excited as it had been a long time since I'd written a song and was beginning to wonder if I still had it in me. The last two songs I'd written and performed were for The Women's Constitutional Convention over six years ago, and it was then that we'd met Kirstie's family. Since then I'd put all of my creative energies aside to deal with the complex and emotional issues of managing a large family inside a polygamous relationship.

After lunch I felt some strength coming back, so Kirstie and I decided to drive to the neighbor's house to make some phone calls. Kirstie wanted to find out how things were with her family in Lovell, and I was anxious to talk to Rosalie about her presentation to the potential investors in the health resort.

On the way down our two-mile winding dirt road, I could hear a song quietly playing on our Subaru's radio. The radio was almost turned off, but I could still recognize the voice of John Denver. I quickly turned it up:

> Singing, good morning America, how are you?
> Saying, don't ya know me I'm your native son?
> I'm the train they call the city of New Orleans
> I'll be gone 500 miles when the day is done

"Can you believe it?!" I cried ecstatically to Kirstie. "They're *actually* playing a John Denver song on the radio!"

I'd concluded that the powers that be had banned all of his music from the airwaves because of his attacks on all their "sacred cows." (If you've ever heard "Raven's Child," you know what I mean.)

Kirstie and I were jubilantly singing the chorus with John when we nearly ran into Karl and Amber coming the other way. I stopped the car adjacent to them, rolled down the window, and turned up the radio so Karl and Amber could hear the music playing.

"Just listen whose playing on the radio!" I shouted enthusiastically, thinking they'd finally believe me that a John Denver renaissance was beginning.

Karl and Amber did not share my enthusiasm…their faces were sullen and grave. Karl said something to me that I couldn't hear over the strains of the song. He motioned for me to turn down the radio.

"He's dead, Jesse. *John Denver's dead!* He died yesterday in a plane crash. It's over, Jesse. He's gone. I just read about it in a newspaper article in town."

His words felt like boulders crashing down on my head. I was stunned. I couldn't believe what he was saying. *No way, could it be true!* It must be another one of Karl's cruel ploys, trying to discredit my spiritual connection with John.

"Is this another one of your *sick jokes!?*" I exploded; disgusted that Karl would stoop so low.

Amber piped in, "Mom, John Denver *really is dead!* Believe me! We *both* read it in the Missoula newspaper!"

I was in a state of shock as Karl related the details of the accident. John had been flying alone in a light plane that crashed into the ocean just off Lover's Point in Monterey Bay. Karl thought it could have been suicide because the day was clear and sunny. I argued that John would *never* do such a thing—if anything, he may have been *murdered*. Regardless, I still couldn't believe any of it until I saw *positive, undeniable proof that John Denver was truly dead.*

Karl knew I was in a state of distress from sickness and shock. He convinced me to turn the car around and follow him home. That evening I went straight to bed without eating, crying, or thinking about anything but John Denver's death.

The next morning after a nightmarish sleep, I grabbed my coat and the car keys and told Karl I wanted to drive down to the neighbor's and call Rosalie to see how our "promo package" went with the investors. Karl wanted me to take Kirstie, but I insisted that I needed some time alone.

My neighbor, Marlene welcomed me and offered a cup of coffee. "No thanks," I responded, "but could I see this morning's paper?"

She handed me the paper and I noticed a small lead-in blurb with a picture of John Denver in the corner of the front page of the Missoulian. I reluctantly turned to the page indicated. It was a full-page article covering John Denver's fatal accident along with a recap of his popular musical history. It only mentioned some of his earlier songs like "Rocky Mountain High" and "Country Roads"—nothing about the *real* John Denver whom I knew and loved.

No mention was made of his more recent and inspiring songs like "Higher Ground" or "The Flower That Shattered the Stone." But these songs were never played over the airways. Those precious gems were reserved only for the dedicated fans who made the effort to purchase the recordings he produced each year.

But did anyone *really* know the John Denver *I knew?* The inspired poet who sang sweet love songs to the heart, from the heart? The prophet who prophesied a path of serendipity for any of us who would simply follow the path of Spirit? What a loss the entire world suffered with the passing of such a gifted voice.

I punched in Rosalie's number on Marlene's phone and numbly talked with an automated operator about a collect billing charge. Rosalie answered after a couple of automated rings.

"Jesse, I'm so glad you called!" Rosalie's voice was filled with concern. "I've been *so* worried about you... I've been feeling your pain. Are you okay?"

"Sure, Rose. You know me. Solid as a rock. Boy, those must have been some mighty powerful prayers you've been saying for me,"

I tried to joke with her but my voice broke. I was referring to our last conversation we'd had over the phone a few days before. I'd been struggling emotionally with the same old issues regarding my lop-sided polygamous relationship; and I'd caved in and shared with her some of my deepest feelings. She promised she would pray for me. The last thing she said before hanging up was, "You really need to get connected with your soul-mate, sweetie." I'd made no response to her remark, but at that point I was open to anything.

We had a tearful, heartfelt conversation about John's passing, and I felt much better after we hung up. Rosalie understood me better than anyone, and I could talk to hear about things I couldn't share with anyone else.

The rest of the day I spent suffering, feeling the reality of John's death. This illusion of loss and separation I felt towards a beloved who'd passed into a different dimension became real to me in the physical sense. But when I transformed it into something spiritual, I knew it was an illusion I was choosing to hold in my mind and heart.

Still, there was the definite disappointment of never being able to share my life story with John face to face. I'd only hoped he'd read what I gave him at the Windstar Symposium a few years before—how his music had led me on a path from being "born again" in "the summer of my 27th year" at his place called Windstar on a "Colorado Rocky Mountain High" where I'd received a true awakening and my vision for Heartsong Living Centers. And then home-birthing Amber in the "month of June" in "a place called Paradise." Of having three more children "born in the Bitterroot Valley" and burying one to remain with the "wild wind for his brother in the wild Montana skies." How it "amazes me" to have lived in a tradition-steeped, Mormon polygamous community and feel that the "wind will surely blow it all away." And the "reaching for Higher Ground" because I can't "live with the things I don't believe in." And just recently beginning the process of "The Flower that Shattered the Stone" starting with my own heart which was shattering again at this very moment.

The story of those remarkable coincidences that correspond to John Denver's songs is something I would only share with a select few who I knew wouldn't think I was crazy. But after hearing my story, none of them could deny the miraculous pattern of coincidences…and neither could I.

But now the reality was so stabbingly painful. I would never be able to physically share that miraculous story with him nor would I be able to honor him with some of *my* love songs sung from *my* heart. Nor would he be able to come and enjoy some "healing time with Mother Earth" here at Higher Ground. These were *very real* disappointments to me, and I was shattered by the pain of sin (my own separation within).

But then I made a conscious choice to come out of my illusion and realize that John Denver was still alive, closer to me now than he'd ever been before. I felt his presence dynamically as I turned my illusion of separation into my resolution of oneness. I resolved that I would write a book about my life's path, get my songs recorded, and build a Heartsong Living Center here at Higher Ground so others could share in the healing time with Mother Earth in the wild Montana Mountains. I would build other Heartsong Living Centers elsewhere so that I could share with others...millions of others...what I'd so desired to share with one person...John.

Wednesday morning I put on my best dress and "made-up" my best pleasant face—to go to a funeral in Pinesdale. Another strange coincidence was that Naomi Powell's husband, John, had died the same day as John Denver. Naomi was my dear friend who had invited me to sing at the Women's Constitutional Convention.

I was comforted by the words and music shared at the funeral of our dear friend who had died at the ripe old age of seventy-six, leaving eight children, forty-five grandchildren, and thirteen great-grandchildren. What a beautiful family legacy, I thought, praising God for my own beautiful family of ten and my loving husband, Karl. John Powell also left a loving, supportive wife, Naomi, who stood as solid as a rock in her faith that death is not the end to life but only the beginning of a new, more exalted existence.

The ushers handed out a poem rolled up and tied with a golden ribbon. As I read its inspired words, I made another resolution: I would live each day fully, as if it were my last, with all the love, joy, and laughter I could possibly find. The poem read:

The Plan of the Master Weaver

Our lives are but fine weavings
That God and we prepare,
Each life becomes a fabric planned
And fashioned in His care,
We may not always see just how
The weavings intertwine,
But we must trust the Master's hand
And follow his design.
For He can view the pattern
Upon the upper side,
While we must look from underneath
And trust in Him to guide...
Sometimes a strand of sorrow
Is added to His plan,
And though it's difficult for us,

We still must understand
That it's He, who fills the shuttle
It's He who knows what's best
So we must weave in patience,
And leave to Him the rest.
Not 'til the loom is silent
And the shuttles cease to fly,
Shall God unroll the canvas
And explain the reason why
The dark threads are as needed
In the weavers skillful hand
As the threads of gold and silver,
In the pattern He has planned.

We are all weavers in the tapestry we call "life." We all bring to life's loom the threads of who we are from another existence. Some bring golden threads of beauty, goodness and truth; while others bring dark and drab threads of self-pity and despair. While some have finished their work at the loom, others must continue. The mystery of life is to find where each of our threads belongs in the fabric of existence...and then complete the task of weaving before the tapestry has a chance to unravel. For there is an element of disintegration, which causes the fabric to unravel before it's completed when we die with our story unexpressed. And that, for me, is the great tragedy of life—of not having the chance to complete the purpose for which we've been sent before the fabric can unravel.

Thursday while straightening my room, I discovered the song I'd written Monday morning before learning about John's death. I read it with amazement as a stream of tears coursed down my face. I shared it with Karl and Kirstie as one last tear rolled down my cheek as a final tribute to the memory of John's physical existence.

Heartsong

Heaven wouldn't be heaven without you
No, it just wouldn't be the same
Not to see you, to touch you, to love you
No, I just couldn't handle the pain

So I sit and I sing you my heartsong
Hoping someday you'll find ears to hear

And I wait, and I watch and I wonder
Hoping someday I will hold you near

It's my heartsong I sing in the morning
It's my heartsong I sing every night
It's the song of two lovers together
Two hearts beating as one...beating as one...take flight

Life isn't worth living without you
Your love makes everything worthwhile
To touch you, to hold you, to love you
To see you break out in a smile

So I listen to hear your heartsong
It plays a tune in my heart
And I still have the faith and the wonder
That someday we'll never be apart

I hear your heartsong in the morning
I hear your heartsong every night
It's the song of two lovers together
Two hearts beating as one...beating as one...take flight

I wondered if there were any clues along the way that would have prepared me for John's death. And of course there were clues—ones I'd missed because of my own darkened illusion that somehow I had to be physically with someone in order to be one *with* them. As I listened to some of John's most recently recorded songs, a voice spoke to me and confirmed his continuing existence. From his Wildlife Concert (which Karl and I personally attended) John shared a prologue to his song, "A Song for All Lovers":

I have a woman friend whose name is Marti Murie, and she is 93 years old. And I think she has done more for Alaska than any other single human being.

And it comes out of not only her love and the experiences she had in that great land and her love for that great land...but out of the love she had for her husband, Olis Murie. And when Olis passed away many, many years ago, the way that Marty kept his love and her feeling for him alive in her heart was to commit herself to saving the land that they both loved so very, very much.

I know a lot of things I could tell you about Marti, but the thing that I want to share with you is that she spoke of Olis always as her beloved. And they loved to dance…the waltz especially. And they danced whenever they could…whenever they felt like it regardless of the conditions. And I have this picture of them out on a frozen tundra of Alaska in each other's arms dancing. And no music except the sound of the wind rushing across that frozen wasteland. Or some place in a forest…or some place beneath the full moon. And so I wrote this song for Marti:

> I see them dancing
> Somewhere in the moonlight
> Somewhere in Alaska
> Somewhere in the sun
> I hear them singing
> A song for all lovers
> A song for the two hearts
> Beating only as one
>
> Imagine the morning
> No longer alone
> The arms of another
> A place to belong
> No longer the struggle
> No longer the night
> Forever becoming
> In the quickening light
>
> To see in the darkness
> To listen within
> To answer in kindness
> To ever begin
> To ever be gentle
> To always be strong
> To walk in the wonder
> To live in the song
>
> I see them dancing
> Somewhere in the moonlight
> In a place of enchantment
> Somewhere in the sun
> I hear them singing

A song for two lovers
A song for the two hearts
Beating only as one

I followed the coverage of John's funeral and how his ashes—his final
mortal remains—were released across the Rocky Mountains. I felt tears come
to my eyes as I was reminded of another one of his songs:

So many years ago
I can't remember now
Someone was waiting for me
I had the answers
To all of my questions
Love was so easy to see
I didn't know...

When I was younger
I should have known better
I thought that nothing was new
Through all the spaces
In all of the changes
What I lost sight of was you
I didn't know...I didn't know

I could see you in
Singing skies and dancing waters
Laughing children growing old
And in the heart and in the Spirit
And in the truth when it is told

My life became shady
And I grew afraid
And I needed to find my way home
I just couldn't see you
I thought that I'd lost you
I never felt so much alone
Are you still with me?

Some how in reason
I lost sight of seasons
Tide rollin' out, rollin' in

Sometimes in evenin'
When daylight was leavin'
I thought I'd never see you again
Are you still with me...are you still with me?

I'm with you in
Singing skies and dancing waters
Laughing children growing old
And in the heart and in the Spirit
And in a truth when it is told

If my faith should falter
And I should forsake you
And find myself turning away
Will you still be there...will you still be there?

I'll be there in
Singing skies and dancing waters
Laughing children growing old
And in the heart and in the Spirit
And in the truth when it is told

Chapter Nineteen

Speaking Wind

The sun hangs low in the western sky illuminating Heartsong's biodome in iridescent gold tones. Some of the younger grandchildren have curled up and fallen asleep cozily on the buffalo robe. Other family members continue to give Grandma Jesse their birthday gifts which hold special meaning—especially those from her thirteen beautiful children who range in age from Ashley, who will turn fifty next year, to Matthew, who will be twenty.

Some of the little ones awaken from their slumber as the gift-giving process begins again. They present their own precious gifts—bouquets and wreaths made from wildflowers; precious stones from their own rock collections; beautiful feathers, which join the one already in grandmother's hair; and pictures lovingly drawn with watercolors, ink or crayons.

Just as all the gifts appear to be given, a distinguished-looking Native American with flowing white hair approaches Jesse, carrying an interesting-looking bundle.

"Oh, Patrick, there you are! Where have you hidden yourself all this time?"

"Oh, I've been here all along, Jesse. It's just that you've been so busy with family and festivities that I didn't feel like intruding."

"Intruding! Oh, Patrick, don't be ridiculous. You know you are just as much a part of our family as anyone else. Come, show us what you have in your hands."

"Patience, Old One, patience. First you must tell the others *our* story... or have you forgotten it after so many years?"

"Forgotten! Patrick, I may be an 'Old One' to you, but the memory of our first meeting is as fresh in my mind as if it were yesterday."

"Oh, Grandma, tell us the story of how you first met Grandfather Speaking Wind," echo a chorus of small voices.

It was Rosalie who first introduced me to Patrick, or "Speaking Wind," as she had learned to call him. She was dating Wallace, who was publishing one of Patrick's books called *The Message*. Rosalie was in the process of reading the manuscript and had also read his earlier book, *When Spirits Touch the Red Path,* when I came down for a visit.

"You've got to read this book…you'll absolutely love it!" she exclaimed, handing me a thin paperback. On the cover, two feathered flutes were crossed in the foreground against a sandstone cliff dwelling.

"Interesting," I remarked. "I hope it's as intriguing as its cover."

I wasn't disappointed. The book took me on a romantic adventure involving an Anasazi tribe of cliff-dwellers in the Mesa Verde area of Colorado. It painted a beautiful picture of their traditions and legends one of which is that they were able to walk into the Fifth World (the fifth dimension) with their coats of skin still on. In other words, the Anasazi tribe learned the process of translation—just as Enoch, Salem, and other tribes of had been taken off the Earth in groups.

But what fascinated me most was the legend that "in the Season of the Long Shadow, the Ancient Ones—enlightened beings from the now extinct Anasazi—would return in skins that weren't red to assist mankind in its great transformation into the Fifth World or New Age. These Ancient Ones would recognize each other and feel drawn to gather together in sacred communion to bring back the sacred knowledge and teachings of the Anasazi."

"So when do I get to meet this intriguing author, Patrick Quirk?" I asked Rosalie, after finishing his book.

"Well, I have his phone number if you'd like to call him. I talk to him all the time by phone. He's helping me with my own spiritual work of healing my 'Sacred Circle'."

She then described the amazing things Speaking Wind, through spiritual intuition, had advised her to do. How it was important for each of us to heal or complete our own "sacred circle" before coming into sacred communion with others. Some of the things she told me were absolutely remarkable. Patrick was able to tune into the spirit world and access precisely the information she needed at the particular time she needed it. And I could tell by her glowing enthusiasm that whatever she was doing was absolutely perfect. I was certainly looking forward to meeting this fascinating "Spirit-Caller" named Speaking Wind…but I was willing to wait until the Spirit brought us together.

About a month later, the Spirit called me to Salt Lake to work on my book, *For Heaven's Sake—What on Earth Are We Doing?*—a fictional account of my vision of the preexistence and manifesting that vision here. I also wanted to visit Delaney who had moved in with her grandparents in Smithfield, Utah to attend high school. I then discovered that Speaking Wind had flown in from Alabama to give a lecture that weekend at a high school in Linden, and I was filled with anticipation to finally meet him.

That evening I arrived at the school with Rosalie and a few of her friends. We waited in the hallway for Wallace, Speaking Wind's editor and escort, who were going to meet us there with him. Wallace had also shown some interest in publishing my book, and we'd become good friends.

When he arrived with Speaking Wind (or Patrick as I would come to call him), our eyes met and there was an immediate recognition of spirit touching spirit—and also a revelation of great purpose in our meeting. He was dressed in Native American leathers, holding an impressive walking stick with animal totems carved into it. Later he explained the significance of the four different animal symbols and their personal meaning to him.

Patrick was immediately impressed by my auric light. He is very adept at seeing and reading auras. "You are doing very well, Little One, very well. You have opened a lot of doors for many people and whatever path you are on, you should stay on it." He then commented that there was one area of my aura that was blocked that needed opening; some of my belief systems were holding me hostage and not allowing the light and truth to penetrate me. He said that we would talk about that later.

As we conversed, he kept looking at me with a strange sort of fascination in his eyes, as if he were trying to remember me from some other time and place beyond this plane of existence. He spoke of a time of awakening that had occurred in the summer of 1992 when many of the "Ancient Ones" had been awakened to who they really are. I thought back to the summer of 1992. I had been on my Vision Quest in the Rocky Mountains near Aspen. Indeed a great awakening had occurred in me—greater than I'd ever experienced before!

Suddenly Patrick looked at me and with a profound smile of recognition. "I can't believe you are here!" he exclaimed. "You are one of the Ancient Ones—but you already know that don't you?! We must talk later, Little One, after my presentation. We will meet for coffee."

I was somewhat overwhelmed when I went into the restroom. As I looked into the mirror I wondered—"Did this Indian Shaman, Speaking Wind, see something in me that I wasn't prepared to see?" I couldn't deny the rapport we shared or my curiosity about what more this Spirit-Caller, Patrick Quirk, would have to say.

For the next hour and a half, Patrick conducted an inspiring presentation about the philosophies of his people—the Pueblo Indians—and the dramatic changes taking place on the Earth Mother. He talked about his own mission in life—to break down the fences or barriers between the White and the Red races so that we could become one human family.

This truly fascinated me, as I felt this same mission for myself as part of healing my own ancestral family. My grandfather on my mom's side was a millionaire and a very visionary man. On his deathbed he had received a vision or revelation from Christ instructing him to "help the Lamanite people." He felt the best way to do this was to establish a foundation to help educate the Indians in the white culture and send them on LDS missions. Although the educational programs were well intended, they created a cultural imbalance—a kind of broken circle—which I felt was part of my destiny to heal, and this fueled my need to understand Native American ways. I also felt that Native Americans had a spiritual quality and depth that Mormons had barely scratched the surface of.

I was anxious to share some of these insights and my family history with Patrick, hoping to create a connection with him that would not only help fulfill our personal visions but also a vision of oneness between the white and red races. But because of a misunderstanding of directions on the driver's part, I missed joining the group for coffee. I was sorely disappointed by the mix-up, which meant I couldn't talk with Patrick until the following morning at Wallace's home.

I took Mom with me as it was a short distance from her home where I was staying. I felt she could speak with Patrick regarding the family foundation, and he could suggest how it might be better directed to meet the needs of the Indians. She was the oldest in the family and president of the foundation.

We met Rosalie there, and she and I listened as Mom and Patrick discussed some of these concerns. I was anxious to help facilitate the changes Patrick suggested as a way to heal the broken circle I felt has been created.

Then out of the blue, Patrick turned to me, his eyes sparkling with laughter, "Little One, you are so much in the Spirit that you are leaving others behind. You must learn to laugh more and not take life so seriously." He continued to talk directly to me as Wallace and some of his friends came to listen to our conversation.

"Most people are following the path of the flesh and can't even hear the path of the Spirit calling to them. I can see that you're already very much in-tune with the path of the Spirit, and oftentimes you are so caught up in it that you tune-out others who are calling to you but who so desperately need your wisdom. Jesse, you need to share with others the things that you know, the beauty that is yours that they see in your face and long for. You must now begin the path of a leader to teach others who see in you what they desire but don't know how to obtain it. You must share with others your knowledge so they can also learn for themselves the path of the Spirit. It is important for you to do this now as part of your spiritual path."

"Patrick, you know that I'm already aware of this. That's why I'm writing a book about my spiritual path. It is easier for me to write about it than to speak about it to others."

"This is good, Jesse," he remarked earnestly. "But you must also learn to speak what the Spirit is showing you. This way you can better help those you come in direct contact with. I see you becoming a great teacher to many people."

"Perhaps, Patrick, but I see them coming to me at my place at Higher Ground, because my home—the land, the trees, the plants and the animals—all have their messages to share."

I was passionate and intense as I placed my hands over my heart. "They are all a part of me and are with me here in my heart. They want to share their voices, too."

Patrick nodded and smiled knowingly, contemplating Higher Ground for a moment. "Yes, this place of yours is a sacred place," he acknowledged. "You have done well, Little One. You have already learned to speak and listen to the Standing Ones and Plant People. They recognize you and accept you as part of them. This is good, Jesse. You must now learn to listen to the Stone People. They, too, have their messages to share. You must learn the sacred ceremony of the circle of stones."

"Patrick, you know that I long to learn *all* the sacred ceremonies of your people, but I've never had a Shaman to teach me these things. I even tried to build a sweat lodge with the help of a friend so that we could have that sacred ceremony. Then I called out in spirit for a Shaman to come and guide us in this ceremony. But none came. Perhaps *you* are that Shaman."

"Perhaps, Little One, perhaps," contemplated Patrick. "I will take it up with the Spirits after I complete my work here in Salt Lake in bringing forth my child. You know, Jesse, writing a book is something like having a child. You first have the pleasure of conception, and then it grows inside of you until it is time for it to be delivered. I feel them all as if they were my own children. You must complete your own work on your child, Little One. It is important for you to do this."

I knew that Patrick was talking about my book. But he paused and then smiled faintly. "I also sense that you are in the process of bringing forth another child besides your book. Am I right, Jesse?"

I blushed as all eyes focused on my belly. "Yes, you're right. Am I already showing? I'm only three months along."

"No, Jesse, you don't look pregnant—except for the glow about you. Spirit told me you were pregnant. Is this your first child?"

I smiled, feeling a flicker of wicked anticipation. "No, Patrick, this is my *tenth* child. Didn't Spirit tell you that?"

I laughed out loud as Patrick's eyes grew round, and he jerked upright in surprise.

"*Ten children!* You mean to tell me that this is your *tenth* child you are carrying? You must be joking, right?!"

"Go ahead," I replied, still laughing. "Ask Spirit if I'm telling you the truth. Would I joke about a thing like that?"

"You're one amazing lady…you know that don't you?" breathed Patrick, settling back into his chair. "You have done very, very well, Little One. But tell me…why have you chosen to birth so many children when you could use your time helping the other children who are already here who need your help so desperately?"

"Because bearing children is also part of my spiritual path," I explained passionately. "I feel the greatest gift I can give to Spirit is to provide bodies as temples to house spirits. Each child I have born called to me in spirit for embodiment. How can I refuse when there are so many women who cannot or will not provide bodies for spirits? Spirits must have a way to get here as they have been promised. I feel that someone must be willing to make the sacrifice of providing bodies for the spirits who cry out for existence. And also to provide a place to raise them so that they can fulfill their own spiritual paths."

"Yes, Jesse, you have done well in providing places for Spirit to dwell. But I don't know where you ever find time to do it all." Patrick sounded genuinely concerned.

"Most of my time is devoted to my children, as this is where I get my greatest joy—loving and caring for them, teaching them the ways of the Spirit. If I can't teach them the ways of the Spirit, then why should I try to teach anyone else? Besides, children are so much easier to lead in the ways of Spirit than adults. Adults are already set in following the path of the flesh. With children there is still hope that they will listen and learn. Perhaps in them there is still hope for the future."

"So is it your hope, Jesse, to bear enough children of your own that you can repopulate the world after all of those who are following the path of the flesh are destroyed?"

I couldn't help laughing along with Patrick, even though I knew his comments were flavored with sarcasm.

"Perhaps, Patrick, but I'm hoping that others who feel the same way as I do will join me. I already have a sister-wife with two children of her own who have joined our family. She's a great help to me, and if it weren't for her taking care of all of my children while I'm down here working on my book, I wouldn't be here talking with you."

"Now, wait a minute!" For the second time in two minutes, I'd stunned Patrick. "You mean to tell me that your husband is married to *two* women?"

Again, I couldn't help but laugh at the shocked look on Patrick's face. "Why look so surprised, Patrick? Your people did it all the time. Didn't most of your chiefs have more than one wife? Look at Chief Joseph—he had two. And hasn't that always been one of men's fondest dreams—to have more than one wife?"

This time Patrick blushed. "Not one of mine. I had a hard enough time trying to keep one wife happy. Your husband must be one amazing guy."

"He is," I replied sincerely.

Patrick changed the subject. "You both have done very well with your place up in Montana, what you call…Higher Ground. That is a good name. A good Native American name. I bet you have some interesting stories to tell about it."

Patrick continued in a sort of spiritual reverie, as if part of him had left to go on a spiritual journey. "Yes, there is good spiritual energy there. Good, clean water. Many of the ancient Standing People have stayed there for many long years to protect this place for a very sacred purpose. You have done well to keep this place sacred."

"Yes, there are many ancient cedar groves on and close to our land." I confirmed. "We have been careful not to allow any unnecessary cutting of the cedars."

"This is good, Little One, this is good. I see that there are nine very sacred spots on your land. Have you found them all yet?"

I mentally counted the sacred spots I'd discovered in the five or so years I'd lived at Higher Ground. I could only recall seven.

"You must find all of them," explained Patrick earnestly. "You must perform sacred ceremony on them to bless the land."

"We've already blessed and dedicated the land to God for His purposes. But I feel there is more to be done in order for it to manifest its purposed vision. I feel I need one of your people to do sacred ceremony there as I don't know how to go about doing it the true Native American way. I don't have adequate knowledge of the spiritual ways to do ceremony on my own. As I told you earlier, I tried to put a sweat lodge together but without much success."

Patrick was quiet for a moment, and then broke out in peals of uncontrollable laughter. Everyone surrounding us couldn't help but join in the laughter, although they were unaware of why he was laughing. I sat in silence, however, as I had a feeling that I was the focus of his laughter.

"Oh, Little One, forgive me, but I just couldn't help myself." He continued to chuckle as if caught up in some hilarious scene from a comedy act. "Oh, it is just too funny to watch you and your friend trying to put your sweat lodge together."

He then began mimicking me trying to hold down one end of a willow while the other end went flying up, struggling to secure them with pieces of string. He mimicked me tying them with knots, just to see them fly apart in all directions. It was all quite amusing but not exactly how I remembered it. I didn't think I'd done that bad a job for my first experience and without instructions.

"Now, Patrick, aren't you exaggerating just a bit?" I commented, feeling somewhat embarrassed about being the center of everyone's amusement. "I guess that's why you were brought into my life, Patrick—to show me the *right way* to do ceremony. I do remember calling out for a Shaman to help. Perhaps you're the one I was calling for to come."

"As I said before, I will talk with the Spirits about this when I get home." He paused, and then added with a final chuckle, "It's obvious you *do* need some help, Little One."

It wasn't until that evening that I was really able to talk with Patrick alone and ask him the one question that had haunted me ever since I'd read his book, *When Spirits Touch the Red Path.* As I'd been writing my own book, I'd become stuck on one point—a question that had filled my soul and begged for an answer. "What was it like to become one in spirit?" Somehow I knew Patrick knew as he'd alluded to it in his book.

All that evening during Patrick's encore presentation at Wallace's house with a few of Wallace's friends and associates, I felt stirrings of spiritual anticipation at the prospects of talking alone with Patrick.

Finally, Patrick and I escaped the crowd to Wallace's balcony and found a stone wall to sit on in the moonlight under a sky full of stars. I was full of questions. I felt like a schoolgirl as intense emotions welled up inside of me as Patrick pointed out the different groups of constellations. A shooting star blazed across the pinpricked galaxy, and we both smiled at each other warmly, reaching for each other's hand. As we sat hand in hand, I could feel an intensity of emotionally-charged energy between us. It was as if two stars had collided and we were now sharing in the illumination and energy from their dynamic fusion.

"Do you feel the energy?" I asked Patrick.

"Of course, Little One. There is great purpose for our paths coming together."

"But what does it *mean?* I don't understand these feelings that I'm having towards you."

Patrick chuckled deep in his chest. "Always asking questions, Little One, wanting to know more. Jesse, you haven't changed a bit."

"What do you mean, Patrick, I haven't changed a bit? Are you trying to tell me that we *knew* each other before...in a previous life perhaps?"

The idea of past lives always fascinated me. I was aware that many religions taught about reincarnation, but I was somewhat skeptical. My own Mormon upbringing discounted the idea that we have more than one life. That *this life* was the time in which we had to work out our salvation. Yet I always felt that I existed before and had acquired acquaintances from other lives...from other spheres of existence. What other way was there to explain the connection I felt with some people? And now Patrick was sitting here implying that *we'd* had a past life together.

My mood changed as Patrick took out a cigarette. "Do you mind?" he inquired, noticing the distraught look on my face.

"To be honest with you, I do," I replied rather abruptly. "I'm really sensitive to cigarette smoke."

"Well, I'll be careful to blow the smoke away from your face. It's kind of a bad habit, you know. I can't seem to get rid of it," Patrick stated, apologetically. "It used to be that the Red Man used tobacco ceremonially... and it was a good thing. But then the White Man came along and added something which made it addicting."

"More Nicotine," I stated, matter-of-factly.

"Yes, Nicotine."

Patrick puffed smoke in the opposite direction and continued. "About our past lives together? Yes, Jesse, we've been together more than once before, and we were *very* close."

I pondered his words for a brief moment, trying to recall in my soul's memory why I felt such a connection with Patrick. He only smiled and puffed clouds of smoke which floated upward into the night sky.

"Tell me, when did you first realize this...um fact? Was it when we first met?"

"Oh, Little One," Patrick laughed, "You still have the same spirit—forever asking questions."

I smiled back in response. "But how will I know the answers if I don't ask the questions?"

"Patience, Jesse, patience. The universe is always unfolding itself to our view, all in its own due time."

We both glanced up to the starlit sky and allowed the silence to speak the emotion that flowed between us. We were holding hands again.

Patrick continued, "I didn't recognize you when we first met in Linden. I recognized immediately that you were one of the Ancient Ones by the intensity of your auric light. But as we spoke together this morning here on the balcony, it all started to come back to me who you were. To tell you the truth, Jesse, *I was quite shocked!* I just couldn't believe it was possible that you were here again in this time and place." He paused, struggling with emotion.

"I still can't believe you are *really* here! Many of the Old Ones have already been awakened to who they really are and what their work is. There was a great awakening in July of 1992, when many of the Old Ones were awakened."

I thought back to July of 1992 when the Spirit had strongly prompted me to go on a Vision Quest in the Rocky Mountains near Aspen. It was during that time that I'd received some of the most astounding revelations of my entire life. Some had opened up a cataclysm in the spiritual realm when I'd acted upon them. As Patrick jarred my memory, I was filled with that same spiritual astonishment that I'd encountered on my Vision Quest.

"I can see by your face, Little One, that you are beginning to remember many things," Patrick smiled good-humoredly.

"Tell me more about our past life together, Patrick. I am only beginning to recall a few faint memories. I always felt like I was an Indian at some other time and place. I've always felt so connected with the Indian way of life. I even tried to learn all the Indian arts and crafts like spinning, basketry, pottery and making moccasins. It almost became an obsession with me. I even coerced my family into living in a teepee while we were building our log cabin in Montana."

"These are good things, Little One. They will help awaken you to who you truly are. It's not the color of skin that makes you a Red Man. It is the quality of your heart. You are as Indian as any Red Man I know. You must learn to follow the path of the Spirit and trust in your heart."

I paused, trying to get a hold of the emotion coursing through my soul.

"But Patrick, my heart is telling me that I want to be *one* with you. How can that be when I'm already married and am a mother of a large family?"

Patrick laughed again at my unchecked honesty. "Little One...you must learn not to ask so many questions. Questions always take you away from the joys of the present moment and put you into expectations of the future. You must learn to be happy with the joys of the present and what we are sharing together—here and now. Do not look to the future at what may or may not be possible."

His voice became more serious. "Also, you must never make a decision in the face of emotion. Emotion is only an illusion of what is truth—of what the heart is saying is truth. You must pass through all of the faces of emotion before coming to a decision of any kind. Then you will make the correct choice."

I sat silently with a million questions running through my mind, crying out for an answer. Patrick would be leaving for Alabama the following day, so I wanted to make the most of our time together. I realized that most of my questions must remain unanswered, at least for the time being. But still, one question begged for an answer—the one answer that I needed in order to continue with my book. Somehow I knew Patrick held the key to this knowledge.

"Patrick." I began, "Without taking away from the beauty of this present moment, may I ask you just one last question? I feel that somehow you know the answer."

Patrick chuckled again, "Of course, Little One. Why should I assume that you had changed any since I knew you last?"

This comment nearly distracted me, but I set it aside to forge ahead with my question. "Well, then, the question I've wanted to ask you ever since I read *When Spirits Touch the Red Path*, is—what is it like to be *one in spirit?* I feel that somehow you hold the answer to this question, and my spirit needs to know in order to continue with my book."

Patrick sighed heavily and his expression changed to one of deep contemplation. I realized that I probably wouldn't receive a direct answer. As the cool October breeze etched its enchantment across our faces, I felt like an actress in some surreal play that stretched from one lifetime into the next, searching for the lines from a long-forgotten script.

Patrick's cigarette was glowing its last red ember, and I knew the script to this romantic scene was about to come to an end—along with the cigarette. "It was always good for us, Jesse," his voice trailed off with the smoke of his last puff. I watched the smoke fade into the night air and wondered if I would ever know the mysteries of spiritual oneness.

The rest of the night was spent mingling with Wallace's friends and associates. As we played games, assisted in healings, and communed verbally and spiritually, the energy between Patrick and me continued to intensify. I could feel a warm current of magnetic energy flow between us each time we were near. I'd never felt that way before, except perhaps when I'd first met Karl. The spiritual connection with him obviously went far beyond this lifetime.

When it became late and most of Wallace's guests had gone home, Wallace offered me a ride to my mother's house. My mom had come to hear Patrick's lecture, but she had left earlier. Patrick volunteered to come along with Wallace to say his good-byes. I was both surprised and glad he did.

As Patrick walked me to the door, I couldn't help but feel a bit nervous. I had played out scenes like this in my high school days, and now, twenty years later, I still felt like an impetuous schoolgirl.

"Patrick, I *am* going to miss you," I said as we stood on the front doorstep. "I feel that we have so much we could learn from each other. Now here you are on your way back home to Alabama, and we've barely scratched the surface."

"Oh, Little One, haven't you learned anything by now?" sighed Patrick. "When Spirits touch the Red Path, they will always have a spiritual connection. Just seek me in the realms of the spirit and I will always be there for you. You have already learned to listen to Spirit. All you must do now is to call to me in the spirit, and I will be there. Just listen for me."

His face brightened as he continued, "And if that doesn't work, Jesse, you can always use the telephone. You *do* have my phone number, and you *do* still know how to use a phone, don't you?"

We both cracked up at the irony of it all. Soon I would be going back to my home in Montana where I lived in the mountains with no phone or electricity. The only *real* way to get a message to me was by postal service or, as we sometimes joked with friends, by smoke signals in case of an emergency. Now, here I was talking about communicating with a Red Man by means of spiritual telepathy. But for the time being, I anticipated using my mom's telephone to keep in touch with Patrick until I went back to Montana.

"You *will* give me a call tomorrow to let me know how your flight was and that you arrived home safely?" I asked anxiously.

"I promise, Little One. Don't worry."

"Can I ask you just one last question before you leave?" I ventured.

Patrick chuckled whole-heartedly, "Sure, Little One. Ask away."

"Why do you always call me 'Little One' when I feel that we are equals? It makes me feel like you are trying to be a father figure or condescending to me."

"I'm sorry, Little...Jesse. I didn't mean it to sound that way." He was genuinely sincere. "Actually it's a term of endearment that I use for those I feel close to. My own spiritual guide called me by that name. I guess it's just been a habit for many years. But if it bothers you, I will call you by whatever name you prefer."

I thought for a moment. "Well, what was the Indian name you used to know me by?"

Patrick put his finger to my lips. "Not now, Jesse. You've already asked *too* many questions for *one* night. Besides...that is something you must discover on your own."

And then, as if Spirit had a will of its own, Patrick pressed his lips gently upon mine, releasing the passion that had been building up between us all evening. My knees went weak as Patrick held me close.

"Good night, Little One..." Patrick whispered as walked off the porch into the night air to join Wallace in the van.

And I was left silently stunned, still asking the question in my mind, "What is it like to be spiritually one?"

Now Patrick was gone and what choice did I have but to take it to the Lord for clarification and enlightenment.

The next day I decided to drive up Emigration Canyon and try out an Indian ceremony Patrick had described in his book called "emptying the bowl." I parked my car on a turn-out near a hiking trail and walked up a steep incline for about a mile. I came to a strange-looking, ancient fir tree that looked like a grandfather "Standing Person." As ceremonially as possible, I selected twelve rocks for my sacred circle—four medium-sized ones for each direction—and smaller ones to go in between each. I also selected another flat rock for an altar to burn a sage offering. Along with the sage, I placed the scrap of paper in which Patrick had written his name, address and phone number as he'd said it's important to use something personal from the person you are saying prayers for. It helps focus the energy.

So, there I was, sitting cross-legged in the middle of a circle of rocks, saying prayers to an almost dead tree and feeling rather self-conscious already when along comes a hiker. Boy, did I feel like some sort of New Age weirdo!

I struggled to refocus and began to pour out my heart to God in this Native American fashion, wondering how and if the old tree in front of me would pick up my prayers like an antennae and send them up through the cosmos on a direct line to God.

After I finished emptying my heart as if into a bowl, I felt somewhat light-headed and definitely lighter-hearted. I knew deep within my soul that my prayers would be answered in some miraculous way. When the process felt complete—when no more thoughts were racing through my mind and my heart was at peace—I ceremonially replaced the rocks where I'd found them and put Patrick's address back into my pocket. I felt lighter than air as I bounced down the hillside to my car and drove back to my mother's house.

A few moments after arriving home, the telephone rang. It was Patrick. "So tell me—what has Jesse been doing on top of a mountain in front of an ancient Standing Person?"

I was amazed by the accuracy of his spiritual ESP. "How did you know where I've been?"

"Nothing is kept secret in the realms of the Spirit. You have done well, Jesse. The spirits are pleased with your efforts. Your prayers will be answered."

"But how?" I inquired.

"Well, first tell me what your prayers were, and then I will tell you how they will be answered?" Patrick teased.

"Well, you're the 'Spirit-Caller.' You probably tapped into the Great Spirit channel and overheard all of my prayers already," I replied wryly.

There was a long pause, then he stated soberly, "Little One...there are some things that are near and dear to the heart that only the Great Spirit can hear. He has heard you and will answer you. Just be patient and remain open. He is aware of all prayers of the heart and will answer them according to each individual's need and desire. We must look to the spirit-that-moves-in-all-things to answer all of our questions. One must not look to another person or source for our enlightenment. They will always fall short and leave us wanting. It is our own path of the Spirit we must learn to follow."

More briskly he added, "Now I must go run some errands before dinner. I will call you first thing in the morning, and we will talk more on this subject. Goodnight, Jesse. Pleasant dreams."

That night as I lay in bed, wrestling with my thoughts and feelings concerning Patrick, I tried to convince myself that these feelings of genuine love for him were *wrong* and that God or the devil was trying to test me to see if I would stand or fall. I prayed to the Lord that if these feelings were evil, they would leave me as I was in fear of committing a sexual sin that would prevent me from reaching eternal exaltation.

The lustful idea of going to bed with Patrick had never entered my mind. I can honestly say I was not attracted to him in the physical sense. I did, however, desire to be close to him—very close—and share in his knowledge concerning the Spirit World. I felt we had so much to share with each other in order to gain a broader view of the whole picture of who we are and what we are doing on this planet. I truly felt that our paths had come together for a purpose yet to be discovered. I was left with a million unanswered questions and the first one was still, "What was it like to be one in spirit?"

I pondered this concept when suddenly I felt a spiritual presence that I knew to be Patrick's. I felt the same warmth and energy I'd felt the night before when we were together—only stronger, more intense. He communicated to me that our spirits were calling out to each other to become one in spirit. He then asked my permission for his spirit to enter my spirit and become one.

What happened next can only be described as pure ecstasy. No other words could come close to communicating the feelings of complete love and joy that I felt towards Patrick—and the entire universe—as our spirits merged and made love to each other in complete communion of oneness. It was Nirvana…boundless bliss! I'd read about this experience before in tantric yoga books as the awakening of the *Kundalini* energies or serpent power. And although I'd felt stirrings of the *Kundalini* as Karl and I had come together both physically and, to a degree, spiritually; I'd never felt the total power of the *Kundalini* surging and spiraling up and down my spine, opening up each chakra or energy center. I felt completely energized and revitalized by each orgasmic current as my chakras were opened up by the love-energy Patrick's and my spirit were sharing. It was more intense than any physical lovemaking I'd ever experienced in my entire life. And unlike physical lovemaking, which sometimes leaves you feeling exhausted and disappointed, spiritual lovemaking was energizing and completely satisfying.

After our spirits made love for several hours into the night, my mind was filled with all sorts of questions about what had just occurred. Patrick's spirit stayed with me for the rest of the night as we communicated telepathically— Patrick's spirit answering my questions to my own satisfaction

The next morning I was still in a state of energized euphoria when the telephone rang. It was Patrick.

"Good morning, Jesse. How did we sleep last night?"

"Oh, Patrick...you know very well how *we* slept last night. Was it as good for you as it was for me?"

"It has *always* been good for us. I already told you that."

"But Patrick...I want you to describe to me exactly how it felt for you so I know I wasn't just imagining it."

"Oh, Jesse. You know you weren't just imagining. Trust in your spirit. Your spirit is very sensitive to these things."

"But why was it that our spirits were able to come together like they did when I've never experienced it before with anyone else?"

"Oh, Little One...forever asking questions! Don't you know that questions can only get you into trouble by taking you out of the present? You had a need to know what it was like to be one in spirit. That need was answered by both of our spirits."

"But it was so...divine. It's hard for me even to find words to describe it. There really aren't *any* words to describe it, are there? You'd have to *experience* it to know."

"And *you* were asking *me* to describe to *you* exactly what it was like? Jesse, sometimes words just aren't adequate. That is when we must learn to listen to Spirit. I will call you again tonight and we can talk more about this then. In the meantime...have a delightful day."

And I *did* have a delightful day. The spiritual lovemaking we had experienced that night had opened me up to a whole new realm of enlightenment I never knew existed. All of my senses had been spiritually awakened, and I could see auras and energies surrounding people, animals, plants, even insects. In fact, all of existence had a life-force of its own, which I could sense through spiritual eyes and also tap into. My hearing became more acute as each sound held a vibration of its own, which I could differentiate and understand its spiritual quality.

And tastes...wow! My taste buds were opened up to a whole new taste sensation. As I ate an omelet that morning, I was thrilled by my ability to identify each ingredient by its own unique vibration. Mushrooms, olives, broccoli, cauliflower, eggs and cheese—each contained a different vibratory taste, which I relished as a unique gift from God.

My spirit was soaring that day, as if I had truly been born-again—born into a new world that I never realized existed until now. I tried to share all of this newly discovered enlightenment with Rosalie, who was more than a bit curious to know what had happened to me. But the more I tried to explain it to her, the more I realized that what Patrick had told me was absolutely true. You just can't explain it—it has to be experienced!

Throughout the day, I felt Patrick's spiritual presence as we danced the "dancing butterflies" courtship dance. I could spiritually listen to him tell jokes, which he would do at the most inappropriate times, usually when I was having a conversation with someone, and I would laugh out loud, while others were thinking I'd lost my mind.

That night I was anxious for Patrick's phone call so as to discuss the day's events.

"Hello, Jesse. How was your day?"

"Wonderful!" I exclaimed. "And how was yours?"

We then shared and confirmed to the other what was *really* happening in the Spirit realm.

"Didn't you love the way Wallace reacted to the joke I told you while you were talking with him?" Patrick teased.

"Oh, you should have seen his face, Patrick. When I started laughing out loud right in the middle of his sentence, I think he thought I was crazy. I tried to explain what was going on—but then he *really* thought I was crazy!"

"Oh, Wallace is a good egg. He's almost ready to be awakened. Perhaps you can help him with this, Jesse."

"Me! Are you joking, Patrick? How can *I* possibly help to awaken Wallace?"

"Oh, it's something you will learn to do soon, Jesse. It's all part of your path. In fact, Jesse, it was *you* who taught *me* about these things in our past life together. I find it quite amusing that it is *I* who am teaching *you* this time around. Our spirits have had fun playing together. But now it is time to rest and relax. I have a wonderful tape I bought today with music depicting the four elements—earth, air, fire and water. I would like you to listen to it with me."

"And so how do you propose to do that, Patrick? Play it through the phone?"

"Oh, Little One," Patrick laughed. "You do still have much to learn."

With that he hung up the phone and I was left to wonder what in the world he was talking about. But Patrick was right. It was time for rest and relaxation. I undressed and slipped between the sheets. Almost immediately Patrick's spirit entered the room and asked permission to be one with me again. There was no hesitation in my acceptance, and as we joined in spiritual communion, pure ecstasy filled my soul again. After a few moments of awakening the *Kundalini* and experiencing a few spiritual orgasmic rushes opening all of my chakras, Patrick's spiritual energy or vibration began to change.

At first they became like that of the earth—firm and solid—penetrating me as if a mountain were being thrust up through the Earth in volcano-like eruptions. It was powerful energy, breaking open each chakra with a penetrating orgasmic thrust. And wow, was it satisfying! I had never felt so firmly rocked with each powerful spiritual orgasm.

Then the energetic vibration changed and became like that of air, totally different, with breezy, finger-like currents of air caressing me, pulsating a beautiful windsong to my soul. I felt lovingly caressed, as if I were being stroked by Patrick's spiritual fingers. It was like the spirit of the wind inviting me to join in a oneness celebration of breezy ecstasy—and I did—feeling the orgasmic rushes move up and down my chakras.

Again the vibrations changed to that of fire. I felt the intense fire of the *Kundalini* energy, igniting me with flames of passionate, fiery orgasms. Ah... it was so explosively irrepressible...so warm, so alive! My soul was on fire with Patrick's fiery thrusts that I felt I would explode into flames!

Finally, the energy vibrations changed to that of water—cool and calming, with wave after wave of liquid passion filling my soul to over-flowing. Like the flow of the river to the sea...like the fountain of living waters being poured inside me. I felt the flood of Patrick's spiritual energies pulsing my chakras open. My spirit was overflowing with the love Patrick flowed inside me.

And though my energy centers were blown wide open, it was all I could do to contain all of it—the energies of earth, air, fire and water. My heart began singing praises to God for the gift of grace he'd given me...to experience making spiritual love with Patrick.

As for Patrick—all I could do as he brought me deeper and higher with each spiritual climax to a greater awakening was to express his name over and over again in spirit, telling him how much I loved him!

As the week progressed and we experienced spiritual oneness together each night, our conversations over the phone became more frequent and more intimate. Patrick had a sense of the hilarious, which I truly enjoyed. He mentioned that my religious beliefs had made me quite sterile, and he was attempting to bring more laughter into my serious world. And he was quite successful at it, I must admit.

He also convinced me that part of my problem was that some of my "belief systems" were based on a false premise—that the Book of Mormon was an actual history of the Native Americans rather than a plagiarized version of another book written by a Baptist preacher named Solomon Spaulding. The facts were that Spaulding had written a fictional history of the Native American culture, and Joseph had falsified it, convincing many people that it was received by God on golden plates. The Native Americans know where their spiritual roots come from—not from a visitation from Christ—but from an actual visit from a female prophetess named the White Buffalo Calf Woman. That is why the Native Americans are a matriarchal society rather than a patriarchy—to keep everything in balance as Spirit intended.

The Mormons, with all of their falsehoods, had again created an imbalance on this continent; not to mention the other Christians who were guilty of trying to convert all the so-called "Indians" to their religious persuasions. It was all very overwhelming to me, but it all made so much sense. I knew, however, that it would take me time to adjust to these "new beliefs."

He also mentioned that the moment of our coming together that night at Wallace's place had awakened the chief of the Sioux Nation from a deep sleep, wondering what had just occurred. After Patrick told him of our meeting, he and other spiritual leaders from various other tribes Patrick had talked with were anxious to meet me. I didn't know quite how to react to all of this unexpected publicity, so my first reaction was—what do I wear? Patrick laughed as he remarked, "Whatever you'd like, Jesse. It really doesn't matter as they just want to meet *you*."

And so Patrick made preparations for the two of us. He planned for me to fly out to his home in Alabama for a huge pow-wow to meet all his friends. He also wanted me to help him with the final editing of his book, *The Message*. After that, we both planned to fly to Montana to perform sacred ceremony at Higher Ground. He had spent an entire day fasting and calling to the Ancient Spirits to see what ceremony he would be allowed to perform. In his utter amazement, after many long hours of Spirit-Calling, he was given permission to perform a very sacred, three-day ceremony called, "The Seven Steps to Returning to the Sacred Oneness." It involved several sweat lodge ceremonies, vision quests and other sacred ceremonies. Only those who prepared themselves for it would be encouraged to attend. It promised to change their lives, so they would never be the same again. Patrick said the Ancient Ceremony was destined to shift the entire planet.

Many people from Rosalie's and Wallace's group of friends in Salt Lake desired to attend this sacred ceremony and planned to meet us in Montana. The only problem was—Karl didn't know *anything* about *any* of this. He hadn't made any phone calls to me during the two weeks I'd been in Salt Lake. I figured he'd been too busy with Kirstie and the children to drive to the neighbor's to make a collect phone call. And I was unable to call him. I attempted to send an urgent telepathic message to him to call. But he wasn't receiving *any* of my messages.

That night the phone rang. It was Patrick. We discussed our plans for my airplane flight. I told him I'd already received the tickets in the mail. As I anticipated the prospects of our being together physically in the next day or so, our conversation turned more intimate.

"Patrick," I began. "What is it like to make love in the spirit *and* the flesh at the same time?"

"I really don't know, Jesse. I've never had the opportunity to experience it. But there you go again...asking questions that will get you out of the present moment. Haven't I told you before..."

But before he could finish his lecture on staying in the present, I interrupted. "You know, Patrick, the most fascinating thing about making love to you in the spirit is that spiritually we are both the same sex. You are not male and I am not female. We have just chosen these disguises for ourselves in the physical world, but in reality—in the spiritual world—we are both alike and can make love as either male or female. Don't you find that incredible!"

"Yes, Jesse. You are beginning to understand."

That night Karl broke his two-week silence and called. As I began sharing with him all the wonderful news about my new-found friend, Patrick, and what we'd been able to experience together, I could immediately tell that Karl wasn't sharing my enthusiasm. In fact, the more I talked about Patrick and what we'd planned during the next few days, the more I felt his jealousy and anger at not being included in all of this. I explained that if I could have talked to him, I would have included him every step of the way. But in his choice of separation and isolation from me, I'd had to make my own decisions following the direction of the Spirit.

But Karl was convinced that I was being directed by the *wrong* spirit, and that I needed to *come home immediately* before I got myself into some *serious trouble*. I told him that I would return home when the Spirit directed me to and asked him to respect my right to make decisions on my own. I told him I would be flying to Higher Ground with Patrick from Alabama in a few days or so, after I completed the work with him I'd commissioned to do. I asked him to please plan to meet us at the Missoula airport and help with the preparations for the sacred ceremony on the land. I expressed how important I felt the work was that I was doing with Patrick. But the more I spoke of our plans, the more adamant Karl became against it. His tone became threatening. He said that he would meet me or anyone else I had invited to *his* property with a shotgun and would escort them off the land—especially if they were Indians dressed in leathers.

Our conversation deteriorated to the point where there was no hope for any further rational discussion. I hung up the phone in utter frustration, but I was still determined to carry out my plans...come what may. I knew if God was behind it, everything would turn out as planned. I just needed the faith to carry it through.

My frustration with men and male ego was at its peak as I drove my daughter, Delaney, back to Cache Valley to Grandpa and Grandma Clark's, where she was staying while going to high school. We'd spent a wonderful weekend together, but she needed to be back to school the next day.

Then on the way back home, I plugged in one of my favorite meditative tapes, Carlos Nakai's *Canyon Trilogy*, to release some frustrations and get centered. As I listened to his sultry Native American flute with the musical strains reverberating off canyon walls; my own spirit cascaded into a mystical awareness, connecting me more deeply to Mother Earth than I'd ever experienced.

As my spirit became one with the spirit of the Earth, I had overwhelming feelings of deep sorrow. I identified this pain as that which all mothers go through in bearing and nurturing their offspring. But the pain that was expressed from the spirit of our Earth Mother far surpassed any which I'd ever experienced or could possibly imagine. Certainly, as a mother of many children, I'd experienced total exhaustion, neglecting my own needs, as I directed my energies toward fulfilling those of others. But never before had I felt the intense despair of being totally exploited, raped, and ravaged by those I loved and cared for; giving all of myself—my body, my energies, my spirit, my entire soul—so that they could have a joyful existence. The Mother Spirit did not expect anything in return for her self-sacrificing gifts of life. But instead of gratitude—to be pillaged in this manner was an abomination greater than any I'd felt could exist. The atrocities that we, her children, had inflicted upon our Mother were reprehensible, unforgivable.

And the worst part was that I, as a human being—part of the human family—was just as guilty as anyone else! My sin was my own unawareness of being out of touch with the mystical oneness, thinking that what I did personally had no appreciable effect on the entire whole. Each time I'd taken more than I needed for my own joyful existence, I had created an imbalance in the web of life. Each time I exploited others to serve my own carnal desires, I exploited the Earth Mother. Each time I neglected to live up to my highest integrity, I had compromised the integrity of the whole.

I wept bitter tears…tears of regret as I understood that I knowingly and unknowingly, helped to create the "dis-ease" that Mother Earth was suffering. My tears flowed for more than two hours after I drove home. Then, sitting in my bedroom, I vowed that, through this blessing of being awakened to my oneness with Mother Earth, I would remain aware of any violations I might create in the future. I also repented of all the violations I had committed in the past and vowed to do everything in my power to awaken others to this mystical concept of oneness so that they, too, could repent of their separations within.

Just as this process of repentance felt complete, Patrick called. My voice must have held residual pain from my intense experience because he immediately asked what was wrong. I shared with him, to the best of my ability, my experience of connecting with the spirit of Mother Earth. I then told him of my earlier conversation with Karl and his hard-heartedness. I told him how I detested the male ego which had become totally out of control. He remained silent as I began to reprimand him for his own exploitations of our Earth Mother, for his self-indulgence in food, tobacco and sex. I reminded him that of *all* people—he as a holy man, a *Shaman*—should have known better.

Patrick's voice became cold and distant—something I hadn't experienced from him before. Without responding to my statements, he promptly demanded that I return my airline tickets. The more I tried to reason with him, the more adamant he became that things were out of balance and that our relationship could no longer continue. We could remain only friends.

"Friends!" I exclaimed. "You want to just be *friends?*" At Patrick's insistence, I abandoned my argument that *it had already gone well beyond friendship* and that I desired more than anything to continue our relationship. But if *he* wanted to manifest the illusion of separation, what could I do? *I* refused to live in the world of illusion! Yet I felt at a lose as to what to do. Both men I had grown to love were at war with each other and I felt trapped between the two of them with no where to turn.

So I returned the airplane tickets and did not go to Alabama. I did not meet with the gathering of Elders. We did not perform the sacred ceremony of "Returning to Oneness" at Higher Ground.

For several years, Patrick and I had no formal communication by phone or by mail, although I tried desperately to contact him. But on occasion, when we'd both returned to the reality of our oneness, we enjoyed the ecstasy of spiritual lovemaking.

And yes, I found out the answer to my question of what it was like to make love in the spirit and in the flesh at the same time. On my return home to Karl, I taught spiritual oneness to him. All I can say is—WOW! When spirit and body are inseparably connected there *is* a fullness of joy!

Chapter Twenty

Communion

The sun is setting low on the horizon as Grandma Jesse finishes telling her story. The grandchildren stir restlessly on the buffalo robe as she motions Grandfather Speaking Wind to continue with the rest of the story; sharing the gift he cradles carefully in his arms. Patrick sits down cross-legged on the buffalo robe next to Grandma Jesse and begins.

"For centuries, the legend has been told of how two young braves from the Lakota tribe of the Sioux Nation went out to hunt. As they were out stalking the buffalo, a strange light approached them from the distant plains. As it got close enough for them to see what caused the light, a beautiful woman appeared, clothed in brilliance and carrying a strange bundle.

"One man, who had evil thoughts to possess the beautiful woman, ran forward attempting to draw her to himself. The other man watched as a cloud of smoke descended upon the man. When it lifted, nothing was left of him but dry bones.

"The other man, whose heart was pure, knelt in fear as the buckskin-clad woman approached him. She spoke to him telling him not to be afraid, but to return to his people and prepare them for her coming. This was done, and the beautiful maiden appeared in their midst, walking among them in a sunrise, or clockwise direction and singing a strange but beautiful song.

She then held forth her bundle and said (and at this point Speaking Wind holds out his own bundle): "This is a sacred gift and must be treated in a holy way. In this bundle is a sacred pipe which no impure man or woman should ever see. With this sacred pipe you will send your voices to Wakan

Tanka—the Great Spirit, Creator of All—your Father and Grandfather. With this sacred pipe you will walk upon the Earth which is your Grandmother and Mother. All your steps should be holy.'"

Patrick then unwraps the ancient bundle to reveal two buckskin pouches. From one he removes a catlinite pipe bowl; from the other, he removes a magnificently carved stem with feathers attached. They have the appearance of being old—very old—and everyone present can sense that something *wakan* (very holy) is near.

"The bowl of the pipe is red stone which represents the Earth—the mother of us all. A buffalo is carved in the stone facing the center and symbolizes the four-legged creatures who live among us as brothers and sisters."

Then he lifts the stem and holds it up next to the bowl and speaks:

"The stem is wood and represents all growing things. Through this stem is breathed the Holy Spirit which is the breath of life. Twelve feathers hang from where the stem fits into the bowl and are from the Spotted Eagle. These represent the winged ones who live among us."

Then Patrick joins the bowl of the pipe to its stem.

"All these things are joined to you who will smoke the pipe and send voices to Wakan Tanka. When you use this pipe to pray, you will pray for and with everything. The sacred pipe binds you to all your relatives—your Grandfather and Father, your Grandmother and Mother.

"The red stone represents the Earth Mother on which you live. The Earth is red and the two-legged creatures upon it are also red. Wakan Tanka has given you a red road—a good and straight road—to travel. And you must remember that all people who stand on the Earth are sacred.

"From this day, the sacred pipe will stand on the red earth, and you will send your voices to Wakan Tanka. There are seven circles on the stone which represent the seven rites in which you will use the pipe.

"The Buffalo Calf Woman then instructed the people to send runners to the distant tribes of the Sioux Nation to bring in the many leaders, the medicine people, and the holy men and holy women. This they did, and when the people had gathered, she instructed them in the sacred ceremonies. She told them of the first rite—that of the Keeping of the Soul. She told them that the remaining six rites would be made known to them in visions. As she started to leave, she said:

"'Remember how sacred the pipe is, and treat it in a sacred manner, for it will be with you always. Remember also that in me are four ages. I shall leave you now, but shall look upon you in every age. In the end, I will return and again smoke the peace pipe with you and teach the last rite—the sacred marriage ceremony of joining Earth to Heaven.'"

"The Sioux begged the Spirit Woman to stay with them, promising to erect a fine lodge and give her a fine man to provide for her, but she declined their offer:

"'No, the Creator above, the Great Spirit is happy with you—you the grandchildren. You have listened well to my teachings. Now I must return to the Spirit World.'"

"She walked some distance away from them and sat down. When she arose, she had become a white buffalo calf. She walked further, bowed to the four quarters of the Universe, and then disappeared into the distance.

"Her sacred bundle was left with the people. Until today a traditional Sioux family, the Keepers of the Bundle, have guarded the bundle and its contents on one of the Sioux reservations. They have waited until the day when the pipe would be returned to its original owner and all the rainbow tribes—red, yellow, black and white would smoke it together. Then the Buffalo Calf Woman would show them the sacred marriage ceremony, which would build the rainbow bridge connecting Earth to Heaven.

Patrick finishes speaking and then stands. Ceremonially, he hands the ancient peace pipe to Grandmother Jesse, who acknowledges the gift with a grateful smile and nod of her head. She stands and beckons for everyone to stand with her.

"You, my beloved brothers...go and build the ceremonial fire upon the altar before the sun sinks in the western sky. And you, my beloved sisters... gather all the things from the table and from the ground to prepare for the sacred ceremony."

All is done just as Grandma Jesse directs, and they all return to gather around her.

"You musicians...you who have learned to play the sacred flute and drums. Get your instruments and find a spot to sit and play over by those trees," she directs, pointing to a stand of tress at the edge of the summit.

When this is done, she directs the grandchildren to form a circle around her and hold hands. Then another circle is formed around them by the Elders—the grandparents and godparents of these little ones. The Grandma Jesse instructs the rest of the family of friends to form a third circle around the perimeter.

"Come, Speaking Wind...fetch me an ember from the ceremonial fire so that I may light the sacred peace pipe. By the way, Patrick, you did bring the sacred pipe tobacco?"

Patrick smiles and nods. Together they pack tobacco into the ancient catlinite pipe bowl. He then walks to the altar where the fire is burning brilliantly in the pre-dusk light, removes a long, flaming stick, and brings it over to Grandma Jesse.

With it she lights the pipe and hands it to Patrick to make sure it is in good smoking order. He breathes in the first few puffs and then hands it back to Jesse to begin the sacred ceremony. Everyone drops their hands to their sides and stands silently as Grandmother speaks.

Turning toward the eastern horizon, she holds the sacred pipe up with both hands toward the sky.

"To Squaw Peak in the East, where the sun rises each day reminding us that our Father in Heaven shines light down upon all his children—all his creations—to warm them with the light of his love. We, as your children, offer thanks to the element, fire, for our continued existence. And we call to the Yellow Race of two-leggeds to join us in this sacred circle of love."

Patrick then throws a pinch of tobacco toward the east as a gift offering to the element, fire.

Grandma Jesse then makes a quarter turn clockwise to face the southern horizon and again holds the peace pipe up to the sky:

"To the Clark Fork River in the South, where the children of the water swim freely, and where fresh water flows so that we might partake of its refreshing and life-giving properties. We offer thanks to the element, water, for our joyful existence. And we call to the Black Race of two-leggeds to join in this, our sacred circle of love."

Patrick throws a pinch of tobacco southward to honor the water element. Jesse then makes a quarter turn towards the west.

"To Stark Mountain in the West—where the strength of the Earth protects us and gives us a firm foundation on which to stand and exist in this physical plane. We offer thanks to the element, earth, for our continued existence. And we call to the Red Race of two-leggeds to join with us in our sacred circle of love."

Patrick throws a pinch of tobacco in the western direction as a gift offering to the element, earth. Jesse makes a quarter turn to face north and lifts the sacred pipe towards the sky:

"To the North, where the buffalo herd runs free once again and the breath of life fills the souls of all of God's family, giving us life as the Spirit-which-moves-in-all-things. We give thanks to the element, air or Spirit, for our continued existence. And we call to the White Race of two-leggeds of the North to join us in this sacred circle of our love."

Patrick reaches into his pouch for a gift offering and tosses some tobacco northward for the element air.

Grandma Jesse again faces west and begins to puff on the pipe to cause it to smoke again. And as smoke begins to billow out, she blows a few puffs into the western sky. The sun is sinking low behind the horizon of Stark Mountain, creating a rosy glow across the sky. With both arms extended, holding both ends of the ancient peace pipe, Grandma Jesse continues her prayers to the Great Spirit in the sky.

"With this smoke I send prayers to our Father in Heaven, his son, Jesus Christ, and the Holy Spirit—who are one God—and ask to be joined with you in love, peace and Holy Communion. I ask that all creatures of the Earth and all races—yellow, black, red and white—be joined in this Holy Communion."

As she finishes her brief but heartfelt prayer, she hands the pipe to Patrick. He then takes a puff and blows smoke into the fiery evening sky. "To the Great Spirit—we send this smoke up to you with our prayers. We ask to be joined with you and all of our ancestors who have gone before us in sacred communion." He puffs the pipe again and hands it back to Grandmother Jesse.

Jesse hands the pipe to Grandfather Karl who also smokes the sacred pipe and begins his prayer. "Our Father in Heaven who watches over all that we do and say. We thank thee for this precious gift that is ours this day. We ask thee to hear the words of our hearts and answer us according to thy will. We ask for all humankind to be sealed up in this sacred circle of love—that we may join this circle of love here on Earth with the circle of love which exists in Heaven. Amen."

Karl puffs on the ancient peace pipe again and then hands it back to Jesse. Jesse motions to Patrick for more tobacco. Together they fill the pipe's bowl and Patrick puffs on it to get it to smoke. He hands it to Jesse who then passes it to the circle of Elders so all who wish to do so may join them in communion prayer. This they do, according to their own will and desires, saying prayers and puffing smoke from the ancient peace pipe.

Then the sacred pipe is handed to the outer circle of Jesse's family and friends to join in the Holy Communion with the others, as they wish. The musicians seated outside of the sacred circle are also given the opportunity to partake in the Holy Communion prayer.

Finally the pipe is handed back to Jesse, and she helps her small grandchildren who, by this time, are intensely curious about what it's like to smoke the amazing peace pipe. They are given the opportunity to try to produce a puff of smoke out of their mouths. Although most of them cough and choke during the attempt, they all have a delightful time trying. They are also encouraged to say their own prayers to the Great Spirit in the sky and to follow the ascension of the smoke.

Grandma Jesse then takes the ancient pipe and empties its smoldering contents upon Mother Earth, allowing all the elements—fire, water, earth and breath—to be joined with her in Holy Communion.

"Begin the music!" she announces, after the magnificent peace pipe is carefully wrapped up again into its original bundle—this time still assembled as one whole rather than as separate pieces.

Grandfather Speaking Wind carefully takes the bundle and places it on a special rock altar next to the smoldering fire. He returns to join Jesse and the rest of the Elders, holding hands in the Elder's circle.

The music of the native flutes and drums fill the air with mystical, magical strains—inviting everyone present into the circle dance of communion. The three circles begin to revolve. The first of children rotates in a clockwise direction. In the middle, the Elders' circle moves in a counter-clockwise direction. The outside circle of family and friends rotates clockwise. It's as if they are all gears in a gigantic human gyroscope.

Dancers lift their voices, singing and chanting whatever emerges from inside them during their spontaneous praise to the Great Creator. As everyone joyously, jubilantly sings and dances their own passionate heartsong to the rhythm of the flutes and drums, an energy field of rainbow auric light begins to form all around them. The light gains in intensity until it creates a huge, rainbow-colored energy vortex ascending upward into the sky. Everyone continues singing and dancing, infusing the mystical auric light with their combined ecstatic energies.

Then, as if through the dynamic intent of everyone's heart, voices are heard coming down from Heaven singing strains of a familiar song:

> The Earth is our Mother just turning around…
> With her trees in the forest
> Her roots underground
> Our Father above us whose sigh is the wind
> Paint us a rainbow
> Without any end…

Everyone singing and dancing in the rotating spirals looks upward, and tears fill their eyes as they behold concords of brilliant angels descending from Heaven to join them in the sacred circle-dance of light and love.

Heaven has opened its door and angels—past loved-ones who have crossed over to the other side of the veil—descend in their own heavenly rainbow vortex to join the earthly vortex which the family of friends has created. And when the two vortices come together in Holy Communion, the combined fusion of energy creates a supernova of pure light reflected in rainbow colors.

The brilliance instantly transforms the Elders back to their prime age of twenty-three by some energizing process of translation. Grandfather Speaking

Wind's long, white hair is transformed to shiny black and his etched face becomes handsome and youthful. Grandma Jesse and Grandpa Karl become their radiant, youthful selves ready to receive the precious gift, which is offered to them. A brilliant light-being, whose countenance resembles that of Jesse's father, holds a tiny infant in his arms. As he hands the child to Jesse, she recognizes it to be her precious infant son, Jadon. Tears flood her face as she receives him into her welcoming embrace. Karl holds them both in his arms, crying joyous tears, as they continue to slowly dance with their precious son held between them. The music continues as a familiar lyrical voice is heard singing...

> I see them dancing
> Somewhere in the twilight
> In a place of enchantment
> Somewhere in the dawn
> I hear them singing
> A song for all lovers
> A song for the two hearts
> Beating only as one...

They all look up again as the light-being with the transcendent voice descends through the spiraling vortex of light. John Denver has returned in a resurrected form and is still singing.

Karl takes Jadon from Jesse's arms as John, holding out a radiant arm, offers to dance with Jesse—who is also aglow with light. Dancers and singers continue to dance to the tune as a chorus of angels sing:

> Imagine the moment
> No longer alone
> The arms of another
> A place to belong
> No longer the struggle
> No longer the night
> Forever becoming
> In the quickening light
>
> To see in the darkness
> To listen within
> To answer in kindness
> To ever begin
> To ever be gentle

To always be strong
To walk in the wonder
To live in the song

I see them dancing
Somewhere in the moonlight
In a place of enchantment
Somewhere in the sun
I hear them singing
A song for two lovers
A song for the two hearts
Beating only as one

No one knows how long they all danced in communion celebration atop Marriage Mountain as time and space no longer exist. The polar shift has taken place, and all things have become as one. No longer is there any fear for tomorrow as pain and sorrow no longer exist. Each new day is filled with love, joy and peace for it truly is the dawning of a New Day—the age of enlightenment...the Millennium.

The Beginning

About Heartsong

Heartsong is the voice deep inside each and every one of us yearning to be heard.

It is the song of the heart expressing divine gratitude to our Creator—God—the Spirit-which-moves-in-all-things—Jesus Christ—whatever you conceive this mystical force to be.

It is the song of the heart expressing deep felt love for our Creator—for each other—and for all of Creation—no matter what form it has chosen to manifest.

Heartsong is the gift of the heart which we all give to each other whenever we reach out and touch Heaven…and bring a bit of Heaven back to Earth to share.

Heartsong is my gift of Heaven I share with you—the reader.

And to all of those who have offered their heartsongs to me in order for this gift to manifest—I give sincere thanks.

If you would like more information on how you can assist in manifesting Heartsong Living Centers, please write me at:

Heartsong Healing Center
4749 S. Holladay Blvd.
Holladay, UT 84117

Or email me at: heartsong @webpipe.net

All proceeds from this book go towards manifesting the Heartsong Living Centers and The Sacred Paths Foundation.

Author's Note

The world doesn't need another prophet…given the history of what we've done to *all* of our prophets. When I first wrote this book in 1998, I felt I was on a mission from God to give his message to the world so we could be healed from our sins (separations within). I sent my manuscript to over thirty publishers with the same results—rejection. I shared my manuscript with several friends. Many read it and it changed their lives in dramatic ways. Others simply discarded it—they didn't have time to read it.

Today I write for my own personal healing. I made a commitment to myself and others to finish this book and get it published. I revised the original manuscript as I come from a totally different place now. I no longer feel the need to heal the planet. The planet is perfect just as it is. It is a playground allowing us to create whatever reality we wish to create. All of our choices are here. This has been its purpose—to give us choice. We can choose to create good things or bad…and we do.

I am choosing to create my own reality for good. I am currently the owner and manager of Heartsong Healing Center in Holladay, Utah where I indulge in my life's passion—bodywork and water therapy. You are welcome to come visit. I also purchased land in Central Utah where I'm currently developing Heartsong Living Center—a sustainable eco-village. Three of my children still live with their dad in Montana while some have moved out on their own, gotten married, or are going to college. I'm remarried to a special man named Brad Bird, and like the words to a favorite John Denver song:

> Life is so good
> Life is so good these days
> My life is so good these days…
> My life is so good.

I hope your life is *so good* and if you get something out of reading my book—it *is good.* Perhaps when I complete my Heartsong Living Center you can come out and visit me and we can sing songs, share massages, and come together in heartfelt communion. I look forward to that. Blessings—Janae aka Jesse